UNDERDEVELOPMENT
IN KENYA

Underdevelopment in Kenya

THE POLITICAL ECONOMY OF NEO-COLONIALISM
1964-1971

COLIN LEYS

Professor of Politics
University of Sheffield

UNIVERSITY OF CALIFORNIA PRESS

BERKELEY AND LOS ANGELES

University of California Press
Berkeley and Los Angeles, California

First Paperback Edition, 1975
ISBN 0–520–02770–1 [paper]
ISBN 0–520–02731–0 [cloth]
Library of Congress Catalog Card Number 74–76387

Printed in the United States of America

4 5 6 7 8 9 0

Contents

For Gudrun, Tom, Patrick and Sally

Acknowledgments

Several institutions and many individuals helped me to write this book. The universities of Nairobi, Glasgow and Sheffield provided me with rewarding intellectual contexts, and the Rockefeller Foundation in New York and the Social Science Research Council in London also supported me financially. I am specially grateful to Professor James S. Coleman of the Rockefeller Foundation for encouragement and endless kindness, and to Professor W. J. M. Mackenzie of Glasgow University who went out of his way to help me write up my material after leaving Kenya.

Many people have contributed to this study whom I cannot thank individually here as I should like; my obligation to them all is very great. But it is a pleasure to be able to acknowledge the stimulus I received from colleagues in Kenya, and in particular Henry Bienen, Michael Cowen, Frank Furedi, Göran Hyden, Kenneth King, John Nellis, John Okumu, Lawrence Smith, Tony Somerset, Gary Wasserman and Rodney Wilson. Three people, Professor Mackenzie, Jitendra Mohan and my brother Roger Leys have also helped me very generously in trying to think more clearly about the significance of what has been happening in Kenya and elsewhere in the third world. Although the final product will satisfy none of them, they have taught me a great deal and saved me from many errors. I should also like to thank Selina Coelho and Festus Geoffrey for much kind practical assistance, and Mrs Shelagh Clark for skilfully typing the text.

One debt which every student of Kenya incurs is to a number of very able and hardworking people in public life who are very much alive to the implications and importance of the main issues raised in this book. Many of them will disagree with much of what I have written (and I must absolve them and anyone else I have named from any responsibility for either the views or the errors it contains); but I am none the less deeply grateful to them all.

Tables

List of Abbreviations

ADC   Agricultural Development Corporation
AFC   Agricultural Finance Corporation
COTU   Central Organization of Trade Unions
DFCK   Development Finance Company of Kenya
DN   *Daily Nation* (Nairobi)
EAS   *East African Standard* (Nairobi)
FKE   Federation of Kenya Employers
HFCK   Housing Finance Company of Kenya
ICDC   Industrial and Commercial Development Corporation
KADU   Kenya African Democratic Union
KANU   Kenya African National Union
KAU   Kenya African Union
KCC   Kenya Co-operative Creameries
KFL   Kenya Federation of Labour
KNFU   Kenya National Farmers' Union
KNTC   Kenya National Trading Corporation
KPU   Kenya People's Union
KTDC   Kenya Tourist Development Corporation
NCC   National Construction Corporation
NKG   New Kenya Group (later New Kenya Party)
NHC   National Housing Corporation
SN   *Sunday Nation* (Nairobi)
SRDP   Special Rural Development Programme

Preface

This book began as an enquiry into the relationship between the 'private sector' of the Kenyan economy and the pattern of national development since independence was formally attained in 1963, a subject which seemed curiously neglected in comparison with the literature on Kenya in the inter-war years. But as the work progressed it became clear that it really posed some fundamental questions about the significance of independence for the mass of the people, and that instead of filling a gap in the existing literature it was necessary to try to disengage oneself from many of its presuppositions.[1] First it was necessary to realize that the relation between the 'private sector' and the pattern of post-independence development could not be understood in purely Kenyan terms, but was the outcome of international forces as they had operated over several generations, and continued to operate, on the land area and collection of peoples we know as Kenya; as Baran put it, the question of 'whether there will be meat in the kitchen is never decided in the kitchen'. Secondly, the original formulation of the problem in terms of 'the private sector', and even more fundamentally, in terms of 'the economy' as something distinct from 'the political system', soon appeared not merely artificial but as a positive obstacle to grasping the reality involved. This was not merely a question of being willing to transgress 'disciplinary' boundaries, but of trying to establish a standpoint from which all the concepts in terms of which the Kenyan experience had hitherto mainly been described could be critically reconsidered. But this meant, thirdly, that to try to answer the questions which posed themselves appeared as an unavoidably political act, involving a decision about the interests and the political practice which the

---

1. In this respect I have followed in the footsteps of E. A. Brett whose *Colonialism and Underdevelopment in East Africa* (Heinemann, London 1972) is a landmark in the reinterpretation of Kenya's pre-independence experience.

framework of enquiry should try to embody. The more I thought
about it, the more it seemed to me that the comparative neglect
of the topic in the existing literature, i.e. not asking these questions,
was also a political act, however reluctant most social scientists
might be to accept this.

Difficulties soon arise for anyone who openly abandons the
convenient fiction of 'value-freedom', according to which the
social scientist's analysis is independent of his political commitments. However the need to do so has become increasingly
hard to escape as the result of the actual record of conventional
'development theory', whose supposedly neutral concepts (such
as 'modernization', 'political development', and the like) have
proved not only to embody the dominant relationships of advanced
capitalist societies but also to be largely sterile as tools for understanding what is happening in the third world.[2] Among their
major deficiencies both 'political development' and 'economic
development' theories have had in common a marked dis-
inclination to distinguish clearly between the different interests
at stake in the countries of the third world, let alone to make the
antagonisms between them into the central focus of enquiry. Their
focus has rather been on 'nations', and even more on the 'leader-
ships' of 'nations', seen as confronting various obstacles to 'development' – 'development' being treated as an ultimately universal
good. This perspective presupposes that the 'leadership' is more
or less representative, or at least more or less benevolent; or
failing this, it presupposes that there is no 'serious' alternative to
the existing 'leadership', or at any rate none with which it is the
business of 'development theory' to be primarily concerned. And
since it does not start out from an analysis of the way in which
different 'patterns of development' embody the dominance of
different combinations of class interests, in practice it tends to
take as given the interests which the 'leadership' represents, and
more or less thoroughly reflects these interests in the concepts it
uses, the questions it asks and the answers it offers.

Some people have concluded that the trouble lies in not having
tried hard enough to find a social scientific standpoint truly

2. For a recent critique of these concepts see Jose F. Ocampo and Dale L. Johnson,
    'The Concept of Political Development', in James D. Cockroft, Andre Gunder
    Frank and Dale L. Johnson (eds), *Dependence and Underdevelopment* (Doubleday, New
    York 1972), pp. 399–424. Frank's more general earlier critique, 'Sociology of De-
    velopment and Underdevelopment of Sociology', is reprinted at pp. 321–97 of the
    same volume.

independent of all the interests involved in the predicament of the third world. Others, however, have come to the conclusion that Marx and Mannheim were right in arguing that the 'categorial apparatus' of social knowledge necessarily reflects and embodies personal and class interests, and that the researcher in effect chooses which interests his concepts and methodology shall try to embody and reflect.[3] This is also my position. It does not of course restrict the range of choice. One may choose a conceptual framework which embodies the dominant relationships and class interests more or less frankly. Anyone who doubts this may consult, by way of illustration, an on-the-whole well-informed article on Kenya by an anonymous contributor ('The Looker-On') to *Blackwoods Magazine* in March 1971, which begins:

> Seven years after casting off the gyves of the oppressor, Kenya is still standing up to independence better than any other country south of the Sahara. There has been no breakdown of law and order, no revolution or military *coup*, no economic collapse . . . there is a good atmosphere in the country.[4]

And it ends: 'Provided they keep their mouths shut and a suitcase packed, Europeans can still live there with great pleasure and a fair profit.'[5] One is tempted to say that 'Looker-On' reveals the 'inner secret' of conventional development theory as it applies to Kenya. The alternative, it seems to me, must be to try to adopt a conceptual framework which as far as possible embraces the interests of those who are exploited and oppressed in the third world, and tries to disclose 'the necessity and at the same time the conditions of transforming industry as well as the social structure'

---

3. The expression 'categorial apparatus' is Karl Popper's, but his attempt to refute Mannheim by showing that the view that social knowledge is conditioned by the personal and class situation of the social scientist involves a paradox, i.e. is strictly nonsense, seems to me unconvincing; and the widespread acceptance of this supposed refutation has helped to stifle the serious study of the social and material determinants of social knowledge. See Karl Popper, *The Open Society and Its Enemies* (Routledge, second edition, London 1952), Vol. II, Ch. 23 and Ch. 24, notes 7 and 8 (2) (a); also Martin Landau, *Political Theory and Political Science* (Macmillan, New York 1972), pp. 34–42. On the other hand Popper's solution to the problem of achieving 'objectivity' is much less unacceptable than Mannheim's.

4. *Blackwoods Magazine*, March 1971, p. 273.

5. ibid., p. 284.

through which their poverty and subordination are perpetuated.[6] This is certainly not easy, and it is not made any easier by the fact that so many people see it as a departure from the sort of academic 'impartiality' which includes among its virtues the fact that it hardly ever involves saying anything upsetting. Unfortunately once one sees that that kind of impartiality is suspect, this cannot really be helped. Since not all the interests involved are mutually compatible, everyone must choose those which he would like his work to try to serve.[7]

While we are on this subject it may be appropriate to mention the question of certain words and concepts used in the book. People who can swallow words like 'charisma' and 'integration' (or indeed 'modernization') without flinching sometimes have a surprisingly strong aversion to some others, such as for instance 'class', or 'oppression'. It is true that many of Marx's central concepts have suffered from crude usage and dogmatic repetition, and that the accounts of Marxism familiar to many people are deformed versions, produced by both sides in the Cold War. But some of these concepts we need, and one of the most striking pieces of evidence that dogmatism is not the exclusive prerogative of Marxists is the extraordinary resistance that still exists to the idea that there are classes and class struggles in Africa, let alone that they may be of central importance. I have tried to use a minimum of technical terminology of any kind; but where, for instance, the sense of the situation requires one to refer to people who own particular means of production and exploit the labour of others, and who act politically to defend this relationship and the advantages it gives them, I have referred to them as part of a bourgeoisie.[8]

A theoretical framework which does address itself directly to the questions with which this study is concerned, is to be found in

6. The quotation is from *The German Ideology* in the version published by L. D. Easton and K. H. Guddat (eds), *Writings of the Young Marx* (Doubleday, New York 1967), p. 419.

7. Impartiality is of course not the same thing as objectivity; cf. Hugh Stretton, *The Political Sciences* (Routledge, London 1969), p. 157: 'Won't the interventionist's . . . hopes and fears, his values and his ideological blinkers, distort everything he does . . .? I concede that they can, and that they often do; and further, that the way to guard against these ill effects is to practise about one half of the conventional wisdom on the subject of scientific objectivity. But it is difficult, as Mr Wanamaker said of the wasted half of his advertising budget, to know which half.'

8. One is sometimes tempted to adopt Eric Berne's device of writing obscene words backwards or sideways (thus: ssalc, eisioegruob, noisserppo, etc.) so that it becomes possible to maintain a rational discussion about what they denote

the work of 'underdevelopment' and 'dependency' theorists. The perspective of 'underdevelopment' is largely derived from Marxism but those who have adopted and contributed to it include non-Marxists, and 'neo-Marxists' as well as Marxists with differing conceptions of the nature of Marxism and differing conceptions of the relation between theory and practice, not to mention specific differences about the interpretation of particular situations and about political strategy and tactics.[9] We may therefore speak of 'underdevelopment theory' (or 'dependency theory'), but not yet of 'a theory of underdevelopment' (or even of 'theories of underdevelopment', in the proper sense of the term 'theory'). What we have is rather a 'perspective' – a way of looking at the predicament of the third world which directs our attention to structures, mechanisms and causal relationships largely or wholly neglected by, and mostly contradictory to, conventional development theory. To my mind underdevelopment theory represents an immense advance, politically and intellectually, over conventional development theory, in spite of some very serious defects of its own. But whether it leads in fact to better understanding and valid strategies of development can only be known by applying it to particular situations, which is what is attempted, in an admittedly halting fashion, in this book.

In view of the rather general nature of most 'underdevelopment theory' it seemed necessary to begin by trying to outline its main theses and their implications, and this forms the main subject of Chapter 1. During the years since 1970, when this study was begun, the relevant literature has expanded rapidly, and much that was then relatively inaccessible has been published in various collections.[10] There have also been some important theoretical

---

9. An exceptionally clear and lively survey of many of the different strands involved is provided by Aidan Foster-Carter's 'Neo-Marxist Approaches to Development and Underdevelopment', in E. de Kadt and G. Williams (eds), *Sociology and Development* (Tavistock Publications, London 1974), pp. 67–105. Although I do not accept all the author's interpretations, his paper stands out in the literature by reason of its range and perceptiveness, and anticipates several conclusions arrived at much more laboriously and less incisively in the course of the present study.

10. These include: Roger Owen and Bob Sutcliffe (eds), *Studies in the Theory of Imperialism* (Longman, London 1972); K. T. Fann and D. C. Hodges (eds), *Readings in US Imperialism* (Sargent, Boston 1972); Giovanni Arrighi and John S. Saul, *The Political Economy of Africa* (Monthly Review Press, New York 1973); and Henry Bernstein (ed.), *Underdevelopment and Development* (Penguin, Harmondsworth 1973). A valuable earlier collection is Robert I. Rhodes (ed.), *Underdevelopment and Revolution* (Monthly Review Press, New York 1970).

developments within underdevelopment theory, so that trying actually to make use of it for understanding an equally rapidly developing situation was often difficult and extremely uncomfortable, to the point where I felt a more than usual sympathy for the railwayman in the story, who was asked how to get to Carlisle, and replied that if he were trying to get there, he would start from somewhere else. Today what is really called for is not an outline but an extended critique of underdevelopment theory, but that is a different and long-term undertaking.[11] I have in the end left Chapter 1 substantially as it was originally written, partly as a benchmark for the subsequent analysis, and partly for the benefit of readers who would like to remind themselves of the main elements of underdevelopment theory, and some of its implications and shortcomings. It also briefly discusses the Marxist foundations of underdevelopment theory, and even more briefly indicates the way in which I have used the term 'neo-colonialism' to denote both the particular historical phase and the particular political and social relationships which obtained in Kenya in the 1960s.

'Underdevelopment' is actually a term I would be glad to do without. At one time 'underdeveloped' meant, in UN parlance, 'insufficiently developed', or what is now called 'less developed'. The state of affairs in the 'underdeveloped countries' was thought of as being due to a lack of capital, know-how and other inputs which had led to 'development' in the advanced industrial countries. Critics of this view argued that on the contrary, the predicament of the 'underdeveloped' countries was due to the application to them of western capital, know-how and political power, often over several centuries, in ways which had structured (and continued to structure) their economies and societies so as to continually reproduce poverty, inequality and, above all, political and economic subordination to the interests of western capital. If Andre Gunder Frank was not the first to subvert the original meaning of 'underdeveloped' by writing of the 'development of underdevelopment' he was certainly responsible for condensing the essential argument involved into this succinct polemical form.[12]

But as others have also pointed out, there are two important

---

11. A forthcoming study by Jitendra Mohan will make a major contribution to this critique.

12. Andre Gunder Frank, 'The Development of Underdevelopment', in his *Latin America: Underdevelopment or Revolution* (Monthly Review Press, New York 1969), Ch. 1. See also Foster-Carter, op. cit. (note 9), p. 69.

reasons why we should really dispense with the term. One is that the historical circumstances of all the different countries exposed to imperialism have differed so widely, according to the stage which capitalist development had reached, both on the world scale and within the particular imperialist power which imposed itself on them, when they were first exposed to the imperial impact; and according to the situation which existed within each subject area – including its scale, natural resources, the nature of the previously existing social formation, and so on. Consequently in so far as 'underdevelopment' refers to the substantive consequences of imperialism, the resulting characteristics of the 'underdeveloped countries' economies, social formations, political structures, and so on, its connotation is almost impossibly wide. Chad is underdeveloped, and so is India and so is Brazil. Secondly, and even worse, in so far as it connotes a concept of *development* it is purely that of the capitalist development of the imperial powers; yet their path of development is one which underdevelopment theory sees as being either undesirable or impossible (or both) for the underdeveloped countries of the third world today. It would be better to speak of various kinds of development under imperialism, such as colonial and extractive, settler-colonial, neo-colonial, and so on, including many different contemporary forms of 'associated dependent' development;[13] and of various kinds of more autonomous development, both capitalist and socialist. But for the time being we probably cannot do without 'underdevelopment', since it has acquired a definite currency.

---

13. For the last of these see especially the work of the Latin American 'dependency' theorists, for instance Fernando Henrique Cardoso, 'Dependency and Development in Latin America', *New Left Review*, 74, July–August 1972, pp. 83–95.

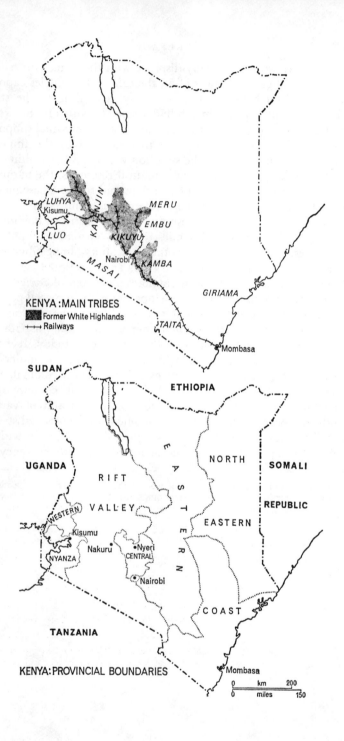

KENYA: MAIN TRIBES
▓ Former White Highlands
+—+—+ Railways

LUHYA
Kisumu
LUO
KALENJIN
MERU
EMBU
KIKUYU
Nairobi
KAMBA
MASAI
GIRIAMA
TAITA
Mombasa

SUDAN
ETHIOPIA

UGANDA
RIFT
VALLEY
WESTERN
Kisumu
NYANZA
Nakuru
Nyeri
CENTRAL
Nairobi
EASTERN
NORTH
EASTERN
SOMALI
REPUBLIC

TANZANIA
COAST
Mombasa

KENYA: PROVINCIAL BOUNDARIES

km   200
0
miles 150
0

CHAPTER 1

Underdevelopment and Neo-colonialism

Anyone looking for the origins of the theory of underdevelopment must begin his search in the writings of Marx and Lenin. Marx took a keen interest in the effects of British capitalism on India, China, and Ireland; and Lenin not only wrote a detailed study of the development of capitalism in Russia down to 1899, but also formulated a general theory of imperialism. But Marxism is a revolutionary doctrine, and Marx, Lenin, Bukharin, and Luxemburg, 'the principal Marxist creators of the theory of imperialism',[1] were European revolutionaries. Although their vision included some countries on the periphery of the international capitalist system, their prime concern was with the revolutionary prospect in Europe and European Russia. Writing to Kautsky in 1882 Engels made it clear that he took it for granted that the socialist revolution would come in Europe and North America first, and that 'semi-civilized countries' would 'of themselves follow in their wake; economic needs, if anything, will see to that'. 'But', he added, ' . . . as to what social and political phases these countries will then have to pass through before they likewise arrive at a socialist organization, I think we can today advance only rather idle hypotheses.'[2]

This was common sense; but as a socialist revolution has not yet occurred in western Europe or North America, whereas a revolutionary situation exists in many parts of the former colonial empires, a major theoretical development has been required.

In its most general aspect the evolution of Marxist thought on these matters is part of the history of international communism and well known; but the precise point of departure of current

---

1. The phrase is from T. Dos Santos, 'La Crise de la Théorie de Développement et les Relations de Dépendance en Amérique Latine', *L'Homme et la Societé*, No. 12, April–May–June 1969, p. 58.
2. S. Avineri (ed.), *Karl Marx on Colonialism and Modernisation* (Doubleday, New York 1969), p. 473.

underdevelopment theory from Marx's and Engels's own discussion of the impact of capitalism on India, China and other parts of today's 'Third World' is less well known, and worth trying to clarify.

There are two distinct sides to Marx's treatment of the periphery of the international capitalist economy. On the one hand, he saw the initial plundering of the backward regions as part of the process of 'primitive accumulation' of capital, on a par with the forcible appropriation of peasant landholdings by large landowners in Europe, whereby sufficient volumes of capital were accumulated in individual hands to lay the foundations for the transition from merchant capitalism to industrial capitalism.[3] On the other hand he saw the destruction of the stagnant, non-evolutionary social formations summed up in the blanket term 'Asiatic despotism' as a pre-condition for the emergence of the 'semi-civilized' peoples from the 'prehistory' of mankind – i.e. for their attainment of industrial communism.[4] This destruction could only be brought about by capitalist penetration from outside, especially when backed up by direct imperial rule, as in India; destroying the old communal economies and social systems along with the moghuls and emperors, introducing private property in land, destroying traditional manufacturing, forcing the creation of a market for industrial products.

But what is really important, from the point of view of the ex-colonies today, is what Marx thought were the positive effects, as opposed to the necessary destructive effects, of capitalist exploitation as it continued to affect the colonies. His views on the situation in India, where the process in question was most advanced, were quite clear. In his article 'The East India Company – Its History and Results' he described how the English cotton manufacturers gradually came to depend on the Indian market: until 1850 cotton sales in India accounted for a quarter of British cotton exports, and an eighth of total British exports of all kinds.[5]

---

3. *Capital* (Allen and Unwin, London 1949), Vol. I, Part VIII, especially chapters 26, 31 and 32. On the later significance of colonial rapacity for capitalism in the metropolis, see Avineri, op. cit., Introduction pp. 18–19.

4. ibid., *passim*, and especially section (iv).

5. ibid., pp. 99–108, and especially at pp. 106–7. This and some of the subsequent passages from Marx dealing with India have been commented on from a similar point of view by several other writers, and the connection with Marx's thoughts on Ireland is also specifically made by Foster-Carter (op. cit., see Preface, note 9, p. 71); see also M. Barratt-Brown, *Essays on Imperialism* (Spokesman Books, London 1972), pp. 63–7.

At this point, he said, they began to find that their sales stagnated and even declined because of the low purchasing power of the Indian population, and they also wanted to foster an alternative source of supply of raw cotton in India, to reduce their dependence on American production. They therefore sought to 'apply capital to India' (i.e. to invest there), but this brought them into conflict with the East India Company's 'moneyocracy' and 'oligarchy', who stood to lose by the changes which such investment would entail. The power of the Company was broken and the 'millocracy' were allowed to get on with 'the transformation of India into a reproductive country', and for this purpose 'to gift her with means of irrigation and internal communication.' 'They intend now drawing a net of rail-roads over India', Marx went on, 'And they will do it. The results must be inappreciable.'[6]

What Marx meant by 'inappreciable' was spelled out two pages further on:

> I know that the English millocracy intend to endow India with railways with the exclusive view of extracting at diminished expenses, the cotton and other raw materials for their manufactures. But when you have once introduced machinery into the locomotion of a country, which possesses iron and coals, you are unable to withhold it from its fabrication. You cannot maintain a net of railways over an immense country without introducing all those industrial processes necessary to meet the immediate and current wants of railway locomotion, and out of which there must grow the application of machinery to those branches of industry not immediately connected with railways. The railway system will therefore become, in India, truly the forerunner of modern industry. This is the more certain as the Hindoos are allowed by British authorities themselves to possess particular aptitude for accommodating themselves to entirely new labour, and acquiring the requisite knowledge of machinery.'[7]

It thus seems clear that in 1853, at least, Marx thought that a process of industrialization was bound to occur in India as a result of investment by British capitalists. This conclusion is only reinforced by his qualification that the process would not benefit the masses directly.

---

6. These quotations are from Marx's better-known article, 'The Future Results of British Rule in India', published three weeks after the article on the East India Company: Avineri, op. cit., p. 134.

7. ibid., p. 136.

All the English bourgeoisie may be forced to do will neither emancipate nor materially mend the social condition of the mass of the people, depending not only on the development of the reproductive powers, but of their appropriation by the people. But what they will not fail to do is to lay down the material premises for both. Has the bourgeoisie ever done more?

By 'reproductive powers' which the people must appropriate in order to emancipate themselves Marx could only mean industrial capacity. Even though he added that these things would happen 'at a more or less remote period', he made it clear that he had no doubt at all that they *would* come about, when he said 'we may safely expect to see . . . the regeneration of that great and interesting country' as a result.

This stands in almost complete contrast to the view of Paul Baran – who has good claims to be regarded as the most influential founder of contemporary 'underdevelopment theory' – for whom India was the classic example of a country which had been *prevented* from developing and regenerating: which experienced only the destruction of her traditional economy and society, and after that nothing but 'the chronic catastrophe of the last two centuries'. The reason for this, according to Baran, was that the capital accumulated in India was not invested there: 'there can be no doubt that had the amount of economic surplus that Britain has torn from India been *invested in India,* India's economic development to date would have borne little similarity to the actual somber record.'[8] Baran cited only two passages from Marx's writings on India, neither of them relevant to this central issue, which rather suggests that he thought Marx had simply been mistaken. But if Marx was mistaken in thinking that the forces which he thought were driving English capitalists to invest in India would lead to a cumulative cycle of further investment there, where exactly did the mistake lie?

The main reason, he says, why Western capitalists 'breaking into India, China, the countries of South East Asia, the Near East and Africa' did not generate a cumulative process of capitalist development there was that either they found 'established societies with rich and ancient cultures', or 'the general conditions and in particular the climate were such as to preclude any mass settlement of western European arrivals. . . . Consequently in both cases

---

8. Paul A. Baran, *The Political Economy of Growth* (Monthly Review Press, New York 1957), p. 148.

the Western European visitors rapidly determined to extract the largest possible gains from the host countries, and to take the loot home.'[9] The 'removal of a large share of the affected countries' previously accumulated and generated surplus' as a result of this motivation plays a central, if not *the* central part in Baran's thesis, and in the last analysis it seems to be the only thing which really divides him from Marx. He follows Marx in emphasizing the destruction of the traditional economies and societies by the wholesale seizure of land for capitalist production for exports, and the opening up of domestic markets to imported manufactures, and he also acknowledges that capitalism 'forced the diversion of some of their economic surplus to the improvement of their systems of communication, to the building of railroads, harbours and highways, providing thereby as a by-product the facilities needed for profitable production'. All this 'provided a powerful impetus to the development of capitalism', but 'this development was forcibly shunted off its normal course, distorted and crippled to suit the purposes of Western imperialism'.

In Baran's account these distortions have their source largely in the nature of the wealthy classes in the periphery countries which are able to survive from pre-colonial times, or which are created under colonial rule; they do not wish, are not able, or are not permitted to develop into autonomous bourgeoisies, developing the capitalist mode of production in their own countries. Instead they form, together with the educated salariat, part of the structure through which the transfer abroad of the bulk of the surplus is assured even after colonial rule is over.

In Baran's view, therefore, Marx's mistake would appear to have been a failure to think through the difference it made in the long run that the owners of the capital invested in India lived in England.

Against this it can be pointed out that Marx qualified his long-term optimism about India, remarking in one place that British rule there had been 'swinish', and suggesting later that the destructive effects – and hence obviously the subsequent constructive effects – of capitalism in India and China were not really as certain as his earlier articles on India had asserted, because of the resistance of the pre-capitalist modes of production it encountered there:

> To what extent [merchant capital] brings about a dissolution of the old mode of production depends on its solidity and

9. ibid., p. 142.

internal structure. And whither this process of dissolution will lead, in other words, what mode of production will replace the old, does not depend on commerce but on the character of the old mode of production itself. . . . The obstacles presented by the internal solidity and organization of precapitalistic, national modes of production to the corrosive influence of commerce are strikingly illustrated in the intercourse of the English with India and China.[10]

Moreover, in their analysis of the situation in Ireland ('the first English colony', 'artificially converted into an utterly impoverished nation'), Marx and Engels sketched a theory which at first sight seems rather inconsistent with the thesis of the articles on India. In Ireland, Marx wrote (this was in 1870),

the English bourgeoisie . . . has in the first place a common interest with the English aristocracy in turning Ireland into mere pasture land which provides the English market with meat and wool at the cheapest possible prices. It is equally interested in reducing . . . the Irish population to such a small number that *English capital* (capital invested in land leased for farming) can function there 'with security'. It has the same interest in *clearing the estate of Ireland* as it had in the clearing of the agricultural districts of England and Scotland . . .[11]

This contrasted rather sharply with the earlier articles on India, the English bourgeoisie were seen to be investing in India in order to sell to India: 'You cannot continue to inundate a country with your manufactures unless you enable it to give you some produce in return.' Marx did not explain why the motivation of the English bourgeoisie was apparently so different in the two cases, although there are many clues to what he probably thought, particularly in his consistent emphasis on Ireland as a source of cheap labour for English industry, driving down wages and keeping the proletariat divided and mystified by racialism; but it is evident that Marx's thinking about the impact of British capitalism on the rest of the world provided for a good deal of the complexity of real life, and that Baran's important emphasis on the part played in under-

---

10. *Capital* (Progress Publishers, Moscow 1966), Vol. III, pp. 332–3. Compare Marx's comment in a letter to Engels in 1853 that in his article on 'British Rule in India' 'the destruction of the native industry by England is described as *revolutionary* . . . As for the rest, the whole rule of Britain in India was swinish, and is to this day.' Marx–Engels, *Selected Correspondence* (Moscow 1953), p. 102.

11. Marx to S. Meyer and A. Vogt, 9 April 1870 (ibid., pp. 285–6).

development by surplus transfer need not necessarily be seen as involving a radical departure from Marx's ideas.

In fact we need not really doubt that if Marx had lived another twenty-five years he would himself have revised and synthesized his analyses of Ireland and India, and also of China and the Middle East, and would have produced the sort of underdevelopment theory towards which Marxists have been working in the last twenty years or so. The ingredients are largely there and, especially when his dominating concern with the proletarian revolution in Britain led him to see a revolution in Ireland as a prior condition for it, one sees that he could easily have knitted it all into a consistent theory if he had been concerned with the revolutionary possibilities of the colonies and semi-colonies themselves, rather than being interested in them primarily because of their significance for the prospects of revolution in the metropolis.[12]

The fact remains that he did not do this; he left a lot of loose ends, apparent inconsistencies and unanswered problems, and although he anticipated much that is now an essential part of underdevelopment theory – for instance the growth of monopoly capitalism – the world has not stood still, and the relationship of advanced capitalist countries with the ex-colonies has evolved in many ways. Underdevelopment theory is thus partly a correction and partly an expansion of Marx's interpretation of history, an extension of his method and central ideas to a problem which, in a world scale, was still in embryo at his death: the failure of the countries of Asia, Africa, and Latin America to follow a path of autonomous capitalist development, leading to their 'regeneration' after they had been brought within the capitalist world economy. Above all in this perspective the countries of the third world no longer figure as sources of primitive capital accumulation, or as outlets for surplus capital, or in any other way primarily as aspects of the history of Europe or North America. On the contrary, underdevelopment theory is – or should be – precisely a theory of *their* history, a theory of the contradictions in the development of their modes and relations of production under colonialism and imperialism, contradictions which are expressed today in the

---

12. His programme for Ireland set out in a letter to Engels in 1868 could hardly sound more contemporary: 'What the Irish need is (1) Self-government and independence from England (2) An agrarian revolution . . . (3) Protective tariffs against England. Between 1783 and 1801 every branch of Irish industry began to flourish. The Union which overthrew the protective tariffs established by the Irish Parliament, destroyed all industrial life in Ireland . . .' (ibid., p. 236).

growing polarization of these countries between authoritarianism on the one hand, and revolution on the other.

UNDERDEVELOPMENT THEORY IN OUTLINE[13]

The starting-point of underdevelopment theory is the period in which any given region of today's 'third world' began to be progressively incorporated into a permanent relationship with the expanding capitalist economy. Sometimes the initial relationship was largely one of simple plunder and extortion, though generally represented as trade (as in the case of the slave 'trade'). But even where the trade rested only on exchange the essence of it was that it was conducted on very unequal terms, mainly because it was backed up by superior force on the side of the capitalist 'traders'. The 'profits' formed part of the original or primitive accumulation

---

13. A bibliography on the questions raised in this section would now fill a book; and as I have in no way tried to reproduce the work of particular writers, so as to reflect their emphases and qualifications, but only to sketch a coherent outline of what seems to be common ground for most of them, it would be inappropriate to cite them in detail. My main original debts, however, were: Paul A. Baran, *The Political Economy of Growth* (Monthly Review Press, New York 1957); Andre Gunder Frank, *Capitalism and Underdevelopment in Latin America* (Monthly Review Press, New York 1969); Michael Barratt-Brown, *After Imperialism* (Heinemann, London 1963); Hamza Alavi, 'Imperialism Old and New' (*Socialist Register* 1964, pp. 104–26); Jitendra Mohan, 'Varieties of African Socialism' (*Socialist Register* 1966, pp. 220–26); the work of Giovanni Arrighi and John S. Saul, now collected in their *The Political Economy of Africa* (op. cit., see Preface, note 10); Samir Amin, 'The Class Struggle in Africa', first published in *Revolution*, Vol. I, No. 9, January 1964, pp. 23–47, and 'The Development of Capitalism in Black Africa', *L'Homme et la Société*, No. 6, 1967, pp. 107–19; and several of the papers included in R. I. Rhodes (ed.), *Underdevelopment and Revolution* (op. cit., see Preface, note 10). Of the more recent contributions which have influenced some other parts of this book, though on the whole not this chapter, I would particularly mention Tamas Szentes, *The Political Economy of Underdevelopment* (Akademiai Kiado, Budapest 1971); Charles Bettelheim's Appendix I to Arghiri Emmanuel, *Unequal Exchange* (New Left Review Editions, London 1972), pp. 271–322; Ernesto Laclau, 'Capitalism and Feudalism in Latin America' (*New Left Review*, 67, May–June 1971, pp. 19–38); Pierre-Philippe Rey, *Colonialisme, neo-colonialisme et transition au capitalisme* (Maspero, Paris 1971), and the same author's *Les alliances de classes* (Maspero, Paris 1973). Unless one can read Spanish and Portuguese much of the work of the 'dependency' school is still inaccessible, although its much greater emphasis on the industrialization which takes place in underdeveloped countries has begun to have a salutary effect in correcting some of the more deterministic versions of the underdevelopment thesis. A useful review is P. O'Brien, 'A Critique of Latin American Theories of Dependency' (Institute of Latin American Studies, University of Glasgow, March 1973, mimeo). A recent challenge to some received ideas of underdevelopment theory is Bill Warren, 'Imperialism and Capitalist Industrialisation' (*New Left Review*, 81, September–October 1973, pp. 3–44).

of capital in Europe, which was necessary before capitalist accumulation based on wage labour could occur. Later, and in some cases from very early on, trade was supplemented by investment (for example in gold-mining or plantations), which needed to be reinforced by direct rule, or colonialism, so as to make possible the enforcement of contracts, protection of title to property, forced labour, and so on.

The main effects were the same, with or without direct rule: first, the extraction of the surplus of the 'periphery' countries – that is, what is produced over and above what is needed for the peoples' subsistence and for maintaining their stock of productive equipment – for use in the metropolitan countries;[14] and second, the emergence of new relations of production in the periphery countries, based on their progressive exposure to, and domination by, capitalism. In particular, new social strata and ultimately social classes were either brought in (through colonial settlement), or created from among the indigenous population, which had an interest in organizing and facilitating the new economic activities involved (trade, mining, crop production, and so on). In the course of time these strata or classes became powerful enough to render direct rule by the metropolitan power unnecessary. Moreover, as primitive accumulation gave way to capitalist accumulation (in which the apparently 'natural' forces of the market for labour are sufficient to ensure that the surplus is appropriated by the capitalist), the need for the continuous and overt use of force by the government to back up the process of accumulation declined.[15] This facilitated the replacement of direct colonial administration by 'independent' governments representing local strata and classes with an interest in sustaining the colonial economic relationships. To the extent that the state in the metropolitan countries was a

---

14. The concept of 'surplus' used here and generally by underdevelopment theorists is due to Baran, and corresponds to what he calls 'actual surplus', 'the difference between society's *actual* current output and its actual current consumption' (op. cit., p. 22). Elsewhere his concept of 'potential surplus' – 'the difference between the output that *could* be produced in a given natural and technological environment with the help of employable productive resources, and what might be regarded as essential consumption' (p. 23) becomes theoretically important also. As Baran notes, these are 'macro' concepts, and neither is uniquely related to Marx's concept of surplus value.

15. Referring to primitive accumulation in Europe, Marx wrote that it was 'nothing else than the historical process of divorcing the producer from the means of production. It appears as primitive, because it forms the prehistoric stage of capital and of the mode of production corresponding with it.' (*Capital*, Vol. I, p. 738.)

'committee for managing the common affairs of the whole bourgeoisie', the state which emerged in the periphery country was a sort of sub-committee. The social strata which the neo-colonial state represented were dubbed by the Chinese Marxists 'comprador elements' after the cadre of professional inter-mediaries who dealt with the foreign trading houses in the coastal enclaves.

As Baran insisted, the fact that in most cases it was a largely foreign bourgeoisie which appropriated the surplus did make a decisive difference to what followed. Whereas in the metropolitan countries the bourgeoisie either consumed or invested their profits there, generating additional demand and further investment, in the periphery countries this was not the case. Such local demand as was generated locally was also largely satisfied by imports from the metropolitan countries, so that this also failed to stimulate secondary investment. The result was not complete stagnation, but growth largely confined to the sector or sectors producing primary products for export. The economies of the periphery acquired their well-known 'external orientation', with very weak links between the different domestic sectors, and very strong links between the primary-producing sectors and overseas markets and suppliers.

From the first, there was a further fundamental difference between the operation of capitalism at the periphery and its operation in the metropolitan countries, namely its monopolistic character; or rather, whereas industrial capitalism in the European metropolitan countries embarked on its most rapid period of ex-pansion and became the dominant mode of production under con-ditions of relatively free competition among capitalists, this did not occur at the periphery. This is very important for explaining why such economic surplus as is retained locally continues to have so little effect in generating domestic development after capital be-gins to be invested locally. For there are several ways in which local people can expect to appropriate *some* surplus in the condi-tions of 'periphery capitalism': for instance as local employers of labour, especially rich peasants, who appropriate surplus value from their workers; as local peasant producers who own their means of production and generate a surplus with them; local middlemen of various kinds; and so on. In many periphery coun-tries such activities soon accounted for a substantial part of the money economy, which meant that a significant part of the surplus was locally appropriated, and might therefore have been expected to give rise to a corresponding growth of internal demand and domestic investment, even though on a scale reduced by the share of the surplus which was appropriated and expatriated by foreigners. The reason why this happened only to a very limited extent was the presence of monopoly elements in the relationship between the metropolis and the periphery (the word 'monopoly' is used here broadly, to refer to more or less exclusive control over resources or markets and the prevention of free competition).[16]

To begin with there was the imperial monopoly of force. Later, the colonial powers created legal monopolies such as monopolies in the purchase and export of primary products, in the importation and distribution of consumer goods, in the provision of shipping for exports and imports, in the collection of savings and the provision of credit, in the use of wage labour, and in many other things. The effect of all these monopolies was to permit indigenous employers, traders, and so on, to appropriate a share of the surplus only by increasing the exploitation of the workers or the peasants, which was not always possible; and to leave the peasant producer with little or no surplus.[17] With the end of colonial rule some or all of these monopolies came to an end, but by then their place had been taken by new forms of monopoly which were less 'primitive' (in Marx's sense) and less vulnerable to mere political change.

These are of two main kinds, corresponding to two stages of the 'development of underdevelopment'; monopoly in international commodity markets, and monopoly in industrial technology. Both of them are due to the past accumulation of capital in the metropolitan countries and the export of capital from the periphery countries, which taken together have conferred on the former a cumulative advantage in bargaining power. In relation to commodity markets, it takes the form of superior information and know-how, a limited number of actual buyers (who increasingly control the wholesale and retail outlets as well), and a general ability to deploy capital in the manipulation of stocks. It also takes

---

16. While the concept of monopoly used here is close to Lenin's in his *Imperialism, the Highest Stage of Capitalism*, the historical phenomenon referred to is not identical. Lenin's attention was fixed on the large combines, trusts, etc., which arose from the process of concentration in industrialized capitalist states. At the periphery monopoly was a cardinal feature of capitalism from the outset, though the actual amounts of capital involved, and the size of the concerns, could be very small.

17. The discussion of the successive historical forms of monopoly in Chile is one of the most persuasive and suggestive parts of Andre Gunder Frank's statement of a general theory of underdevelopment in *Capitalism and Underdevelopment in Latin America* (op. cit., note 13), Part I.

the form of a technological capacity to find substitutes for the products of tropical agriculture, which has kept down the prices of many of them in spite of growing demand.[18] In relation to industrial technology, it takes the form of know-how, embodied in machinery for mass production, based on constant innovation in product lines and the constantly accelerating technological change which this both requires and makes possible.

Both forms of monopoly *could* in principle be broken, or the advantage they conferred on the metropolitan countries could be greatly reduced, by the pursuit of deliberate counter-strategies on the part of the periphery countries; to take the most obvious examples, by combination among commodity producers, such as the Organization of Petroleum Exporting Countries (OPEC), or by conscious disengagement from dependence on imported industrial technology, and reliance on much simpler, home-made technology, such as that symbolized by China's communal steel foundries in the Great Leap period of 1958–61. But these theoretical alternatives are likely to be pursued only in rather special circumstances of the sort which in fact produced OPEC, or by revolutionary regimes such as China's;[19] and that the 'comprador elements' which were produced in the periphery countries under colonialism, and which subsequently acquired a large measure of

---

18. This does not imply that there has been a deterioration of the terms of trade for underdeveloped countries arising from this cause; recent work suggests that there has in fact been no long-term deterioration of the terms of trade of Africa, Asia and Latin America (cf. Angus Hone, 'The Primary Commodities Boom', *New Left Review*, 81, September–October 1973, pp. 90–92). But there is little doubt that some commodities, including sisal and cotton, would have fetched higher prices but for synthetic substitutes.

19. Hone (loc. cit., note 18) concludes: '. . . in the future the terms of trade could well be improved for the developing countries should they make use of the considerable opportunities for "producer-based" agreements on production and export targets. Usually these are only successful if a small number of producers are developed and are difficult to administer if developed economies control a large share of production. But the International Tin and Olive Oil Agreements have worked successfully for more than 10 years and there could well be producers' agreements for jute, copper, pepper, natural rubber, palm oil and coconut oil.' But the spectacular rise in commodity prices, and especially the rise in oil prices secured by the Arab governments in 1973, should not be allowed to obscure the real difficulties which producers of other commodities confront in raising prices by agreements. Nor should we forget that some underdeveloped countries, including some of the largest, may well lose rather than gain from such price changes, especially if they are major oil users; or that the gains from improved commodity prices are not necessarily enjoyed by the mass of the people in the 'gaining' countries. This depends on the way production and sale is organized, and on the nature of the regimes in power.

political power, generally play an integral part in maintaining the existing patterns of trade and industrial dependency. All governments of periphery countries would of course prefer better terms of trade and less dependence on foreign technology, but in most cases the social strata and classes which they represent have not been willing to make the sacrifices which a serious attack on these patterns would imply. It is artificial to point to the existence of theoretical alternatives, without recognizing that the *status quo* is underwritten by the social classes which underdevelopment has created and brought to power in the periphery countries.

The metropolitan countries' monopoly of industrial technology assumes critical importance only when industrial production begins to be undertaken in the periphery countries. This has taken place for different reasons, according to time and place, for instance during periods of depression in the metropolitan countries, leading to a severe drop in the demand for primary products, or during major wars, when domestic demand for manufactured goods in the periphery could not be supplied from the metropolis; but above all, as a result of political independence under nationalist leadership at the periphery, leading to a demand for industrialization. Previously industrialization was mainly limited to processes necessary for the export of commodities, or to making products for domestic use which enjoyed 'natural protection' because they were bulky. But with the adoption of import-substitution policies by means of protection the stage appears set for a progressive sequence of industrial investment, which should in due course become self-sustaining and lead to full-scale industrialization. But in most cases the results have been disappointing. The reasons for this are seen to be (*a*) the existing pattern of demand; (*b*) the ownership and monopoly character of the investment; and (*c*) the technology resulting from both (*a*) and (*b*) above.

(*a*) The existing pattern of demand is heavily influenced by the fact that local income distribution is skewed towards a small, partly expatriate section of the population. Often the total population is so small (within the national boundaries drawn by rival imperial powers) that even if it were wealthy it could not absorb enough of any sophisticated product to justify local production on an economic scale; in fact, incomes being extremely low, markets are even smaller; and being highly unequal, markets are smaller still. Yet these are the markets there are; the mass of the population is able to afford only a very few of the cheapest products of modern industry. The opportunities for profitable investment, therefore, even with high levels of protection, tend to be very narrow; investment can often only be made profitable if a single plant is given a monopoly of the market, so that for this reason alone the industrial sector which emerges tends to be monopolistic in character from the outset.[20] Moreover, the nature of the product is frequently such that a high proportion of the inputs used in production must be imported. This means that the 'external orientation' of the economy tends to be reproduced in the industrial field: the 'backward linkages' of the new industrial investment are largely with overseas suppliers, not domestic ones.

(b) The new investment is largely undertaken by foreign capital; and moreover by foreign capital in the age of the international corporations, which represent the culmination of the process of concentration in the advanced capitalist countries which Marx foresaw and Hilferding recorded. These are the organizations which have developed the sophisticated technology required for supplying mass markets (of which the high-consumption sectors of the population of the periphery countries form a part). Import-substitution – in the literal sense of producing domestically the same products which have formerly been imported – means in practice that these organizations set up highly protected subsidiary factories to manufacture in the periphery what they formerly exported there. These organizations also tend to be vertically integrated: they produce the goods needed for each stage of production, from processing raw materials to packing the final product. Even when an input might be produced locally, it often pays firms of this type to import it, partly because the extra cost of producing the small quantity needed for production in a subsidiary overseas after they have supplied the needs of their main factories will be very small, and partly because importing their own products provides opportunities for internal pricing policies which enable them to take their profits at whatever point in the total 'stream' of supply is most advantageous to them. Apart from the fact that this reinforces the 'external orientation' of the new industrial sector, preventing it from stimulating a cumulative process of domestic investment, the expatriation of surplus becomes a leading characteristic of the industrial sector in all its

20. This obvious but important point, and some of those which follow, have been developed by Meir Merhav in *Technological Dependence, Monopoly and Growth* (Pergamon Press, London 1969).

aspects.[21] What is more, because of the political risk of nationalization, or more generally of instability, high profit-levels are sought;
and because the periphery countries are competing for the investment, they mostly have to accept this.

(c) What has been said so far brings out only indirectly the critical
importance of technology, and the metropolitan countries' monopoly of it. One of the reasons why foreign firms, rather than local
entrepreneurs, tend to dominate the industrialization process at
the periphery is that they have the know-how and the capital
which are required: technology embodied in machinery, and resources to supply it. Their employment of this technology, developed for advanced industrialized countries, means that the
new manufacturing sector is capital-intensive; it does not generate
large increases in employment but leads to the creation of a
relatively small, semi-skilled labour force that is paid high wages
(in relation to the incomes of the mass of the population) in order
to reduce labour turnover and secure compliance with management needs. This also limits the impact of industrialization on
domestic demand, and tends to reinforce the existing demand for
relatively sophisticated consumer goods with a relatively high
import content.

In most African countries, the absence of an established landlord class, or of other elements in the indigenous population with
capital accumulated from other forms of economic activity, tended
to leave no alternative but industrialization through the agency of
foreign firms. But in Asia and Latin America the accumulation of
wealth from agriculture by a landlord class, or from trade by a
local merchant class, meant that the creation of an indigenous
industrial bourgeoisie was not ruled out. Various reasons, all more
or less valid in one situation or another, have been advanced for
the comparative failure of such a class to fulfil its classic role as the
leader of an autonomous industrial revolution. The experience of
much of Latin America, where a substantial indigenous bourgeoisie exists, but where the goal of an autonomous capitalist
development has continued to elude policy-makers, has led to the
variant of underdevelopment theory which accounts for this in
terms of the central concept of 'dependency'. Technological

---

21. For an early survey of the mechanisms used by international firms in India see
Hamza Alavi, 'Imperialism Old and New' (op. cit., note 13); further documented
in Michael Kidron, *Foreign Investments in India* (Oxford University Press, London
1965).

dependency plays a central part in this analysis. In its barest essentials the point is that, given the existing pattern of local demand, a local capitalist class at the periphery, even with ample help from the state, cannot enter the industrial field without using technology developed in the industrialized countries. This technology is owned by private foreign companies; it can be bought, at a price (in terms of royalties, commissions, management contracts, and so on). But as it is being constantly revolutionized in its countries of origin, it must be constantly bought again; in effect it has to be hired. The costs of this process are not negligible. They can easily exceed net profits. It follows that the price-levels of the new industries established in the periphery on this basis must reflect these payments, which further restricts their markets. In the meantime, dependence on imported technology also tends to entail imported inputs, almost as much as if the investment were made by foreigners.[22]

Only two lines of escape from this ultimate dependency on the metropolitan monopoly of technology appear to exist. One is to reproduce the metropolitan countries' capacity to make technological innovation (that is, roughly, the Japanese path), basing industrial strategy from the start on breaking into the international market for manufactured products. It is very doubtful if this option now exists for the great majority of underdeveloped countries. The other is to opt for a much simpler 'home-made' technology, manufacturing purely for the domestic market, or the markets of other underdeveloped countries with like-minded regimes. This strategy, however, requires a different pattern of demand: mass markets for less sophisticated goods, which in turn could only be based on a very different class structure and a different kind of political leadership. In other words it implies radical social changes at the periphery.

But the process of underdevelopment does not suggest that such changes are likely to occur in an evolutionary fashion. By the 1960s in Africa, and much earlier in Latin America and most of Asia, new social strata – embryonic classes or parts of classes – corresponding to the phase of import-substituting industrialization, had emerged alongside those already formed around the

---

22. Not quite as much, because a local entrepreneur may not wish to take advantage of the opportunity provided by importing inputs to transfer capital overseas, and in any case he will have to do it by 'over-invoicing' with the connivance of his supplier, which is not always as easy or cheap as an internal accounting operation within a single firm.

exporting and trading sectors. In particular, various petty bourgeois strata providing services to industry; in some countries, a local industrial bourgeoisie, usually however playing a subordinate role in partnership with foreign capital; industrial workers; an expanded state economic bureaucracy, concerned both with the general management of the economy and with particular industrial sectors involving state participation; indigenous managers of the local subsidiaries of international companies. Only one of these new strata, the industrial work-force, had any more interest in a major redistribution of purchasing power than any of the older elements represented by the 'comprador administrations' which were in power. The industrial wage-workers, however, were spread over a very wide range of skills, working conditions and wage levels, which together with high rates of unemployment made them organizationally weak. Where a radical union leadership emerged it was rarely strong enough to withstand co-optation by management or the government, often coupled with repression. All the other new elements in the configuration of political forces have individually privileged positions within the status quo, which a radical change would be likely to jeopardize.

Consequently, the line of escape from technological dependency through a re-orientation of production based on a radical redistribution of purchasing power has rarely been contemplated, let alone actually pursued. Instead metropolitan capitalism has had no difficulty in establishing relationships with the new groups or classes which appeared on the scene in the industrialization phase. A new process of social and political integration takes place between domestic interests and foreign capital, at various levels; the incorporation of local personnel into executive jobs in foreign firms, the financing of local politicians by foreign firms, the provision of custom and agencies for local small businessmen, the supply of 'technical assistance' and especially economic advice by capitalist governments, the provision of carefully designed capital aid, military assistance, and so on, all of which progressively articulate the periphery with the centre, and strengthen the position of the 'comprador' regimes.

In short, the phase of industrialization at the periphery of the capitalist system does not lead to an autonomous process of capitalist development, but to a further consolidation of underdevelopment. The population of the towns increases, but urban employment does not keep pace with it. *Per capita* incomes barely rise, the gap between them and *per capita* incomes in the metropolitan countries grows wider, and income distribution inside the underdeveloped countries remains so unequal that the real incomes of the majority may well decline. Although industrialization usually proceeds under the banner of import substitution, the import bill rises and the surplus flows abroad through new channels. In the end, all that has happened is that a new industrial 'enclave' has been established in the economy, but without any tendency to set in motion a chain-reaction of investment and employment which will eventually make it burst out of the enclave and transform the economy as a whole. On the contrary, the society has been 'locked into' its subordinate role in the international capitalist system by new means.[23]

SOME LIMITATIONS OF UNDERDEVELOPMENT THEORY

At least this is the conclusion which might seem to follow from what has been said so far, which is (I think) not unfaithful to a large part of the 'underdevelopment' literature. Yet it is a curiously static conclusion, and seems to depend rather mechanically and one-sidedly on a combination of primarily economic factors, some of which seem to some extent contingent, and capable of being at least partly mitigated, in conditions which it is quite possible to imagine; altogether a strange outcome for a body of theory to which Marxism has contributed so much, and therefore a useful point at which to consider some of the limitations of 'underdevelopment theory' which are responsible for this sort of result.

First of all, it does tend, especially in its rather mechanistic versions, to go beyond suggesting reasons why many third world countries have not 'developed' (in the ways expected and hoped for by the 'developmentalists') to seeming to offer a *model*, and hence a theory, of the actual path of third world development – 'underdevelopment' – which is a far more ambitious and difficult task. As Warren has noted, a latent 'stagnation' thesis does often seem implicit in underdevelopment theory, although neither the

---

23. Some underdeveloped countries, or rather their capital cities or main ports, may also serve as staging points in the chain of exploitation, drawing in surplus from neighbouring countries while themselves being in turn exploited by more distant metropolitan centres; this idea of a chain of exploitation stretching from the rural hinterlands of the most backward colonies or semi-colonies through such 'periphery centres' to the metropolitan capitals was well captured by Frank's metaphor of 'satellitization' in his *Capitalism and Underdevelopment in Latin America* (op. cit., note 13). Nairobi and Mombasa constitute a case in point.

theoretical achievements of this literature, nor the facts of the modern history of the third world generally really make this plausible.[24] Underdevelopment theory does suggest reasons why, in many third world countries, capitalist development has not followed and will not follow the same sort of course, or with similar social and political consequences, as it did in the advanced metropolitan countries; but it does not show that no capitalist development can occur in them at all, or even that no country in today's 'third world' can ever become in some sense an 'advanced' capitalist country, pursuing as 'autonomous' a path of capitalist development as many countries which are today regarded as 'advanced' and relatively autonomous capitalist countries.[25] Underdevelopment theory simply does not furnish convincing grounds for such a claim, and this should not be seen as its thesis. What it does is only to try to explain the actual patterns of development – capitalist development of a kind – which have occurred and are occurring throughout most of the third world. As I have already suggested, it is a weakness of the term 'underdevelopment' that it does refer to so many different stages and forms of development, although this should not be made a pretext for ignoring the force of either its general perspective, or the particular analyses which it puts forward.

A closely related point is that the orientation of underdevelopment theory towards capitalism itself is sometimes ambiguous. This is more obviously true of 'dependency theory' than of 'underdevelopment theory'; as O'Brien aptly remarks:

> Sunkel and Furtado are perhaps more squarely [than Dos Santos or Cardoso, whom he takes as the other two leading representatives of dependency theory] in the reformist ECLA tradition which wants national development without the class struggle and independence without revolution. Much writing on dependency seems to leave one with the vision of the desirability of an anti-imperialist, populist leader uniting his people under a technocratic State.[26]

---

24. Bill Warren, 'Imperialism and Capitalist Industrialisation' (op. cit., note 13).

25. Warren is also correct, I think, in detecting a straw man in the notion of 'autonomous' or 'independent' capitalist development which some underdevelopment theorists hold to be impossible for the countries of the capitalist periphery.

26. P. O'Brien, 'A Critique of Latin American Theories of Dependency' (op. cit., note 13), p. 15; Andre Gunder Frank suggests where this leads in his critique of Furtado in 'The Brazilian Pre-Revolution of Celso Furtado' (*Latin America: Underdevelopment or Revolution*, op. cit., see Preface, note 12), pp. 333–9; and in his attack

Underdevelopment theorists, by contrast, see capitalism as being unlikely to be capable of providing the masses of the third world with the basic necessities and decencies of life in any foreseeable future, and are generally committed to the view that a revolutionary socialist alternative is necessary. But the latter position cannot be deduced from the former and, in any case, what is meant by 'necessary' here? The most serious limitation of underdevelopment theory seems to me to concern precisely this point.

One way of seeing this is to note the heavily economistic character of most underdevelopment theory. Social classes play an important part in it, yet rather abstractly and passively, not as protagonists in intensifying struggles providing its central dynamic. Political power, control of the state, is also seen to be important, but again somewhat abstractly, not as a pervasive dimension of the struggles between classes and of the structures of oppression which permit one class to exploit another, and which indeed are bound up with the very formation and development of classes. Imperialism features in underdevelopment theory too, of course, but once more, in a rather disembodied form (a clue to this is provided by the frequently-used expression 'economic imperialism'): the real contemporary history of the third world, the familiar grand strategies formulated with regard to it and carried out by the leading industrial powers – global systems of military alliances, continent-wide programmes of civil and military 'reconstruction', regional schemes of 'institution-building' and active patterns of bilateral diplomacy and intervention on behalf of compliant regimes and forces, and against revolutionary ones – all this tends to be treated in underdevelopment theory as part of the supplementary context, rather than as central. The significance of all this is that in one critical respect underdevelopment theory tends to resemble 'development theory' – it concentrates on what happens *to* the underdeveloped countries at the hands of imperialism and colonialism, rather than on the total historical process involved, including the various forms of struggle against imperialism and colonialism which grow out of the conditions of underdevelopment. It is striking, in fact, that in so much of the literature on underdevelopment comparatively little attention is still paid to the countries which have actually succeeded in snap-

---

on Helio Jaguaribe in *Lumpenbourgeoisie: Lumpendevelopment* (Monthly Review Press, New York 1972), Ch. 9.

ping the ties of dependency and beginning to liquidate the legacy of underdevelopment – notably China and Cuba;[27] and when we consider the process through which this was actually accomplished, a process of struggle culminating in armed struggle, we are reminded of how 'passive' the perspective of underdevelopment can easily become. The way of China and Cuba (or of the liberation movements in Africa) may not be the only way, but it is clearly much too important a way not to occupy a central place in any view of underdevelopment which is seriously committed to ending it. And what about other ways? To put the matter simply: what is needed is not a theory of underdevelopment but a theory of underdevelopment and its liquidation.

But a theory of this kind implies nothing less than a theory of world history from the standpoint of the underdeveloped countries, a theory of the oppression and liberation of these countries; something not only very far beyond the scope of this chapter, but still in a fairly rudimentary stage of development, however keenly the need for it may be felt by anyone who approaches the problems of a particular underdeveloped country with these questions in mind. The case-study in this book is limited by (among other things) the limitations of underdevelopment theory as it actually exists.

SOME OBJECTIONS

In spite of these limitations, the evident, even if vague, revolutionary implications of underdevelopment theory seem to account for a good deal of the resistance to it among 'developmentalists'. The impulse behind the vast programme of practical and academic activity involved in the business of 'development' is essentially liberal, democratic and generous. It is painful for anyone who has been involved in it to entertain the possibility that this whole programme may have functioned primarily to help

---

27. It seems to me that this is one respect in which Foster-Carter's notion of 'Neo-Marxism' conflates what are in fact rather distinct streams of thought. He writes that 'Neo-Marxism as an academic phenomenon is largely a response to the way in which people like Mao and Ho have changed the world – and also to the concomitant failure to change the world of other people, such as Rostow', op. cit., (Preface, note 9, p. 8). I think that underdevelopment theory might well be defined as primarily a response to the latter rather than the former stimulus, and that those who have been most affected by the examples of China or North Vietnam are by and large not particularly concerned with underdevelopment.

make the subordination of the third world to metropolitan capitalism more palatable and permanent. One reaction to this unhappiness is to caricature underdevelopment theorists as 'advocates' of revolution (as if revolutions had ever resulted from advocacy) and even as wishing to see the masses of the third world suffer more, in order to make them more revolutionary. They are accused of lacking humility, with the apparent implication that it is more humble to advocate only measures which are consistent with the existing system in general.[28]

A more substantial kind of objection, however, is directed towards the nature of the 'revolutionary break' which underdevelopment theory implies. Some critics appear to think it impossible even to imagine a socialist alternative for the periphery countries, as if the various revolutions that are in progress in various parts of the third world, and those which may be attempted in the future, can be known in advance to be doomed to failure. Others, without claiming clairvoyance, none the less see difficulties which it is worth while briefly exploring. These fall into three main categories.

First, it is pointed out that in many countries revolutionary attempts to break away from the capitalist system have failed, and that the practical difficulties involved are in all cases immense. There is the hostility of the metropolitan powers when their nations' capital is appropriated and debts are repudiated, the hostility of comprador groups or classes, the unsuitability of the civil-service structure and the bourgeois outlook and class-interest of civil servants, the lack of solidarity among wage-workers, the limited education of the peasantry, the shortage of revolutionary cadres, the continuing dependence on metropolitan markets, the impossibility of dramatic or early improvements in living standards, and so on: in short, all the social and economic consequences of underdevelopment which operate in a vicious circle to keep the country locked into its place in the capitalist periphery or pull it back there against all efforts to extract it. To all this underdevelopment theory can make no reply, except to point out that only people who are not hungry, sick, hopeless, or despised could imagine that it is anything more than a statement of what

---

28. See Gustav F. Papanek, 'Development Planners, Ethics and Objectives', in the *Bulletin* of the Institute of Development Studies, Vol. 2, No. 2, January 1971, at p. 34, and Dudley Seers, 'What types of government should be refused what types of aid?' in the *Bulletin*, Vol. 4, Nos. 2/3, June 1972, pp. 6–15. See also the reply to Seers by T. J. Byres in the same issue.

must be overcome in order that underdevelopment may be abolished.[29]

Secondly, there is a more explicitly normative objection that a revolutionary break with capitalism will involve bloodshed and suffering and will call for a large degree of enforced collectivism in return for what may be a faint chance of success. The probable social cost of revolution, in other words, is held to be higher than that of underdevelopment. This, however, is a matter of judgement, and it is easy for people who are secure and affluent to judge wrongly.[30] It is an old argument, and Hinton, writing on the Chinese revolution, did well to recall Mark Twain's comment on those who pitied the plumage but forgot the dying bird in the French Revolution; there were, he said, two terrors to be borne in mind, not just one:

> ... the one lasted mere months, the other a thousand years ... a city cemetery could contain the coffins filled by the brief terror which we have all been so diligently taught to shiver and mourn over; but all France could hardly contain the coffins filled by the older and real Terror – that unspeakably bitter and awful terror which none of us has been taught to see in its vastness or pity as it deserves.[31]

Yet the argument is really beside the point. Revolutionary situations are not created by intellectual analyses. 'Comprador regimes' are apt to be authoritarian; the real offence of underdevelopment theory is probably that it points this out and at the same time undermines the faith in the efficacy of capitalism at the

---

29. Moreover although such obstacles have in places proved serious and even decisive, in other places they have proved much less absolute and decisive than many people expected. To see them as absolute, rather than relative and capable of being reduced and overcome in the course of time, seems to express a political commitment rather than a lesson of history.

30. Radical middle-class intellectuals are apt to be criticized by conservative middle-class intellectuals for being officious, sentimental and paternalistic in their judgements on these matters, as if it were obvious that conservative middle-class intellectuals were never insensitive, indifferent or cynical. The operative principle seems to be an implied demand for class solidarity. There is no doubt a great deal of guilt underlying the work of many middle-class radical intellectuals. A shrewd colleague suggested that both the 'development' theorists of the late 1950s and early 1960s and the 'underdevelopment' theorists of the late 1960s and early 1970s have been driven by essentially the same guilt-ridden motives, and indeed may occasionally be the same people – for instance myself. This seems very likely; but exactly what should be inferred from it is less clear.

31. Quoted in William Hinton, *Fanshen* (Vintage Books, New York 1968), p. 101.

periphery which plays such an important part in the protective ideology of such regimes.

Thirdly, it is observed that the idea of a revolutionary break with the international capitalist system implies, for many countries, a decision to curtail drastically their imports of advanced manufacturing technology and hence really to give up the goal of ultimately competing in the mass markets of the advanced industrial countries. To many people this seems defeatist, yet we have to ask: is there a real alternative? There are many reasons for doubting whether the process of 'international decentralisation by the big industrial groups' will lead to continuing and sustained all-round growth even in the limited parts of the third world in which it has been a source of rapid industrial expansion in recent years;[32] even if it did, it is very doubtful if the advanced industrial countries would open their markets fully to competition from the underdeveloped countries which were in a position to offer it. In fact, with the exception of certain countries which are partly integrated into the United States economy for political reasons (Puerto Rico, the Philippines, Taiwan, South Korea) the vision of 'catching up' with the advanced industrial nations has proved to be an ever-receding mirage, as the gap has grown steadily wider; and this links the issue with the increasingly severe problem of finite world resources. One does not have to be a prophet of doom to see that the idea that the whole planet will one day produce and consume at the rate of the USA today – let alone at the rate the USA will then have reached – is nonsense. The real alternatives for an underdeveloped country may indeed be either to play a very subordinate role in the international capitalist system, with little benefit to the majority of its people, or to seek an independent role in an alternative system of poorer but non-capitalist countries, a role which promises less, but might be more capable of fulfilling its promise.

The sort of objections we have been considering are less important in themselves, than in the fact that they often constitute the real but unspoken force behind other, more substantial criticisms, which seem to concern purely issues of logic and proof. As subsequent chapters pursue, in effect, the question whether underdevelopment theory 'works' in a specific historical

---

32. The expression is from Celso Furtado, *Economic Development of Latin America* (Cambridge University Press, Cambridge 1970), p. 252, who none the less sees the goal of development for Latin America as consisting in completing the transition to being major exporters of manufactures.

context, this is a point worth keeping in mind. Tom Kemp's remarks about the objections raised against Marxist theories of imperialism are apposite:

> Evidence is always subject to varying appraisals and in this field no one sheds his pre-suppositions, or even prejudices, all protestations to the contrary [notwithstanding]. In the tangled network of social actions the sequence of cause and effect which seems clear to one observer may simply not exist for another. It must be recognised, also, that a strong reluctance exists, or is built up, in capitalist society to the ideas and conclusions which are comprised in the Marxist theory of imperialism, as in Marxism as a whole . . .
>
> However prone many of the epigones [of Marx and Lenin] may have been to dogma and oversimplification, the fact that their opponents had nothing better to offer than contrary dogmas and assumptions must not be overlooked. How else can one explain the readiness with which serious historians and others accept that somehow it was the demonic forces of 'democracy', or the will of statesmen, or the soap-box ravings of fire-eating propagandists which were the driving forces in arms races, wars, empire-building and other aspects of 'imperialism'? How can they 'prove' these assertions? In fact they offer no proof . . .[33]

The case is the same with underdevelopment theory. Many of the objections raised against it will not be overcome by argument or by the presentation of evidence. They spring from a deep attachment to the ideology of 'development' and they will go into the 'museum of antiquities' only as a result of radical changes in the periphery countries.

NEO-COLONIALISM

Of all the real deficiencies of underdevelopment theory the most troublesome for the purpose of this particular study was the substantial absence of a systematic theory of the state or of the nature of politics in conditions of underdevelopment. Some observations are offered on this point in Chapter 7, but it seems desirable to try to clarify one general point at the outset, namely the way the term 'neo-colonialism' is used in this book.

---

33. Tom Kemp, *Theories of Imperialism* (Dobson, London 1967), p. 163.

The term came into general use in Africa when the humiliating limitations of formal independence began to be widely understood by African nationalists around the year 1960, Africa's 'year of independence'. It was the subject of a very clear and fairly lengthy resolution at the All-African People's Conference held in Cairo in 1961, which defined it as 'the survival of the colonial system in spite of the formal recognition of political independence in emerging countries which become the victims of an indirect and subtle form of domination by political, economic, social, military or technical means'.[34] The term is the central concept of books by Nkrumah and Woddis, neither of whom depart substantially from the definition adopted at Cairo, and I have no wish to do so either.[35] However there are some points which do need to be briefly clarified.

First, for obvious reasons neither the All-African People's Conference nor Nkrumah (whose book appeared in 1965) mention, let alone analyse, what the outsider, especially with the advantage of hindsight, sees to be absolutely central to neo-colonialism: the formation of classes, or strata, within a colony, which are closely allied to and dependent on foreign capital, and which form the real basis of support for the regime which succeeds the colonial administration. The Cairo resolution condemned 'puppet governments' as 'manifestations' and 'agents' of neo-colonialism, and Nkrumah wrote of 'neo-colonial States' and their 'rulers' who, he said, derived 'their authority to govern, not from the will of the people, but from the support which they obtain from their neo-colonialist masters'.[36] But puppet regimes in such a literal sense of the term are rare indeed. Woddis, writing after the fall of Nkrumah and from outside the third world, pointed in a different direction: 'If . . . the old system of colonial rule was, in essence, an alliance between external imperialism and local pre-capitalist forces, then neo-colonialism generally represents a new alliance, one between external imperialism and sections of the local bourgeoisie and petty-bourgeoisie.'[37] It is not necessary to accept all of Woddis's views on the subject in order to agree that neo-colonialism cannot

---

34. Reprinted in Colin Legum, *Pan-Africanism: A Short Political Guide* (Pall Mall Press, London 1962), p. 254.

35. Kwame Nkrumah, *Neo-colonialism: the Last Stage of Imperialism* (Nelson, London 1965), and Jack Woddis, *An Introduction to Neo-colonialism* (International Publishers, New York 1967).

36. Kwame Nkrumah, op. cit., p. xv.

37. Woddis, op. cit., p. 56, see note 35.

really be made into a useful concept unless the role played in it by domestic classes is central. We can then speak of neo-colonialism not only as a particular mode of imperialist *policy* applicable to ex-colonies (which it is, and which the Cairo conference characterized) but also as a characteristic form of the political, social and economic life – or of class struggle – in *certain* ex-colonies, i.e. those where the transition from colonialism to independence permitted the relatively efficient transfer of political power to a regime based on the support of social classes linked very closely to the foreign interests which were formerly represented by the colonial state. This was not the case in all colonies, in Africa or anywhere else. Elements favourable to neo-colonialism no doubt exist within all ex-colonies but they have not always had the opportunity to gain an exclusive or even a major share of state power at independence. In the case of some colonies, on the other hand, and I think Kenya was one of them, we may speak of neo-colonialism as a specific phase or episode in its development, and as characterizing its social formation, because the conditions for it existed – indeed they were more or less carefully prepared in the years prior to independence.

On the other hand neo-colonialism in the sense of a phase in the development of particular ex-colonies must, I think, be recognized as likely to be temporary and transitional. Unlike Woddis, who called neo-colonialism 'a temporary tactic of declining imperialism', I am not confident that imperialism is declining; and unlike Nkrumah, who called it 'the last stage of imperialism', I see neo-colonialism as a stage which is inherently likely to give way to other forms of imperialism, as the result of two linked processes. On the one hand, neo-colonialism reproduces and further extends underdevelopment, giving rise to new forms of class struggle which 'an indirect and subtle form of domination' may prove inadequate to contain, giving way to more direct and crude forms. On the other hand, the process of neo-colonial underdevelopment seems bound to modify, and to be increasingly likely to disturb, the initial close relationship between domestic and foreign ruling classes which is its essential feature. Under most circumstances this implies that it is likely to give way to forms of 'dependent capitalist development' which resemble the old 'colonial system' less and less closely.

CHAPTER 2

The Colonial Economy and the Transition to Neo-colonialism in Kenya

It is tempting to begin with the 'comprador' administration of Seyid Said at Zanzibar in the 1840s, when the coast of East Africa, and the interior to the south of Kenya, were first fully incorporated into the rapidly expanding system of world trade. But the interior of Kenya, and consequently its coastal areas too, were actually to be incorporated in a decisively different way as a result of the building of the railway from Mombasa to Lake Victoria, which was completed in 1901.

The railway was built with loan funds, provided by the British Treasury, to provide strategic access to the head-waters of the Nile. To repay the loans and to terminate the annual grant-in-aid paid by the Treasury to meet the cost of administering British East Africa, the land had to be made productive. At the turn of the century several million acres of high-altitude land, much of it close to the line of rail, appeared virtually unused.[1] The colonial administrators of the time, some of whom had South African backgrounds, gradually came to see extensive white settlement as the means of bringing this land into production. The settlers would invest capital and produce crops; the railway would earn revenue by carrying them to the coast, and by carrying the imports inland they would earn abroad, and the government would finance its activities by levying tariffs on these imports. In practice this formula did not work so straightforwardly. But the settlement programme was persevered with.

Kenya began to play the classic role of a country at the periphery of the capitalist system, exporting primary commodities and importing manufactures. It is obvious that no other role was at

---

1. Part of this land, close to Nairobi, was actually owned by Kikuyu families who happened to have been driven back from it temporarily at that time by loss of human and animal life from epidemics. All the land was in any case the collective domain of various tribes, especially the Masai, who moved across the Rift Valley with their herds according to the seasons.

Table 2.1

White Settlement in the Kenyan Highlands[2]

	1903	1915	1920	1934	1942	1953
'Settlers' (approx.)	100	1,000	1,200	2,000	3,000	4,000
'Occupied' acreage	?	4·5m.	3·1m.	5·1m.	6·3m.	7·3m.

first possible. What matters is how the system of ownership and control adopted under colonial rule in Kenya operated to make this role self-perpetuating once it had ceased to be inescapable.

The highlands were 'alienated' to Europeans; that is, Europeans bought the land at nominal prices from the colonial administration. But at first they had neither the knowledge nor the capital to farm it very differently from the Africans on their land.[3] They had not, moreover, come to Kenya to work as peasants. Their 'farms' were extremely large – an average of over 2,400 acres per 'occupier' in 1932. There was therefore only one solution, to make the Africans work for them. This the Africans had no reason to do, unless the Europeans had been willing to pay in wages more than Africans could earn from farming on their own account. But such wages would have meant little or no profit for the Europeans.

2. Figures for 1903 and 1915 from M. P. K. Sorrenson, *Origins of European Settlement in Kenya* (Oxford University Press, Nairobi 1968), pp. 45 and 145; for 1920 and 1934, *Agricultural Census*, cited in E. A. Brett, *Colonialism and Underdevelopment in East Africa* (Heinemann, London 1973), p. 175; for 1942 and 1953, Report of the *Inquiry into the General Economy of Farming in the Highlands* (the Troup Report) 1953, p. 4. These figures must be interpreted with caution. Sorrenson's figures for settlers are approximations, those for 1920 and 1932 are for 'occupiers', those for 1942 and 1953 are for Europeans engaged in farming (i.e. including some Europeans employed by occupiers). It also seems likely that Troup's figures were inflated: R. S. Odingo, in *The Kenya Highlands: Land Use and Agricultural Development* (East African Publishing House, Nairobi 1971), p. 140, gives the 1948 European population engaged in agriculture as 2,871. It should also be noted that the land figures are 'occupied' acreages in the highlands. The total alienated acreage was over 10 million by 1953.

3. On the character of European farming in the inter-war years see R. Van Zwanenberg, 'Primitive Colonial Accumulation in Kenya 1919 to 1939', unpublished D.Phil. thesis, University of Sussex 1971. F. Furedi, in his paper 'The Kikuyu squatter in the Rift Valley: 1918–1929' (Institute of Commonwealth Studies, 1972, mimeo), also emphasizes the labour-intensive nature of most European farming in the early days, and notes that cultivation by 'squatters' on the European farms was accepted in 1918 as part of the 'improvements' which the European landowners were required to show each year to fulfil the conditions of their titles.

Therefore Africans had to be compelled to work, partly by force, partly by taxation, and partly by preventing them from having access to enough land or profitable crops to enable them to pay taxes without working for wages.[4] Eventually, the African population in their homelands rose until by the mid-1920s it became less and less necessary to use force and it was gradually abandoned. From then on population pressure plus taxation assured that enough Africans would be available to work on the modest portion of the alienated land which the European farmers actually endeavoured to make use of. As a contemporary observer put it:

> The very reason that was held to justify the alienation of land to Europeans was the fact that the country was half empty of people. In point of fact the number of Africans dispossessed by the alienation is comparatively trifling, perhaps no more than 50,000. There really was room for colonisation. There really was more land than the Africans of Kenya could use. But that very land was in excess of their needs is precisely the the area which the Government has for twenty years by every means in its power been trying to make them work upon for the profit not of themselves but of European grantees. The whole situation is essentially absurd. . . . The real cultivators of the 335 square miles of alien land under cultivation are of course the fifty or sixty thousand employees who work for wages, employed, most of them, in growing crops which they could and often do grow just as well at home.[5]

Even with the early extensive use of compulsion to procure cheap labour many of the early settlers failed and it was soon clear that a more elaborate system of state support was needed to keep the smaller, less capitalized settlers on the land. As Brett has shown in detail, this gave rise to a highly elaborate system of economic discrimination, whereby Africans paid the bulk of taxation, while the Europeans received virtually the entire benefit of government services – railways, roads, schools, hospitals, extension services and so forth – in addition to being subsidized through the customs tariff (especially after 1923) and having

---

4. This period of Kenyan economic history has been extensively discussed in the literature, but see especially Brett, op. cit. (note 2); M. Dilley, *British Policy in Kenya Colony*, second edition (Cass, London 1966); N. Leys, *Kenya* (Hogarth Press, London 1924); W. Magregor Ross, *Kenya from Within* (Allen and Unwin, London 1927).

5. Leys, *Kenya*, op. cit. (note 4), p. 177.

privileged access to profitable markets, both external and internal.[6]

The result was a spectacular distortion of the economic structure, which lasted broadly until 1939. Down to 1912–13, African production had accounted for at least 70 per cent of exports. By 1928 it accounted for less than 20 per cent, and from 1925 the absolute value of African export production declined as the 'reserves' increasingly relapsed into subsistence farming to support their increasing populations.[7] The reasons have been described as 'obscure', but at least one of them does not require a great effort of historical understanding.[8] By the mid-1920s more than half the able-bodied men in the two largest agricultural tribes (the Kikuyu and Luo) were estimated to be working for Europeans.[9] Within the space of a generation they had effectively been converted from independent peasants, producing cash crops for the new markets, into peasants dependent on agricultural wage-labour. On the other hand the wages they received were extremely low. Wrigley states that shortly before the first world war the African population 'shared to some degree' in the prosperity of the times which 'made it easy for most of them [the Africans] to earn money incomes considerably in excess of the taxation imposed on them'.[10] This is certainly a remarkable definition of shared prosperity, but even so no evidence is offered to support the statement that incomes were 'considerably' in excess of taxation. Bearing in mind the many policies which discouraged African cash crop agriculture and kept African non-wage incomes low, the relation between African wage income and taxation soon after the first world war is of considerable interest:[11]

6. Brett, op. cit. (note 2), Ch. 6; in 1925 and 1926 Africans paid 60 per cent of total taxation in Kenya according to official estimates: see *Proportionate Taxation in Kenya 1925 to 1927* (Department of Statistical Research, British East Africa, mimeo, n.d.).

7. C. C. Wrigley, 'Kenya: The Patterns of Economic Life', in V. T. Harlow and E. M. Chilver (eds), *History of East Africa*, Vol. II (Clarendon Press, Oxford 1965), p. 243.

8. ibid., p. 244.

9. Leys, *Kenya*, op. cit. (note 4), p. 179.

10. op. cit., p. 226.

11. These calculations are derived as follows. Africans registered in employment are taken from Leys, *Kenya*, op. cit. (note 4), p. 178, citing official figures reported in the Nairobi press. The editor of the *East African Standard* (cited in Leys, *Kenya*, p. 206) estimated in 1921 that the annual African wage-bill was £1·5 million, of which a half to two-thirds was paid in cash, and I have used the latter assumption. African tax payments are taken from Brett, op. cit. (note 2), p. 192, based on the *Report . . . on the Financial Position . . . in Kenya*, p. 260a.

Africans in registered employment	approx.	145,000
Cash wages paid to Africans per annum	approx.	£1,000,000
Direct and indirect taxes paid annually by Africans (average 1920–3)	approx.	£750,000
Annual African cash income from wages net of taxation	approx.	£250,000

On Wrigley's figure of 12–14 shillings per month for agricultural workers in 1924, the total African cash wage-bill would perhaps have been closer to £2 million per annum, yet this would still have implied an average cash income from wages net of tax of roughly £9 per employee per annum, and less for workers who only worked part of a year.[12] The fact was that Africans working for wages usually paid hut and poll taxes for those who could not (including for instance old men and widows), and it was widely agreed among district officials down to the mid-1920s that more African labour could not be drawn out of the reserves without the risk of a disastrous decline of food production there. If retained African cash income per head rose appreciably during this period (and this is doubtful), it was evidently due not to wage labour but to cash-crop production, which was generally discouraged[13]. After this time population pressure began to make itself felt and real wages paid on European farms subsequently rose little, if at all, declining sharply with the depression in the early 'thirties and barely keeping ahead of the cost of living once the farmers had recovered from it. In short, African purchasing power under this system was kept about as low as was possible, short of not paying for labour in cash at all.

A measure of the consequences for the pattern of internal

---

12. Wrigley, in 'Kenya: The Patterns of Economic Life' (see note 7), p. 238, does not state the source of his figure for agricultural wages. According to Leys, 'A report by the private recruiting agency that works among the Kikuyu, published in the local Press in February 1924, shows that the standard wages in the Kikuyu province were then still 8 shillings a month without food.' (*Kenya*, p. 206.) He thought most Africans in employment worked a full year and that three to four months of this went to providing cash for their own and others' direct taxation. F. Furedi states that official correspondence, farm files and interviews, show wages for casual labour in 1924 to have been 8 shillings per month plus *posho* (maize flour rations) (private communication).

13. Except for periodic campaigns to compensate for European farmers' crop failures: see Brett, op. cit. (note 2), pp. 205–6.

demand is provided by the customs-revenue statistics for 1925–7, when it was estimated that Africans paid on average 2·1 shillings per head annually in duties, and Europeans 477 shillings, even though the tariff adopted in 1923 had substantially increased duties on various items of African consumption, notably cheap textiles.[14] Local manufacturing was impossible under these conditions, apart from the basic processing of commodities for export, and the processing of food produced by European farmers for the local European and Asian market under protective tariffs, which created an effective monopoly.

Even these industries, such as dairies, would in several cases not have been profitable without additional markets in Tanganyika and Uganda, which were largely the result of expanded *peasant* production in those territories, and which were handed over to the Kenyan producers by the application of the protective tariffs to them as well.[15] Kenya had already become a 'periphery centre' for its region. Under common currency arrangements the large gap between its imports and its exports was financed by its neighbours' trade surpluses, the railway rates charged for Ugandan cotton exports helped to subsidize the specially low rates charged for settler maize exports, and savings and insurance premiums were also channelled through the banking and insurance system from branches in those territories to headquarters in Nairobi. These deposits and payments, however, did not contribute much to internal demand in Kenya, being largely remitted to London.

MONOPOLY

From what has already been said it is obvious that the essence of the colonial economy in Kenya was that it rested on monopolies, to an extent not found in all other African colonies. In fact it is much easier to indicate where there was a degree of competition than where there was monopoly. There was competition between Indian importers of consumer goods, and between Indian wholesalers and retailers, and between Indian buyers of some lines of peasant produce, such as cotton, hides, etc. There was competition

---

14. *Proportionate Taxation in Kenya 1925–27*, op. cit. (note 6), and Brett, loc. cit.

15. Mervyn Hill, in *Cream Country* (Kenya Co-operative Creameries, Nairobi 1956), records how with the onset of the depression Lord Delamere secured the agreement of the 'representatives' of Tanganyika and Uganda before the Governors' Conference of 1930 to continue duties on imported foodstuffs in order to maintain the protection given to Kenyan farmers in those countries' markets.

between Indian building contractors, road hauliers, repair work-shops, furniture-makers and the like. There was some competition between European importers of machinery and equipment, and consumer goods for the luxury end of the European market, though this was limited by exclusive agency arrangements. In short, there was competition wherever it benefited the Europeans as consumers and did not hurt them as producers. Everything else was organized and regulated under some degree of monopoly.

Europeans had a monopoly of high-potential land in the high-lands under the white-highlands policy. (Later, it was to be asserted that, after all, 80 per cent of the country's high-potential land lay in the former reserves;[16] but the effect of the original policy of containing the agricultural tribes within reserves, and of depriving them of access to capital, roads, paying crops, and so on, was that the land the Europeans held was capable of being farmed profitably, while the Africans' land, much of which may have had better soil or more reliable rainfall, was not.) Europeans also got a monopoly of agricultural labour through the hut- and poll-tax system, reinforced by a Masters and Servants ordinance which bound the African worker to serve out a contract on pain of imprisonment, and after 1918 by a Resident Labourers ordinance, which converted the 'squatter' labourer into a kind of serf, bound to work for the owner of his plot for a minimum of 180 days a year. Europeans also monopolized government services. The branch railway lines were sited, with one exception, through European farming areas, and a rating system was adopted which involved carrying European-grown maize, wheat and other temperate foodstuffs at cost, while making very high charges for carrying African-grown exports such as cotton, and imports for African consumption, such as cotton piece-goods. Roads were built by local councils. Those in the European areas were financed by central government grants, those in the African areas by taxes on African produce. With short-lived exceptions, agricultural exten-sion and veterinary services were almost wholly devoted to European farming.

European farmers also had a monopoly of the most profitable crops (especially coffee, which Africans were prevented from growing on a significant scale until the mid-1950s) and the most profitable markets. Control of marketing by means of a system of legal monopolies of buying and selling became particularly

16. *Development Plan 1966–70* (Government Printer, Nairobi 1966), p. 125.

extensive after the slump of 1929–31 had exposed the extreme vulnerability of the settler mixed-farms.[17] Profitable internal markets for temperate-zone foodstuffs such as wheat, dairy products, and bacon, were secured by a protective tariff coupled with legislation to fix prices in such a way that high domestic prices could not be undercut, so that the profits realized on domestic sales could then be shared out among all producers to offset the much smaller profits and even losses made on exports from the output of the large farmers. After the second world war similar measures gave the European maize-farmers an effective monopoly of sales in the towns, and a substantial subsidy from consumers to cover the losses made on maize exports.[18]

The system of monopoly was not confined to European-settler farming. The banks operated a cartel to eliminate price competition. The railways had a virtual monopoly of the transportation of imports and exports through a system of road-transport licensing, and through their effective resistance (until after 1960) to the building of a tarmac road linking Nairobi to the coast. The shipping companies operated a cartel which fixed freight rates. Monopoly, in the sense of a significant degree of exclusive control over some resource – land, labour, capital, technology (including crops), or markets – generally conferred by the state through a law or through executive action, permeated the entire sphere of operations of European (or white, as opposed to Indian) capital in Kenya.

The mere existence of monopoly in this sense did not distinguish Kenya from any other colonial economy. What was distinctive was the attempt, which has to be made in any colony involving substantial settlement by the colonizing power, to create an enclave of the metropolitan society within the colony.

---

17. On the control of marketing generally see M. Yoshida, 'The Protected Development of European Agriculture in Kenya before the Second World War', *Journal of Rural Development*, 1971, pp. 76–102, and M. Yoshida and D. G. R. Belshaw, 'The Introduction of the Trade Licensing System for Primary Products in East Africa, 1900–1939' (East African Institute of Social Research Conference Papers 1965, mimeo).

18. The maize sold in the towns was of course sold to Africans, and represented a direct subsidy from them to European farmers. Clayton estimated that in 1963 Africans bought £5m. worth of arable products from European farms, while European farms paid £5½m. in wages. Thus a large part of African wages in the European farm sector came back to the European farmers indirectly in the shape of subsidies, apart from anything else (E. Clayton, 'A Note on the Alien Enclave and Economic Development', *East African Economic Review*, Vol. X, No. 1, June 1963, pp. 35–40).

These arrangements called for an extensive set of institutions for managing their details. This was most notable in the agricultural sector, with its system of settler-controlled marketing and regulatory boards, production committees and land boards in every area of the highlands, and the quasi-private, quasi-public, quasi-co-operative and quasi-company organizations which handled particular products, especially the Kenya Farmers' Association (KFA) (which both purchased grain and distributed seed and implements, and also built up a near-monopoly of grain milling), and the Kenya Co-operative Creameries (KCC), which controlled and handled the Europeans' dairy output. But in the peak period of settler dominance in politics, i.e. from the mid-1920s until the late 1940s, settler control of policy through committees of the legislative council and government bodies of all kinds was so commonplace that these more permanent and specialized institutions appeared as only part of a larger system of monopoly management which really included the whole administrative apparatus of the country, from the railways' management to the district officers enforcing the labour and tax laws.

THE LARGE-SCALE MIXED FARMS

Naturally this elaborate apparatus was supported by a similarly elaborate economic ideology, and especially by the carefully fostered myth of the importance of the European 'mixed' farms. These farms – the farms situated in areas suitable for both arable and cattle farming – were mostly 'smaller' farms (in Kenyan-highland terms), and supported the bulk of the settlers: the large ranches, and the large coffee, tea and sisal plantations supported many fewer Europeans per acre, and it was the way of life of the Europeans in the 'mixed'-farm areas, with its supporting services of schools, hospitals and roads, that was the focus of settler politics. That way of life and those services were impossible without the special structure of monopoly of crops, marketing, labour, transport, etc.; accordingly the mixed farms were represented as making a unique contribution to the economy as a whole.

But this was a myth. It is doubtful if the mixed farms, as opposed to the ranches and the coffee, tea and sisal estates, ever accounted for much more than half of the total value of non-African farm output, and their share was even lower if one excludes some so-called mixed farms which were primarily very large-scale ranches, but which happened also to contain some arable land.[19] The mixed farms' contribution to output was also very inflated by the protection given to many of their products. With the subsidy element removed, the value of their output would have become an even smaller proportion of the total. Where they could not enforce a monopoly of production, for instance in maize, the staple food of much of the African population, their share fell to a small fraction of the total output, and without their control of the urban market maize production would almost certainly have become a purely African affair, even without the diversion of a single extension worker into the African reserves.[20] And if one systematically subtracts from the value of the mixed farms' output the value of the further subsidies they received from the African population, in the form of services partly financed by the African taxpayer, one soon approaches a very modest if not a negative figure. The same thing is true of export earnings; but it was not until the myth of the importance of the mixed farms had ceased to matter to European political interests that an official mission consisting of Europeans noticed the fact, and pointed out that if one subtracted from the export earnings of the mixed farms the value of the imported inputs into those farms, one also arrived at an insignificant figure.[21] But until independence, and indeed for some time after, the vital economic importance of the large-scale mixed farms was an article of faith in official circles.

This myth was to play an important part in easing the transition from a colonial to a neo-colonial economy.

In the first place, the incoming African political leadership had been conditioned to believe it. They were therefore ready to make critical concessions to the British and to the settlers themselves in order to 'save' the economy by saving the European farmers. The

---

19. The *Economic Survey*, 1960, shows that the average share of plantation crops in the value of total 'large farm' (i.e. non-African areas) output for the three years 1957–9 was 48·5 per cent.

20. Yoshida, 'The Protected Development of European Agriculture in Kenya before the Second World War' (note 17), p. 95, shows that after the failure of the European maize-growers to gain the complete control of marketing that they sought in the mid-1930s, 'with the failure to transfer incomes from other sections of the community, the European acreage of maize declined rapidly. The 233,973 acres of maize harvested in 1929–30 had shrunk to 93,517 acres by the 1939–40 season.' Even with protection after the war European maize production only kept slightly ahead of African marketed output, and in the 1960s large-farm maize output was well under 10 per cent of total production (including subsistence production).

21. See below, p. 87.

first African minister for Commerce, Industry and Communications, Masinde Muliro, told the Nairobi Chamber of Commerce in 1961:

> . . . Nairobi, to a very high degree, is dependent upon the farming community outside Nairobi. So my estimation is that we in commerce and industry will be ensured as long as the farming community is alright. As long as the farming community is not alright, we are not going to be safe in Nairobi. That is why we find that whatever we do, we must get the farming community settled down.[22]

Secondly, the European mixed farms represented a way of life to which educated Africans had learned to aspire. If these farms were also the linchpin of the economy, transferring them intact to individual African owners could be defended as necessary to the national interest. The apparatus of monopoly – the marketing and regulatory boards, in particular – which underpinned the profitability of mixed farming also lent itself to a comparatively easy process of transfer, the settlers co-opting increasing numbers of Africans on to the boards until they passed under the control of African large-farm owners.

Thirdly, acceptance of the myth of the importance of large-scale mixed farming entailed acceptance of the entire system of monopoly, of which it was only the pinnacle. Virtually all Europeans and most educated Africans looked on it as natural. The Royal Commission on East Africa in 1953–5 seemed puzzled by this.[23] The Commissioners seemed surprised by the automatic preference of policy-makers for regulation and control, and their distaste for market forces; or perhaps they just lacked the candour to attack more openly the enormous privileges of the settlers which the monopoly arrangements served. The colonial administration perhaps also hesitated to say what it really thought the Commission's liberalizing recommendations would mean: that is, a golden opportunity not for Africans, but for Asians, who by that time had produced a merchant capitalist class which was poised to become an indigenous industrial bourgeoisie of the classical type. This unspoken assumption was very likely correct, and

---

22. Record of a special meeting with the Management Committee of the Nairobi Chamber of Commerce, 29 November 1961.

23. See especially Chapter 7 of the *East Africa Royal Commission 1953–55 Report*, Cmd. 9475, 1955; the Kenya government's reply, published as *Despatch from the Governor of Kenya commenting on the East Africa Royal Commission Report* (Nairobi 1956), at pp. 20–25, is a clear general statement of the official ideology.

African businessmen were soon to discover the advantages of maintaining the general fabric of state monopoly, which provided them with protected opportunities in the modern sector, rather than of throwing the economy open to a competition which the Asians could quickly win.

Brett has described European settlement as the 'predominant form' of capitalist development in Kenya, in contrast with Uganda, where peasant agriculture prevailed, and Tanganyika, where both forms coexisted. Politically, settlement certainly did predominate in Kenya, but in terms of physical output it was from the first less important than plantation and ranch production. It only appeared to predominate in some commodity markets because they were effectively reserved to it. In fact the settlers were historically an 'epiphenomenon', superimposed on the more fundamental relationship between foreign capital, represented by plantation and ranch production and the urban commercial sector, and African peasant producers and wage-workers. When European political predominance and the settler way of life became impossible, the economic contribution of the mixed farm was suddenly seen to be less vital than had been supposed, and it was increasingly replaced by various kinds of peasant farming. In the meantime, however, the mixed farm had served as a sort of shoehorn, easing African businessmen, civil servants and politicians into an alliance with the more durable and important forms of foreign capital that remained.

With the outbreak of the second world war the colonial economy entered on a period of change which was of great importance for the transition to a neo-colonial relationship. Down to 1940 the economy had been hamstrung by the distortions imposed on it in the interests of the settlers. So long as world commodity prices remained high, growth had been possible on the basis of the exploitation of the African population as taxpayers and wage-workers. But when prices collapsed in the depression, and the settlers were forced to rely on the extremely limited domestic market, resulting from their systematic restriction of African purchasing power, the economy stagnated. Some efforts were made during the 1930s to stimulate it by putting resources into African peasant agriculture, but they were halfhearted (for instance the ban on African-grown coffee was retained in Central Province) and inconsistent (for instance, in an unsuccessful effort to give the Kenya Farmers' Association a chance to get control over African maize sales, so as to make them help subsidize European maize-growers, free competition in produce-purchasing was severely curtailed by an ordinance of 1935). The war intervened before the contradictions of policy could precipitate a crisis, though of course not before African political consciousness had been raised to a higher level by the deprivations of the period.[24]

DEVELOPMENTS IN THE COLONIAL ECONOMY

The war reprieved the colonial economy; and what was more important, the sustained demand which it created, and which unexpectedly continued after the end of war, modified the economy in other ways, so that when the political crisis caused by the Mau Mau rebellion came, it was able to respond adaptively and without the need for a very radical reconstruction.

It is difficult to describe the change which occurred precisely, because of the absence of statistics for the inter-war period. The first census of the African population, for instance, was held in 1948 and showed that there were 5·2 million Africans in Kenya, besides 98,000 Asians and nearly 30,000 Europeans, and it is probable that the growth of the African population was just beginning to accelerate rapidly from an expansion begun in the 1920s, after a previous decline.[25] By 1962 the African population had reached 8·4 million. The first estimate of national income was also made after the war, for 1947, and showed a net national income of £53 million, of which just under half was agricultural output and three-fifths of that, the imputed value of African non-marketed production.[26]

By 1947, however, the country had already experienced seven years of continuous demand. The Ethiopian campaign had led to large numbers of Italian prisoners being held in Kenya, and refugees from Poland and elsewhere were subsequently sent there too. Local purchasing power had risen rapidly, while the shortage

---

24. See especially C. G. Rosberg and J. Nottingham, *The Myth of Mau Mau* (Praeger, New York 1966), Ch. 5.

25. Dilley (see note 4) cites the various rather vague earlier estimates of African population in *British Policy in Kenya Colony*, p. 8. Wrigley cites a careful study by B. Fazan in 1935 which calculated that the Kikuyu and some of the Luo had been expanding at the rate of about 1·5 per cent per annum for about the previous ten years: op. cit. (note 7), p. 255.

26. *National Income and Output of the Colony and Protectorate of Kenya 1947 and 1948* (East African Statistical Department, October 1949).

of shipping had led to a call for Kenya to become not only self-sufficient in foodstuffs, and a source of supply for other theatres of the war, but also as far as possible a manufacturer of its own consumer products. The new demand was reinforced by government measures to guarantee and subsidize prices. There was a major expansion of farm output and of local industrial activity. Consequently the 1947 figures describe an economy already dramatically changed from that of the 1930s, with its narrow domestic market for foodstuffs and its chronically inadequate outlets for exportable cash crops.

But in 1947 the process of change was still only beginning. The run-down of military personnel at the end of the war, and the repatriation of prisoners, was partly offset in 1947 by the influx of personnel to man the Tanganyikan groundnut scheme. Kenya's position as a 'periphery centre' offering superior financial, technical, recreational and communications facilities enabled Mombasa and Nairobi to reap much of the benefit of the £35 million which were spent on the scheme before it was finally abandoned in 1950. Meanwhile commodity prices were sustained by American stockpiling during the Korean War, and then in 1952 the Emergency was declared and a fresh build-up of British troops took place in Kenya. Over the years 1952–9 £55 million was spent on containing the revolt, much of it in Kenya. The cumulative effect of these changes, some of which also stimulated economic growth in Uganda and Tanganyika and so indirectly expanded demand in Kenya still further, was to profoundly alter the nature of the economy.

By 1954 the gross domestic product of the monetary economy had grown to £112m. The share of agriculture and livestock production was now about 18 per cent of this total. Manufacturing accounted for nearly 13 per cent, transport and communications for 11 per cent, wholesale and retail trade for 20 per cent. Ten years later (by 1964) GDP had nearly doubled again, to £212m.[27] Although it was obvious that the prosperity of the non-agricultural sectors still depended heavily on agricultural exports, the expansion had called into being substantial new economic interests which saw that it was the prosperity of agriculture, not of settlers, which mattered.

Before the second world war the whole commercial sector was

---

27. In 1964, however, the share of agriculture and livestock had risen to 21·7 per cent, and that of trade had fallen to 16·0 per cent.

very directly dependent on European agriculture, and especially on the mixed farmers, who were their principal customers for goods, services and credit. Now this was no longer true. In 1958 the total value of non-agricultural assets belonging to organizations and enterprises in Kenya was calculated to be just under £99m. This did not include the value of the assets of individuals, and notably the value of the urban real estate held by Asians. The capital value of the plantations and ranches could also be put at about £25–30m. in 1958. By contrast, the total value of the European mixed farms was about £40–45m., and they were also the main borrowers of the £12m. which was owing by non-African agriculture to the commercial banks, the Land Bank, and other credit institutions. In other words the settlers on the mixed farms probably owned no more than about 15–20 per cent of the foreign assets invested in Kenya by 1958.[28] Once the Emergency had called in question the continuation of the whole colonial economy and the security of foreign investments generally it was not surprising that the newer commercial and industrial interests, and even the ranches and plantation companies, found themselves willing if necessary to abandon the settlers, who had hitherto been allowed to speak for all foreign interests, and to seek an alliance with African leaders prepared to accept the private-enterprise system and allow them to stay in business.

This was the basis of the new 'multi-racial' policy of what became the New Kenya Group, formed in 1959, under the leadership of Michael (later Sir Michael) Blundell.[29]

The New Kenya Group was opposed to what it called 'undiluted democracy' through 'the premature introduction of universal suffrage on a common roll', but it favoured the 'progressive extension of democracy', and so for the first time indicated a willingness on the part of Europeans to contemplate African government. It also accepted the opening up of the 'white highlands' to non-Europeans. Its 'fundamental axioms', on the other hand, included the following: 'The social and political tenets of

---

28. These calculations are derived from the *Survey of Capital Assets Held in Kenya in 1958* (East African Statistical Department, 1960); the Troup report on the *General Economy of Farming in the Highlands* (see note 2), pp. 25 and 26; and the *Kenya European and Asian Agricultural Census 1958*, pp. 27 and 29. Such data are necessarily very approximate, but there is no doubt about the relative orders of magnitude involved.

29. For the background to this see G. Bennett and C. G. Rosberg, *The Kenyatta Election* (Oxford University Press, London 1961), Ch. 1.

the free world shall apply . . .' and 'The rights of private property and the sanctity of contracts shall be respected.'

The Group's diagnosis and programme was summed up in its statement on economic development, which contained the following central passage:

> The inherent problem of Kenya lies in the wide gulf between the living and cultural standards of the well-to-do and those of the poorer majority but this is magnified into a racial problem by the fact that in our country racial and economic difference lie together. The usual historical economic conflict is thus, in our case, exacerbated by race.
>
> *The only solution, in our view, is vigorously to tackle the basic problem of low living standards, so that there may rapidly emerge from the poorer majority people having similar interests and similar ideals, to those economically more advanced.*
>
> To this end, we advocate the allocation of considerable financial resources to enable such people to be trained and where deserving financed, for entry into the fields of commerce, industry and improved farming, as well as into the professions.[30]

The basis for collaboration between European and African interests in making a transition to political independence without any radical change in the economic and social structure was thus tentatively indicated. In December 1959 the New Kenya Group, backed by finance from various firms with interests in Kenya, became a political party.[31]

SOCIAL FORCES

The thinking of the New Kenya Group did not of course crystallize suddenly in 1959. It was the political culmination of a process of reappraisal that began with the progressive collapse of the colonial government's authority from 1950 onwards, leading to the declaration of an Emergency in 1952 and the subsequent military campaign against the forest fighters. In order to see the logic of the New Kenya Group's strategy, we must look briefly at some of the social forces created by colonialism in Kenya.

---

30. *The Challenge of the New Kenya*, the manifesto of the New Kenya Party launched by the group at the end of 1959: italics in the original.

31. The leadership and economic basis of the New Kenya Group has been described in some detail by G. Wasserman in 'The Adaptation of a Colonial Elite to Decolonization: Kenya Europeans and the Land Issue 1960–1965' (Ph.D. thesis, Columbia University 1972), pp. 72–9.

It is convenient to begin by dealing with one group which was in fact to play only a passive part in the transition to neo-colonialism, but whose presence was powerfully felt for all that. Indian traders had largely controlled trade and credit at the coast for perhaps two centuries. They had opened up wholesale and retail trade in the interior before colonial rule, and led its expansion since.[32] They had worked on very low profit margins and had a very high propensity to save. When the prosperity of the war-time and postwar years set in, imports tripled and the bulk of them passed through their hands. Between 1948 and 1962 their numbers rose from 98,000 to 177,000. Their wealth also rose rapidly. Much of it was invested in urban real estate, since they were barred by the 'white highlands' policy from buying land in the highlands, although they had proved efficient farmers else-where (for instance in Uganda). But by the early 1950s the opportunities in real estate and in trading seemed to be saturated, and the more enterprising trading families began investing in the local manufacture of products which they already knew, from their knowledge of the market, could be produced locally at a profit even under existing levels of protection, and which would therefore soon attract some other manufacturer if they did not decide to undertake production themselves. In other words, the Indian trading community (after the partition of India, they became known as 'Asians') had produced the prototype of a national industrial bourgeoisie. A student writing about them in 1962 summarized the situation as follows:

> The profits in industry were generally high, ranging from fifteen per cent to fifty per cent on total investment. In industries where duty protection existed they were especially good. A large part of the profits were usually reinvested in industry. Expenditure on luxury goods and conspicuous consumption was very limited because of the traditional low standard of living and, more important, because they wanted to re-invest everything they earned as long as returns were good. New industries were established with the earnings from

---

32. The economic role of Indians in Kenya has not been adequately treated in the historical literature. G. G. Tandberg remarks that 'when the Arabs ruled the East African coast the Indians were the traders and money lenders. When the Portuguese pushed the Arab traders away the Indians remained. When the Arabs returned the Indians were still there . . .' ('The Duka-Wallah: the Backbone of East Africa's Economy', in S. Pandit (ed.), *Asians in East and Central Africa* (Panco Publications, Nairobi 1963), pp. 48–57. He points out that there was an Indian trader at Lake Baringo in 1885.

the existing industrial organisation. This trend has changed slightly in the last few years as political uncertainty in Kenya has increased, and the position of the immigrant communities has become unclear. Some of the earnings are transferred abroad, mainly as short term deposits which can be returned as soon as stability is attained. Some of the profits are used to establish industries in other countries – other parts of Africa and sometimes, in India and Pakistan. But the commitment to industry is definite. The sons and family members of the entrepreneurs are sent abroad for training and the majority will enter industry.[33]

In 1961 over 67 per cent of all the locally owned industrial enterprises with fifty or more employees were Asian-owned.[34] At this stage, on the eve of independence, Asians probably owned nearly three-quarters of the private non-agricultural assets of the country.

As is well known, the Asians' political leaders had been defeated after the first world war in their attempt to get equality of land rights and political representation with the Europeans within the colonial system; and with few exceptions, they had subsequently stood aloof from the African leaders' attempts to reduce European dominance. As the country's traders and occupants of the middle rungs of the pay and status hierarchy in employment they were natural targets of African hostility. The prospect of substituting Asian economic dominance for European political dominance was thus equally unwelcome to both Africans and Europeans. Consequently a basic assumption – again unstated – of the new strategy adumbrated by the New Kenya Group and in other quarters was that development would not be based on the dismantling of monopoly and the rapid expansion of a competitive industrialization programme based on local capital, but on the adaptation of the monopoly system to make room for some Africans, and on the importation of new capital from Western countries.[35]

---

33. I. D. Chandaria, 'The Development of Entrepreneurship in Kenya' (B.A. thesis, Harvard College 1963), pp. 25–6.

34. ibid., p. 28a.

35. It is interesting that the New Kenya Party's manifesto repeatedly emphasized the importance of new external capital, and also stressed that the 'efforts of the people themselves' were potentially the greatest of the country's resources, but did not call for the fullest use of the country's existing stock of entrepreneurial talent and accumulated private capital by offering more protection and help to local investors.

But the most serious obstacle to this strategy was not the economic strength of the Asians but the potential political power of the African masses. This was primarily, though not exclusively, a question of the Kikuyu masses, who had borne the brunt of the European settlers' monopoly of land and of the enforced conversion to wage-labouring. Prior to 1950, this was expressed in two main forms: 'squatting' and political labour unions.

Recent work by Van Zwanenberg, Furedi and King has clearly established the pivotal significance of squatting in the colonial economy.[36]

Squatters were (and are still) people living on, cultivating and generally also grazing, land that does not belong to them. In the early years of European settlement they were sometimes the original inhabitants of the land which had been appropriated by the colonial administration and 'alienated' to a European settler. More often they were landless people or owners of very small plots, who would have moved on to some unused and unowned land but who now found that the only available unused land was in European ownership. The settlers found that they had far more land than they could use and that they could get cheap, and above all, resident and therefore fairly reliable supplies of labour in return for allowing people to cultivate on their land. By the end of the first world war squatting had become a standard feature of the mixed farms, and expressed precisely the contradiction between settler and peasant agriculture. The settlers had a monopoly of land but little capital and, initially, less know-how. The Africans, on the other hand, and especially the Kikuyu, were confined in their traditional areas but were not provided with the techniques, the crops, the capital or the services to farm them intensively for the market. Consequently their own land soon became overcrowded and overworked, using traditional farming methods. Squatting provided the *ahoi* or landless Kikuyu with land, sometimes on a scale which allowed them to accumulate considerable wealth from farming, normally in the form of herds

---

36. Van Zwanenberg, op. cit. (note 3); F. Furedi, op. cit. (note 3) and also 'The Genesis of African Communities in the "Settled Areas" of Kenya' (Department of History, University of Nairobi, November 1971, mimeo); Rebmann M. Wambaa, with assistance from K. King, 'The Political Economy of the Rift Valley: A Squatter Perspective', paper presented to the Annual Conference of the Historical Association of Kenya (August 1972, mimeo). I am also very grateful to Kenneth King for a chance to consult an excellent unpublished paper summarizing part of his work on this subject.

of sheep and goats.[37] It also provided the settlers with labour. On
the most marginal settler farms 'kaffir farming' – share-cropping
or even tenant farming for cash – was practised, but this clearly
threatened to destroy the whole concept of the 'white highlands'
and was abolished by legislation in 1918, which forbade squatting
except on the basis of an agreement by the squatter to work for
at least 180 days a year for the landowner. The squatter thus
became a tied labourer, although he had to be paid for his labour,
at a much reduced rate.

Although squatters never provided the whole of the settlers'
labour force, their economic significance was considerable. From
the early 1920s onwards the attractions of squatting were progressively reduced; the settlers began to demand more work from
their squatters for fewer benefits, and in order to protect their
newly imported exotic herds from infection they banned squatter
cattle, and in some cases even sheep and goats. Even so it was
estimated in 1931 that squatters were using a million acres of
land in the highlands, or nearly two-thirds as much as the settlers
themselves were using.[38] In 1945, in spite of still further legislation
passed in the 1930s to reduce or even eliminate squatting, 200,000
squatters were counted, of whom a substantial majority – 122,000
– were Kikuyu.[39] Furedi has shown that the dominant motive for
squatting was to obtain land which the squatter could not get in
his home area.[40] By the 1930s they were thus an insecure, uprooted
category of people, and although a few found prosperity, most
were extremely poor and exploited, without access to schooling or
other services. When the leaders of the first major Kikuyu
nationalist organization, the Kikuyu Central Association (KCA),
sought support among the squatters in the 1920s, the squatters,
who were landless, felt no great enthusiasm for men who were
githaka owners (i.e. relatively large landowners in Kikuyu

37. In the early days it could even tempt a relatively prosperous person by its apparently limitless scope for grazing stock, and by the chance to escape from the
growing officiousness of the government-appointed chiefs, from forced service in
the Carrier Corps, from the importuning of missionaries, and so on. See Wambaa,
op. cit. (note 36).

38. Van Zwanenberg, op. cit. (note 3), p. 440.

39. J. H. Martin, *Economic Survey of Resident Labour in Kenya*, 1947, cited in Sir Philip
Mitchell, *The Agrarian Problem in Kenya* (Government Printer, Nairobi 1948), p. 20.
There were also about 56,000 people squatting in Crown forests.

40. In Furedi's sample (see note 3) 68 out of 74 had migrated to the European area
because of landlessness.

country).[41] During the Emergency they were stripped of whatever
livestock they had – their only assets – and deported *en masse* back
to Kikuyu country, without any prospect of finding land or
employment there. Once this had happened it was not surprising
that a number came to play leading parts in the forest fighting,
and those who survived the fighting and detention and moved
back into the Rift Valley afterwards provided much of the support
for the Land Freedom Army, formed in 1960, which posed the
threat of forcible land seizure in the highlands. Even after the
carrying capacity of the Kikuyu country had been greatly increased by the crash programme of agricultural development
carried out there as a result of the Emergency, the ranks of the
squatters were continually replenished and expanded by new
landless people as a result of the rapid expansion of the Kikuyu
population. The 'landless in the Rift Valley' thus came to be seen
as epitomizing the reasons why a major programme of land
transfer from the European mixed-farmers to African peasants
must be the key to any strategy for a transition to independence
which would preserve the rest of the colonial economic structure
fundamentally intact.

Parallel to the predicament of the squatters was that of the
urban wage-labour force. Again, recent work by Stichter has
begun to establish the importance of the politicization of the work
force which resulted from the general reduction of wages during
the depression years, and which culminated in a general strike
in 1939.[42] By this time there was considerable experience of union
organization, and during a second general strike in Mombasa in
January 1947 there emerged a general union, the African Workers
Federation (AWF), which almost immediately showed signs of
eclipsing the Kenya African Union (KAU). The KAU, which
aimed at becoming a mass political organization capable of
securing reforms by constitutional means, had grown out of a
study group formed to support the first African member of the
colonial Legislative Council of 1944; Jomo Kenyatta, the former

41. Wambaa, op. cit. (note 36); for the development of the KCA and its post-war
successor, the Kenya African Union, see Rosberg and Nottingham, *The Myth
of Mau Mau* (Praeger, New York 1966).

42. Sharon B. Stichter has shown how unemployment in the early 1930s swelled the
urban populations (there being no room left in the reserves for the paid-off farm
labourers), and fed the discontents that produced the early union activity of those
years ('Development and Labor Protest in Colonial Kenya', 1971, mimeo); see
also F. Furedi, 'The African Crowd in Nairobi: Popular Movements and Elite
Politics', *Journal of African History*, Vol. XIV, No. 2, 1973, pp. 275–90.

General Secretary of the Kikuyu Central Association, who had recently returned to Kenya after fifteen years abroad, mainly in England, assumed its leadership in 1947.[43] Unlike the leaders of KAU, the leaders of the AWF were relatively uneducated men, close to the ordinary workers. The main leader, Chege Kibachia, was arrested in August 1947 and held in restriction in Baringo, a remote district, for ten years, and it was significant that at a meeting of the KAU held in Nairobi three weeks later Kenyatta advised against a general strike in protest against this, and said that an expert was being brought by the government to form trade unions which would pursue purely industrial aims.[44] Two years later in 1949 the radical unionists' Indian adviser Makhan Singh, a Communist who had twice successfully resisted deportation from Kenya after the AWF was destroyed, formed a successor organization, the East African Trade Unions Congress, in collaboration with Fred Kubai. By 1950 the EATUC had become the chief public focus of mass discontent in Nairobi. The government then arrested Makhan Singh and Kubai. Makhan Singh was deported to Lokitaung, on the Ethiopian border, where he remained until 1961. Kubai was jailed for twelve months. A general strike in Nairobi followed their arrests, but was contained by the use of large numbers of police and troops; the EATUC was banned, and no really popular mass organization remained to take its place.

Political power among the masses in Nairobi and its environs gravitated into the hands of the 'Forty Group', named after the 1940 Kikuyu age-group. Furedi has described how this organization, led by largely uneducated but talented and experienced town-dwellers, gradually came to control the African areas of Nairobi, and between 1947 and 1951 also 'built up an organization which extended into all parts of Central Province and into some areas in the Rift Valley'. Landlessness, unemployment, low wages, low status, accelerating population growth and declining soil fertility in the Kikuyu reserve, combined with settler intransigence and a loss of political initiative by the colonial administration, gave rise to a rapidly deepening sense of alienation. The activities of the Forty Group articulated this. It was their oathing programme, and their political assassinations in and

---

43. The KCA had been banned as a subversive organization in 1940.
44. Makhan Singh, *History of Kenya's Trade Union Movement to 1952* (East African Publishing House, Nairobi 1969), p. 158; see also Sharon Stichter, 'Workers, Trade Unions and the Mau Mau Rebellion', paper presented to the Conference on Workers, Unions and Development in Africa, Toronto, April 1973, pp. 8–9.

around Nairobi which finally precipitated the Government's declaration of an Emergency in 1952; and until 1954, when the government purged Nairobi of nearly all its adult male Kikuyu, the leaders of the Forty Group effectively supplied and sustained the Mau Mau resistance. Summing up this period, Furedi wrote:

> The leaders of the populist movements like Mau Mau/40 Group were successful organisers because they lived near and with the African people. Unlike the educated KAU politicians, there was no gulf separating them from the people living in the locations. . . . The period 1946–54 was one of the most intense periods of radical activity in Kenya's history. This was due to the fact that there existed an organised popular movement led by a group of people who expressed the interests of Nairobi's African people.[45]

After the revolt was suppressed electoral politics were opened up for Africans. The new political leaders who were able to take full advantage of this style of politics were naturally men who had good education and who had not been in detention. From then on, 'the political role assigned to the Nairobi African crowd was to be present at demonstrations and mass meetings'.[46]

The squatters and the Nairobi 'crowd' who finally supplied the majority of the forest fighters epitomized the impoverishment and frustration of the lowest paid and least secure sections of the African population. By the same token, there were others who were relatively secure, and a few who were comparatively affluent. As the Emergency wore on the violence that occurred was increasingly between the uneducated and landless Kikuyu, from whom the forest fighters were overwhelmingly recruited, and the educated and landed families, who preponderated in the ranks of the 'loyalists' and the local 'Home Guard' units. In many respects it must be seen as a civil war, or rather a series of local civil wars, which accounted for a major part of the 13,000 African deaths which were due to the Emergency.[47]

THE TRANSITION TO NEO-COLONIALISM

It was on the educated and propertied, not only among the Kikuyu but among all the politically active tribes, that the

---

45. 'The African Crowd in Nairobi' (see note 42), p. 287.

46. ibid., p. 288.

47. See especially M. P. K. Sorrenson, *Land Reform in the Kikuyu Country* (Oxford University Press, Nairobi 1967), pp. 99–101 and 106–9.

strategy of the New Kenya Group depended. They included chiefs' families, who had been able to acquire land and livestock in the course of wielding executive power on behalf of the colonial administration, and who had frequently had early access to mission education. In general, they included anyone with secondary education, since this not only opened the door to relatively well-paid white-collar work, but also to appointment to Native Local Councils, access to improved government housing, and other tangible advantages.

After the second world war, government policy had increasingly recognized the need to prevent frustration among such people, and as far as possible to attach their interests to those of the colonial regime. This emerged very clearly in the government's response to the African ex-servicemen who returned from their experience overseas and sank their gratuities in the purchase and development of trading plots in the rural areas. The District Officer in Nyeri reported that early in 1949 there were sixty markets and shopping centres comprising 971 commercial plots outside Nyeri township, serving a total population of 208,000 people, or one shop to every 215 people, many of whose breadwinners were absent. Regulations adopted by the local councils at the instigation of the colonial government required the would-be shopkeepers to invest an average of £300 per plot, and it was obvious that most of them would fail. He concluded:

> The Kikuyu have chosen their vocation, and if they fail, as I believe very many of them will, for there are far too many for the district, it will be due to the economic laws and their own shortcomings. But they will not easily be persuaded of this, and will put the blame on Government and the other races of the Colony. The 60 markets, at the worst, might in a couple of years be 60 centres of political agitation, for these traders are amongst the more energetic and vocal of their tribe. I feel we should begin to temper the wind to the lambs that are soon to be shorn.[48]

But it was not until the crisis broke that the reluctance of officials at the centre to disturb their relations with European and

---

48. Report by D. J. Penwill on Trades and Markets in Nyeri, 3–7 January 1949, Trade and Commerce File 6/16/11/2, Kenya National Archives. Penwill was later to play an important role in implementing the land-consolidation policy in Kikuyu country. His use of the term 'vocation' showed considerable political insight. The following summary of the evolution of government policy on African traders is based on the same file.

Asian commercial interests was finally overcome. Then a Cabinet committee on 'African Advancement' was set up to look at a series of measures that had been urged unsuccessfully by the African traders themselves (including Oginga Odinga, the first Vice-President of Kenya after independence) and by district officials for the previous eight years. These included removing the restrictions on loans to Africans (there was a legal ceiling of £50), ways to enable African traders to buy wholesale (many were obliged by lack of capital and resistance from established Asian traders to buy their stocks at retail prices and could consequently make little or no profit) and, above all, means of channelling credit to them. In the end it took the joint efforts of the Governor and Ernest (later Sir Ernest) Vasey, a Nairobi businessman who had been brought in to take charge of Finance in the Emergency, to push through a simple scheme of loans, half provided by central government and half by local councils. The commercial banks also agreed to provide mobile banking facilities in the reserves. The US Foreign Operations Administration undertook to provide loan funds for up to 50 per cent of the cost of a scheme for setting up trained artisans in business.

The much better-known Swynnerton Plan (*A Plan to Intensify the Development of African Agriculture in Kenya*) was also a direct response to the Emergency. It was at last clear that the policy of maintaining the reserves as providers of subsistence foodstuffs for low-paid wage-workers' families had overreached itself, and that unless steps were taken immediately to make the reserves produce wealth for their bursting populations, the conditions which gave rise to the Emergency would become chronic. The plan involved consolidating land fragments into single holdings and issuing registered freehold titles to individuals. The larger leaseholders would then be able to borrow from the commercial banks or from the government on the security of their titles. The political implications were quite explicit: 'Former government policy will be reversed and able, energetic or rich Africans will be able to acquire more land and bad or poor farmers less, creating a landed and a landless class. This is a normal step in the evolution of a country.'[49] By the end of the 1950s the programme had been largely completed in Kikuyu country, and it had been followed up by the provision of extension services and credit and, most

49. R. J. M. Swynnerton, *A Plan to Intensify the Development of African Agriculture in Kenya* (Government Printer, Nairobi 1955), p. 10.

important of all, by the removal of the ban on African-grown coffee. The results were dramatic. The value of recorded output from smallholdings rose from £5·2 million in 1955 to £14·0 million in 1964, coffee accounting for 55 per cent of the increase. The bulk of this change occurred in Central Province, the Kikuyu homeland.[50] Undoubtedly most Kikuyu benefited to some extent from it, but those with larger holdings or salaries which enabled them to buy large holdings emerged as the leading beneficiaries, with a substantial stake in the system which made this possible.

Meanwhile in the field of private industry there were also indications of a changed attitude, especially on the part of the managers of the local branches of international companies. The Nairobi head of the East African Tobacco Company, Philip (later Sir Philip) Rogers, was a case in point. His company sold a third of its output through African retailers in 1955, and had started to build up African wholesalers. Companies with similar interests in selling to the local mass market included the Kenya Breweries, Bata, Elliots Bakeries, and many others, who began at this time to switch to African distributors and create a network of African businessmen who would want to keep them in business. Rogers in particular was active in pressing the government to encourage African businessmen: he told the government's committee on the subject that 'as far as his company was concerned the greatest importance was attached to educating the African as quickly as possible as a businessman'.[51] Rogers was also active in founding the Federation of Kenya Employers, and became its first president. He had previously worked in Nigeria and was one of the few Europeans in Nairobi at this time who seemed to have a clear idea, based on that experience, of what a strategy of collaboration with 'moderate' nationalist leaders implied. He told his fellow employers:

Membership of the Association [the original name of the

---

50. *Development Plan 1966–70*, p. 126. The argument used to rationalize the prohibition on African-grown coffee had always been that it would be of poor quality and prone to disease through lack of proper care. Under the impact of the Emergency this argument suddenly appeared to lose its force, and the 1962 *Economic Survey* recorded (p. 19) that 'while the average price for clean coffee from the Scheduled Areas in 1960/61 was £302 a ton, the equivalent price from the non-Scheduled areas (i.e. the African areas) was £360 per ton. This means that the coffee produced by the African farmers of Kenya is the highest quality coffee produced in the world today.'

51. Report by the Acting Secretary for Commerce and Industry to the Minister, May 1954, Trade and Commerce File 16/11/11.

Federation was the Association of Commercial and Industrial Employers] can, I suggest, perhaps be looked upon as an Insurance Policy and, furthermore, not an Insurance Policy simply to prevent strikes, for strikes are the extremes, an indication of dismal failure by both employers and employees. Our aim must be to build up the whole broad future of industrial relations in East Africa . . .[52]

The fact was that the policy of suppressing political unions could not work unless employers were ready to recognize non-political, industrial unions. With the formation of the FKE the government's own efforts to foster such unions began to have some success, as employers increasingly learned to do business with them. The FKE worked hard on its own account to avoid the formation of what it called 'omnibus' unions, and to induce the workers to form one union for each industry, which would then deal with the purely industrial questions of that industry. In 1960 a review by the Executive Officer of the FKE recorded that they had been successful in this.[53] The credit was actually due at least as much to the government's Labour Department, and – most importantly – to Tom Mboya, the General Secretary of the Kenya Federation of Labour (KFL), which was formed with government support in 1952.[54] Under Mboya the KFL did not always steer clear of politics, but it did not attempt to substitute itself for the unions, or to prevent them being developed with government advice along purely industrial channels. Nor did it call for a radical reconstruction of society, although it did call for nationalization of a range of key industries at independence. As the first African Minister for Labour, Mboya was the architect of an Industrial Relations Charter, signed by both sides of industry in 1962, which pledged the unions to respect the limits and pursue the goals of normal industrial action.

To sum up, then: by the time the New Kenya Group articulated the strategy of collaboration with people emerging from the 'poorer majority', with 'similar interests, and similar ideals, to those economically more advanced', the emergence of such people had already been under way for some time.

The crisis of the Emergency had accelerated the process. It also crystallized the divergence of interest between the settler leader-

---

52. Presidential Address, 11 February 1957, Clarke papers, FKE files.

53. Notes on a Review of FKE Policy, ibid., 28 October 1960.

54. Originally the Kenya Federation of Registered Trade Unions.

ship and the newer commercial and industrial companies. It had made it clear that the system of settler political control and large-scale mixed farming could only be maintained at an unacceptable cost. There would have to be an African government. The mixed farms in the highlands would have to be transferred to Africans, beginning with some of the squatters and other unemployed and landless people from the towns and from the Kikuyu countryside. But provided land transfer could be arranged quickly, yet without a severe drop in production or political unrest, the rest of the economic system need not be affected as long as the incoming African leadership had an interest in preserving it.

This was clear to the commercial and industrial interests in Nairobi, and probably to the plantation companies too. They readily saw that the key problem was to find a formula for the land question. If all the mixed farmers were to run down their farms abruptly the short-term economic effects could jeopardize the continuation of the whole economic system. There would be severe unemployment and a drop in commercial activity. If they abandoned their farms (as some in Trans Nzoia district began to do in 1959) there would certainly be a land-grab; by 1960 landless people were moving onto abandoned or undermanaged farms in increasing numbers, and during the following three years, when the transfer schemes were being implemented, it was in many places frequently a race against time to canalize the rush for land into some sort of settlement scheme before it posed an irresistible threat to the whole white-highland economy. But if any European settlers were expropriated the rest would naturally try to realize their assets and run down their farms. The British government could buy them out, but this was a dangerous precedent. It soon became clear that the essence of the formula must be to have the incoming African settlers purchase the land with funds lent to them by the new Kenya government, which in turn would be lent the money by the British government, and if possible also by the World Bank.[55]

Several objectives were achieved simultaneously by this formula, in addition to satisfying the settlers sufficiently to keep them farming until their turn came to be bought out, as Wasserman has

---

55. G. Wasserman records the anxiety of British officials at this time to involve the World Bank in the land-transfer programme, so as to reduce the risk of any subsequent effort by the independent government of Kenya to default ('The Independence Bargain: Kenya Europeans and the Land Issue 1960-62', *Journal of Commonwealth Political Studies*, Vol. XI, No. 2, July 1973, p. 111).

shown.[56] If there was one claim to individual private property which the African leaders could be expected to reject it was the Europeans' claim to own the land in the highlands. The formula for transfer by purchase meant that those nationalists who felt like this would have to swallow their feelings, or be dropped from the leadership. In addition, acceptance of the formula meant that the new government would be responsible for repaying the loan funds used for the purchase. If the new African settlers sought to escape from their debt for the purchase of the land by having the loan written off or rescheduled, or if they simply defaulted, the Kenya government would be highly unlikely to give in; since it in turn could only escape its debt by renouncing the entire international credit system, on which it would be dependent for capital aid for development expenditure.

This was the formula; it was adumbrated in the New Kenya Group's thinking during 1960, after the first Lancaster House Conference of January 1960 at which the British government finally made it clear that there would be an elected African majority in the next Kenyan legislature. This was brought about at elections held (on a restricted franchise and with some seats reserved for Europeans and Asians) in February 1961. Early in 1962 there was a second conference at Lancaster House to work out a programme for independence. This included an agreement on the land-transfer scheme, on the lines already described.

It may well seem puzzling why the African leaders should have agreed to it, especially since a militant wing of the leading African party, the Kenya African National Union (KANU, formed in 1960), which had the support of all the Kikuyu, had been calling for land transfer without compensation. Among the reasons given by Wasserman are the moderating influence of Kenyatta; the fear of independence being delayed; the hope of changing things after independence; a lack of interest in the detail of the negotiations; a fear that the rival party, the Kenya African Democratic Union (KADU), for whose supporters the land issue was less vital than it was for the Kikuyu, might agree to the proposed scheme first and perhaps manage to get KANU excluded from the transitional government; and finally, the risk of alienating the former forest fighters if they were not provided with land quickly.

All these factors undoubtedly played a part, but the real key to

---

56. ibid.; see also 'The Adaptation of a Colonial Elite', op. cit. (note 31), and Wasserman, 'Continuity and Counter-Insurgency: the Role of Land Reform in Decolonising Kenya 1962–1970', *Canadian Journal of African Studies*, Vol. 7, No. 1, p. 133.

the puzzle perhaps lies in the following passage from a paper by a former squatter, Rebmann Wambaa. After being released from detention in 1959 he was wondering how to re-establish himself on the land in the Rift Valley:

> I knew there were these two possibilities – one that the Rift Valley would be divided free amongst all the tribes, and two, that it would have to be bought. It seemed to me that there were differences between what the constitutional leaders thought and what the fighters were hoping for. But the advice was that we should wait for Mzee Kenyatta to come out of detention and he would decide. There was always this looking forward to Mzee and what he would say. Eventually I thought I would try and find out what the leaders of the Kikuyu people thought; so I approached Gichuru, and asked him in a roundabout way what he thought about these people who seemed to be actually buying land in the White Highlands. He told me it was up to me whether I bought or not. 'But', he said, 'there's only one thing I can say – you will get nothing free.' Now this was back in September 1959.
>
> After talking to some more Kikuyu leaders, I began to see the issue more clearly. The Kikuyu were beginning to think that if the Rift Valley was to be divided amongst the tribes, they would have very little claim. The Maasai would get whole stretches of it to the west of Kijabe, and the various Kalenjin groups would claim much of the rest. The leaders could see that it would be better politics to settle all the major disputes about political matters first; and then eventually open the Rift Valley to all who could afford to buy it. This was quite openly discussed in these terms back in the autumn of 1959. The main leaders therefore all stressed the need to wait for Jomo, but at the same time urged that nothing would be free, and that whatever government was eventually formed, it would not, as Mboya said, be a jungle government. There would be strictness.[57]

The main Kikuyu leaders saw that under a system of private property in land the strata of Kikuyu society which they represented would be able to establish themselves in the Rift Valley. Mboya also recognized that the Luo had no traditional claims to the Rift Valley, and he was also anxious to ensure that power did not pass to the leaders of the forest fighters. They agreed in preferring to see the European-owned land transferred to purchasers, rather than distributed free.

---

57. op. cit., p. 11.

But the KANU leaders' thinking about the land issue must be seen in a wider context that was to have continuing importance in the post-independence period. A country within the capitalist system cannot leave its continued membership of the system long in doubt without an economic crisis. From the moment the British government revealed its intention of giving power to the Africans, at the first Lancaster House conference, in January 1960, the colonial economy entered a crisis from which it did not emerge until well into 1964. When two of the Europeans' delegates flew back to Nairobi during the conference to report what was happening there was an immediate slump on the Nairobi stock market and a standstill in property dealings.[58] A capital flight which had already begun in 1959 now reached panic levels. It was generally agreed that the outflow was of the order of a million pounds a month. Settlers stopped investing in their farms, sold off stock and paid off labour. The building industry came close to a standstill. By the time of the second Lancaster House conference early in 1962, the number of people in employment had fallen by at least 20,000, and was to go on falling for two more years.[59]

The crisis of the colonial economy had a very clarifying effect on the way the various groups perceived their interests. A number of European politicians had been thinking in terms of playing a continued political role, and continuing to influence affairs directly in alliance with the leadership of the 'moderate' tribes, organized from 1960 in the Kenya African Democratic Union (KADU). These ideas were dispelled in the course of 1961.

At the end of that year the Colonial Secretary, Reginald Maudling, visited Nairobi, and the Nairobi Chamber of Commerce leaders told him:

> We did not believe that the economy of the country could recover from its present plight until there was enhanced security for land titles and the sanctity of contract, and that the quicker self-government and independence following it

---

58. Bennett and Rosberg, *The Kenyatta Election* (see note 29), p. 21.

59. The Nairobi Chamber of Commerce's circular letter (see below, pp. 59–60) cited the following statistics. There had been some 325 bankruptcies in the years 1959, 1960, and the first nine months of 1961, with liabilities exceeding assets by a total of some £1·5m. The building societies had become insolvent and were being supported by the Commonwealth Development Corporation. The Stock Exchange index had fallen from 136·4 at the end of 1955 to 96·2 at the end of 1959; it then fell to 61·3 at the end of 1960, and in January 1962 stood at 58·8. Net imports of agricultural machinery for the first seven months of 1961 were 58 per cent down compared with the same period in 1960.

came, the better it would be. We said that there were two
chances under self-government and its following independence:— (1) that the Government, as we believed, would
show itself honourable, efficient and ready to listen to advice;
in which case the economy would slowly recover. . . . The
second chance was that the Government, which we did not
believe would be so, would be corrupt, inefficient and
thoroughly dishonourable. If that happened, we said, the
whole economy would collapse. Either of these possibilities
was better than the vacuum in which most of us were now
trying to survive and save our companies – if not from bankruptcy, at least from very parlous conditions. We therefore
urged him to find a solution as quickly as he could to the
political problems with which he was faced.[60]

In other words, if it was inevitable that KANU under Kenyatta –
hitherto feared and reviled as the convicted 'manager' of Mau
Mau – should form the government, so be it. Rogers, the former
FKE president, had understood this even earlier; in March 1960,
after the first Lancaster House conference, he wrote: 'We are thus
faced with the problem not of governing from power but of
governing by example, influence and persuasion, as we did for
the many years I was on Legislative Council in Nigeria, during
which time the Africans had a large majority.'[61]

To the African leaders the President of the Nairobi Chamber of
Commerce said:

We know that the African leaders do not in their hearts wish
Kenya to revert to the bush and the barbarities of intertribal
war, but they can blame only themselves if some of us are left
wondering whether they realise to what risks their present
immoderate language and behaviour [i.e. talk of free land,
nationalization, etc.] are laying them open, and what the
ultimate reactions may be of a largely unsophisticated and
disillusioned populace.[62]

He followed this up on 29 January 1962 (just before the second
Lancaster House conference) with a circular letter to every
member of the Legislative Council, which set out the statistics of the
economic crisis and spelled out one of the implications as follows:

There is also the important human factor to be considered.

60. Minutes of Annual General Meeting, 27 November 1961; Annexure giving a
statement by the President on the meeting held with the Secretary of State.
61. Letter to Mrs Hughes, 1 March 1960, Hughes papers, Kenya National Archives.
62. Presidential Address, 22 January 1962.

Bankruptcy, the closing down of factories and firms and the continued stagnation or further contraction of business can only add to the already large number of unemployed persons . . . the situation may eventually arise where there will be very little hope of suitable employment outside Government for many men now taking advanced education – men who never can revert to a rural subsistence standard of living and who, bewildered and frustrated, will be stern critics of those who are judged by them to have pursued politics at the expense of the economy.

The African leadership described this as impertinent, but the risk that political power might shift in favour of other people who might be willing to put themselves at the head of the unemployed and landless was probably recognized to be a real one. If a land transfer by means of a loan-financed purchase, and a constitutional guarantee of property rights, were necessary to reduce this risk, it seemed only sensible to accept them. KANU's subsequent renunciation of any break with capitalism, officially proclaimed in 1965 in the Sessional Paper on African Socialism, followed logically from this.

But in any case few of the African leaders in KANU, and probably none in KADU, needed much convincing of the need to restore the dangerously ill colonial economy to health. They were not leaders in the tradition of Chege Kibachia but educated men, many of them relatively young men, such as Mboya, who had entered politics while many of the older leaders were in detention, and few of them were radical in their social or economic outlook. Their education and the whole climate of opinion in which they had moved since school had in most cases been premised on the acceptance of private property and the highly regulated, monopolistic, private enterprise system established under colonialism. They had no thought of effecting any fundamental change in it. A series of foreign missions which visited Nairobi during the period from 1961 to 1963 when the KADU and KANU leaders were in a transitional coalition government, all emphasizing the need for improved conditions for foreign investment, may have reinforced their initial readiness to work within the existing structure.[63] After the pre-independence elections of May 1963,

63. Files in the Kenya National Archives throw some interesting light on these early encounters with the representatives of new sources of foreign capital, which were to become much more important in the post-independence period. The Director of Trade and Supplies reported to his minister in December 1960 that he had just learned that the forthcoming West German mission 'will base its consideration of

when KANU won a large majority and formed a government with Kenyatta as Prime Minister, the new Minister of Finance, James Gichuru, had this to say to the Nairobi Chamber of Commerce:

> One thing that has certainly become commonplace is the observation that our economic development is dependent upon political stability . . . we have, in my view, every reason to feel more confident than ever that it is a question of full steam ahead not only to Uhuru [independence] but into the foreseeable future, and I am glad to see that my view is confirmed by our local Stock Exchange. . . I have said before, and I have no doubt I shall say again, how much importance this Government attaches to new investment, and if any doubts still remain I believe that new measures under consideration [legislative guarantees for foreign investments] will make even the most sceptical potential investor realise how much we do indeed welcome any project which genuinely contributes to our economic well-being. . . . You do not have to go far in Nairobi today to become aware of people in our society, with new tastes, frequently with the money to satisfy them, and themselves creating a new demand amongst their fellows for the better things of life – in fact creating a new market. This development will not be confined to Nairobi. At the same time I hear too frequently of the inadequacy of our distribution system, or the cost of reaching much of this potential market, and incidentally stimulating consumer demands and setting in train the urge 'to keep up with the Joneses' which can contribute so much to our productivity.

financial aid to Kenya not only on pure economic considerations, but also on the wider political aspects of the future of Africa. It will have regard particularly to steps which it might be able to take to counter communist infiltration. This information changed our approach to the type of thing which we might submit to the Mission for consideration . . .' The draft proposals for submission to the Germans particularly emphasized 'the promotion of small business and industry throughout Kenya' (Commerce and Industry File, A106/7). The record of a discussion with a visiting Swiss mission in February 1961 noted that among other things the mission said: 'There is a complete lack of a "Stock Market" in East Africa, though the yield is phenomenal. We must encourage foreign investment in these shares. First some improvement in Income Tax was necessary. Amortisation rates should be raised.' The United States International Cooperation Agency (the forerunner of AID) wrote to the Permanent Secretary for Commerce and Industry in the same month: 'As a result of recent discussions with you and other officials in the Ministry, with Members of the German Mission, and other people, we have decided that such assistance as we will be able to provide, and which the Government of Kenya wishes to employ, could best be directed towards establishing a development bank and the establishing of research and advisory services intended to stimulate sound, profitable expansion of private enterprise in Kenya. Provision in Kenya of courses of training in business management may be a third area of interest . . .' (ibid. note 48).

I suggest that the best way of making good these deficiencies is through the African businessman.[64]

It is in this wider context that Kenyatta's personal role took on the importance which it undoubtedly had. From the moment of his release from detention in 1961 he was completely consistent in his position:

> The Government of an independent Kenya will not be a gangster Government. Those who have been panicky about their property – whether land or buildings or houses – can now rest assured that the future African Government, the Kenya Government, will not deprive them of their property or rights of ownership. We will encourage investors in various projects to come to Kenya and carry on their business peacefully, in order to bring prosperity to this country.[65]

He told the Kikuyu that now 'the time had come to forget the past. People might have been Home Guards or Chiefs, they might have been detainees or in the forests, but they were all brothers and sisters and there should be no revenge.'[66] And in 1963 he told the settlers at a specially convened meeting at Nakuru: 'We want you to stay and farm in this country. You must also learn to forgive one another . . . Kenyatta has no intention of retaliation or looking backwards, we are going to forget the past and look forward . . .'[67]

KANU was a loose party of patrons, not a mass organization, and Kenyatta dominated it from the moment that he accepted the leadership. His steady insistence that private property should be respected, that the settlers should stay, and that the colonial government's consolidation of land and wealth in the Kikuyu country should be left undisturbed, quickly became the official 'line' of the rest of the leadership, and the few more radical KANU leaders were soon isolated. The New Kenya Group itself had been overtaken by the speed of political advance and had disappeared. Europeans had no further public political role to play. But an African leadership with 'similar interests and similar ideas to those economically advanced', which the NKG had looked towards, had indeed emerged, and was in power.

---

64. Speech to the Nairobi Chamber of Commerce on 28 October 1963, NCC files.
65. Jomo Kenyatta, *Suffering Without Bitterness* (East African Publishing House, Nairobi 1968), p. 147.
66. ibid., p. 153.
67. *East African Standard*, 13 August 1963.

CHAPTER 3

Continuity and Change in Agriculture

The linch-pin of the transition from colonial rule was the agreement that the mixed-farm areas in the white highlands should be purchased for African occupation at full 'market' valuation. This fell out as it was planned. By 1970 more than two-thirds of the old European mixed-farm areas had been occupied by an unknown number, but probably with over 500,000 Africans.[1] The remaining third – roughly another million acres – were still in European hands, but would mostly be purchased over the next decade. A further four million acres of ranch land and plantations – coffee, tea and sisal – seemed likely to remain in foreign hands because of their very high capital value.[2] The edge had thus been taken off the

---

1. According to the *Economic Survey 1971* (Government Printer, Nairobi 1971), p. 76, the total farm population on the completed settlement-schemes in 1970 was estimated to be about 300,000. Von Haugwitz's study of 532 plots on five schemes as early as 1967, however, suggests that this could be a large underestimate. Sixty per cent of the plots in his survey were already carrying between ten and twenty persons and over 20 per cent were carrying more than twenty. (H. W. Von Haugwitz, *Some Experiences with Smallholder Settlement in Kenya 1963/64 to 1966/67*, Weltforum Verlag, Munich 1971, Table 20.) In addition 18,000 squatter families had been settled on 4·5-hectare plots, which may be assumed to be carrying smaller populations than those in the 'million acre scheme', but perhaps not less than six persons per plot, or a total of roughly 75,000. In addition 28,000 squatters had been registered but not resettled, according to the *Development Plan, 1970–74* (Government Printer, Nairobi 1969), p. 207, and *Economic Survey 1971*, p. 77; with their dependents these probably accounted for about 150,000 people, of whom perhaps 50,000 would have been on farms transferred to Africans. On the African-owned large farms there had also been a substantial population increase, especially on farms transferred to co-operatives: some of these were *de facto* low-density settlement-schemes. On fifty-five 'problem' farms in Trans Nzoia in 1971 an official report stated that there were 13,400 people on 50,000 acres, with the population rising fairly rapidly. I think it is unlikely that the large farms in African ownership by 1970, amounting to 1·6 million acres, were carrying less than 150,000 people.

2. Of the 3 million hectares in the former white highlands, 1·6 millions were used for plantations or ranches. 'During the new plan period the same conditions which have previously hindered rapid Africanization of ranches and plantations will continue to prevail. For this reason it is expected that only a small proportion of the ranches and plantations will be acquired by Africans in the next few years.' (*Development Plan 1970–74*, ibid., note 1, p. 199).

land hunger of the 'fifties, with a minimum of disturbance to the colonial agricultural economy. Public attention was directed firmly away from the old white highlands to the former reserves; it was now officially declared that the special importance of the white highlands had been exaggerated.[3] The system of agricultural surplus extraction built up over half a century seemed to have been carried over almost intact into the era of political independence.

And yet this system had changed in important ways. The land-transfer programme did not take place in a historical vacuum. The hundreds of thousands of Africans who moved into the former European farms were part of a much larger social and economic transformation – the consummation of the switch from a variety of pre-colonial systems of production and exchange to 'peasant' production throughout Kenya.[4] The need to limit cash production in the reserves, in order to get enough labour for European farms, had diminished rapidly from the mid-1920s onwards, but full freedom for Africans to grow profitable crops, and sustained agricultural extension efforts among Africans, had come only in the 1950s. In 1963 the process was still gathering momentum among the Kikuyu, Embu and Meru; it was in progress, though at earlier stages, in other high-potential areas; in other areas still, it had barely begun. The pattern of land use, crop distribution, technology, farm organization, labour utilization, farm income – in short the whole structure of the emergent 'peasant' farming economy – was in a state of flux. The social relations of 'peasant' production were equally fluid and plastic. To control and mould all these changes, and to fit them into the wider framework of

3. 'The present practice of spending a large proportion of the Government budget on the settlement and development of a limited acreage in former European areas should be phased out and future funds channelled to the development of the great potential of the African Areas.' (*African Socialism and its Application to Planning in Kenya*, Government Printer, Nairobi 1965, p. 37). The 1966–70 *Development Plan* expanded this: 'There is sound economic justification for the shift in emphasis to development of the former African areas; and the former African areas contain 80 per cent of Kenya's high potential agricultural land' (p. 125).

4. The term 'peasant production' will be used to refer generically to the various modes of small-scale commodity and subsistence production, based on household labour, which resulted from the impact of colonialism on most of the Kenyan countryside; see Ch. 6, pp. 170–71. For a general discussion of the concept see T. Shanin (ed.), *Peasants and Peasant Societies* (Penguin, London 1971), pp. 11–15; on peasants in Africa see J. S. Saul and R. Woods, 'African Peasantries', ibid., pp. 103–13. Some discussion of the concept in relation to Kenya may be found in C. Leys, 'Politics in Kenya: The Development of Peasant Society', *British Journal of Political Science*, Vol. I, 1971, pp. 313–43.

periphery capitalism, called for new policies and institutions.

By the end of the 1960s the general outline of these had become clear. The two central policies were the individualization of land tenure, and the differential provision of credit. These were supplemented by a wide variety of institutional mechanisms designed to integrate peasant production into the established capitalist economic framework.

The main architect of the new agricultural system was Bruce Mackenzie, a former settler farmer who had been one of a small group of leading Europeans to join KANU on its formation in 1960. He became Minister of Agriculture under Kenyatta in 1962 and remained in this post until 1970, when he retired from politics. His appointment was designed to reassure the remaining European farmers and secure their co-operation in maintaining output while the land-transfer programme went ahead.

The land-transfer programme mainly involved the movement of a mass of African 'peasant' farmers into the former white highlands. But side by side with this a small stratum of politicians, civil servants and traders aspired to take the place of the European settlers as large-scale capitalist farmers. The mechanisms which had formerly secured the privileged position of European mixed farmers had to be kept in operation in their interests, as well as those of the remaining Europeans; and as a matter of fact, the incoming African large-scale farmers needed even more protection than their white predecessors. New institutions such as the Agricultural Finance Corporation, the Agricultural Development Corporation, the large-scale Farmers' Training Centre and many others were grafted onto the existing structure of agencies, boards and farmers' organizations.

Mackenzie used a number of the remaining European settlers in key positions in the new structure – as chairmen of these two new Corporations, for instance, and of most of the marketing boards. He also drew expatriate manpower from several Western aid agencies into these institutions and into his own ministry. In no other sphere was the transition from colonial political control to one of pervasive metropolitan influence – based on advice, technical assistance and credit – so clearly visible.

The new agricultural system was purpose-made, and exceptionally well backed by external funds and manpower, and on the whole it worked well throughout the 1960s: the tensions and conflicts arising from a process of rapid economic change and social differentiation were mostly moderated and contained. In the longer run the contradictions of underdevelopment would express themselves in agriculture, as in other sectors of Kenyan society. But the policies pursued in the 1960s ensured that when this happened there would be a structure of agrarian interests and an institutional apparatus strong enough to resist pressures for radical change.

INDIVIDUAL TENURE

In Kikuyuland, and in neighbouring Embu and Meru, individual forms of land tenure had existed before colonial rule, although communal forms also existed alongside them.[5] The introduction of the colonial monetary economy accelerated the growth of individual tenure, and spread it to other parts of Kenya (notably to North Nyanza) by putting cash from salaries into the hands of 'chiefs, tribunal elders and the educated minority' who could use their wealth to get land either by direct purchase or by costly litigation.[6] Down to 1952 official policy shrank from facing the consequences of the growth of individual tenure, mainly because officials feared political unrest arising from landlessness.[7] The idea of 'group farms' was considered as an alternative which would make possible the granting of some form of title without disruptive social consequences.[8] But this idea belonged really to the old 'Dual Policy' conception of a pattern of economic development in the 'Native Areas' which would be divorced from that of the white highlands and the towns. It would have had to be imposed by the administration, since the emerging leaders in the reserves were the very people who were acquiring individual landholdings. It had no serious backing among senior officials in Nairobi.

---

5. *Report of Committee on Agricultural Credit for Africans* (Government Printer, Nairobi 1950), Memorandum by W. E. Wainwright and L. H. Brown, p. 30; see also L. S. B. Leakey, 'The Economics of Kikuyu Tribal Life', *East African Economics Review*, Vol. 3, No. 1, July 1956, p. 166.

6. See M. P. K. Sorrenson, *Land Reform in the Kikuyu Country* (Oxford University Press, Nairobi 1967), pp. 40, 44–5; for other areas, see the memoranda published by the Committee on Agricultural Credit (op. cit.), especially at p. 38, showing how servicemen's pay was employed for land purchase in North Nyanza; another writer on that area reckoned that 75 per cent of the people were individual land-owners, and noted also that 'It is still possible for rich and educated people to rob others of their land by means of their wealth and ready wit' (pp. 46–7).

7. Sorrenson, *Land Reform*, p. 70.

8. ibid., pp. 62–3; *Committee on Agricultural Credit*, p. 38.

As the 1940s wore on, however, the changes which were occurring in the colonial economy as a whole forced the issue. The
'clearances' of squatters from European farms as land was fenced
for cattle aggravated the now serious pressure of population in the
reserves, especially in Kikuyu country.[9] Land fertility was declining in many areas. Apart from the threat of political instability,
the necessary complementarity between the white highlands and
the reserves was now threatened by the risk that the reserves might
no longer be able to furnish a subsistence for the families of their
absent agricultural wage-labourers. But it now seemed obvious
that to restore, let alone increase, land productivity in the reserves
there must be long-term investment in the land. This meant
that some form of security of tenure was needed – the very
thing Kikuyu nationalists had been demanding since the early
1920s.

It was significant that the issue over which the question finally
crystallized was the provision of credit. According to Sorrenson,

> As was soon to become obvious, agricultural credit could
> hardly be issued to individuals if the title to land was to be
> vested in some vague entity called the kinship group, the
> community, or the tribe. Yet the issue of agricultural credit
> was essential if farming was to be adequately capitalised and
> improved.[10]

This is probably a fair summary of official thinking at the time,
but its implied assumptions deserve comment. One was that
capital was lacking. This may have been true in Kikuyu country,
reflecting the very high level of exploitation of this most economically active of all Kenyan peoples over the previous fifty years;
opportunities for capital accumulation had been largely confined
to those with non-agricultural incomes.[11] It was less clearly true
of, for instance, the Nandi, the value of whose 'excess' stock alone

---

9. Sorrenson, *Land Reform*, ibid. (note 6), pp. 80–82.

10. ibid., pp. 60–61.

11. Swynnerton saw this quite clearly in relation to the future: 'Were each farmer
with a registered title to his land able to borrow up to this amount (£150–300)
against the security of his title, ultimately borrowing would greatly exceed the
resources of Kenya. However, if the development of cash crop growing is pressed
as intensively as suggested in this plan, the African farmer will in due course be
able to secure a substantial income of his own for reinvestment in his farm and
will therefore not be so much in need of outside assistance.' (*A Plan to Intensify the
Development of African Agriculture in Kenya*, Government Printer, Nairobi 1955,
p. 55).

was estimated at £200,000 in 1945–6.[12] The assumption that credit was essential may have reflected in part the special place of Kikuyu problems in official thinking, but it seems clear that it was also due to the assumption that improved African farming would have to be fitted into the same general pattern as European farming, without disturbing protected, high-price markets. To do this, Africans would need the same sort of capital that Europeans used, and so the same sort of credit.[13] Secondly, there was the assumption that credit would be issued to individuals. Although the Committee on Agricultural Credit for Africans envisaged that co-operative societies would be major recipients of loans, the practical implication of much of the report was clearly that individual farmers would be the beneficiaries and that the object in lending to them was to lead to 'better farming practices generally by multiplying and spreading the examples of properly farmed units'.[14] Thirdly, there was the assumption that the only real security was land. Once again the Committee on Credit stated that 'the main security must be that of personal character' (because of the absence of any general form of individual title for Africans at the time); but the prevailing view was expressed by Chief Magugu Waweru of Kiambu, who said 'Land, of course, is the only reliable form of security.'[15]

In short, once the question was posed as one of bringing the Africans' lands into production for the existing markets without prejudice to established European production, the question of introducing any form of tenure other than individual tenure disappeared from view – with few regrets among the African landowners such as Chief Waweru, who were the only Africans consulted. Before the Emergency, however, official action was para-

---

12. *Committee on Agricultural Credit*, p. 48. Cf. also N. Leys's comment on the Masai: 'In 1913 a Savings Bank was started among the Masai. Whoever was responsible for this idea must have had prodigious faith in thrift as the panacea for social ills when we remember that the live stock owned by the tribes must be worth at least four million pounds.' (*Kenya*, Ch. 2, note 4, p. 115.)

13. ibid., p. 31, Memorandum by the D.C. and Senior Assistant Agricultural Officer, Kiambu: '. . . it is as well to bear in mind that it is virtually impossible to envisage any great advance in the general standard of Agriculture and Animal Husbandry in a Reserve without credit being made available to Africans on terms similar to those available to Europeans.' But it is interesting to note that the Committee, with its one African member dissenting, recommended a rate of interest which would in practice have been almost double that charged to Europeans (pp. 6 and 9).

14. ibid., p. 2 and elsewhere.

15. ibid., pp. 7 and 34.

lysed by fear of the political consequences among the Kikuyu landless in Central Province and the Rift Valley. But once their radical leaders were in detention the opportunity arose to cut the Gordian knot. In September 1953 the government instructed R. J. M. Swynnerton, the Assistant Director of Agriculture, to draw up *A Plan to Intensify the Development of African Agriculture*.[16] It was ready within two months, and spelled out a comprehensive programme of consolidating fragments of land and registering the unified acreage under individual freehold titles, on the basis of which loans could be issued to individuals.

By 1956 this policy was being implemented throughout Kikuyu-land. By 1960 the whole Kikuyu country had been registered. In 1959–60 the programme was extended to Meru, Embu, Nandi and Baringo. By 1965 it was in progress in all Provinces.[17] It was then reviewed and greatly accelerated, with the help of a British loan of £3·4m. The total registered area more than doubled between 1965 and 1969, and between 1970 and 1974 it was expected to increase more than fourfold, from 1·6 million hectares to over 9 million – effectively covering not only most of the agricultural land in Kenya, but a large proportion of the pastoral areas as well.[18]

During the 1970–74 plan, this would consume 16 per cent of development expenditure on agriculture. Why was it given such priority? In 1965, at the request of the Kenya government, the British government sent a mission to review the registration and consolidation programme. It reported that public demand for registration was very largely due to 'continuous and dedicated urging and propaganda', that in many areas there was 'deep and widespread lack of understanding' of the programme and its effects, and that in some places the demand was 'ephemeral'.[19] The mission thought that where the demand existed it was due to fear of losing one's land, and the belief that registration of title would make it secure. As the mission pointed out, the only threat against which registration provides real security is that of losing it through being unable to match a rich man's resources in litigation if the traditional title is obscure; by giving individuals disposable titles it actually made former tribal or clan lands more liable to

16. See Ch. 2, p. 52.
17. *Report of the Mission on Land Consolidation and Registration in Kenya 1965–66* (the Lawrance Report) (Government Printer, Nairobi 1966), Appendix D, Table B.
18. *Development Plan 1970–74*, p. 194.
19. Lawrance Report, p. 23 (see note 17).

pass by private sales into the ownership of people outside the tribe or clan.[20] On the other hand the mission was unable to say that registration of individual title had any clear economic effect, except to aggravate the problem of landlessness. 'We ourselves are certainly in no doubt', they said, 'about the overall benefits which generally accrue to individuals and Government through consolidation and registration.' But on their own evidence, this confidence did not rest on any demonstrable cause-and-effect. They pointed vaguely to 'the changed face of the countryside, which for any resident of Kenya whose memory goes back ten years, must indeed present a vivid picture';[21] hardly a very convincing argument, given the fact that it was precisely in those years that Africans had for the first time been allowed to plant the one highly profitable crop in Kenya at that time, coffee, and that the reserves had received 'massive injections of capital'.[22]

The truth of the matter was, however, that the Lawrance Mission's job was not to assess the objective effects of land registration, but to recommend 'a realistic acceleration' of the programme, as they themselves put it.[23] From their own account of the background to the appointment of the mission, the following facts emerge. The Kenya government was seeking aid for a broad programme of agricultural development. As far as the ex-reserves (now called 'Kenya's peasant farming areas') were concerned, this involved, first, an accelerated programme of land registration, and then the provision of credit and extension services. The British government undertook to finance the former, provided the Kenya government could obtain funds (i.e. from other sources) for agricultural credit. The 'other sources', on the other hand, had made it clear that they would only finance credit for farmers who had freehold tenure.[24] The job of the mission was to draw up and cost

---

20. The report cited the evidence of 'the Ngong area of Masailand where registration of land to individual Masai has resulted in immediate sale to Kikuyu farmers and consequent loss of the land to the Masai tribe, probably for ever' (p. 25).

21. ibid., p. 22.

22. Sorrenson, *Land Reform*, p. 223 (see note 6). Africans outside Central Province, in areas further removed from European coffee estates, had been allowed to plant coffee earlier.

23. Lawrance Report, p. 2.

24. The Lawrance Report does not say who they all were but the 1970–74 *Development Plan* indicates that they were the International Development Association of the World Bank, the United Nations Development Programme, USAID, the Swedish International Development Agency, and the West German government. See the *Plan*, p. 218, where the emphasis on the prior necessity for land registration is twice repeated.

a programme for registering titles to land (at the speed called for by the proposed schemes for agricultural credit) for smallholders and for pastoralists, involving a total of just under £20 million over five years.[25] So the question then becomes one of just why the Kenya government and the aid donors were so determined to tie the provision of agricultural credit to individual ownership of land.

The answer is in the end a simple one. The Lawrance Mission saw clearly that in Kenya in the mid 'sixties, the idea that freehold title gave creditors security by enabling them to foreclose was unrealistic. Yet they noted that the commercial banks had none the less come round to the view that in future they would not lend except on the security of a land title, although they accepted that their real security lay in the loanee having some other source of income on which they could if necessary distrain. The banks thought the 'knowledge that he *could* lose his land if he defaulted' helped to make a farmer take his obligation to repay more seriously.[26] Since the banks had provided as much credit for small-holders as the government had in the previous seven years, their thinking was bound to weigh with the members of the mission. But what probably clinched the matter was the mission's encounter with officials of the World Bank, who were considering providing credit for cattle-ranching by the pastoral tribes. The mission wrote:

> The intention is that the land comprising these group ranches should be registered, because registration is likely to be a con-dition of the grant of external loan money. . . . We were in some doubt as to the real need for registration of group ranch land as a condition of loans. Individual ranches whose land is not registered have already been given credit by the Agricultural Finance Corporation on other security, and ob-viously the pledging of group range land against a loan will not by itself provide any valid security to the lender, for it would clearly be impossible for the lender to sell a large tract of Masailand in default of repayment of the loan. We are, however, convinced after discussions with representatives of the World Bank, that registration of group ranches is a pre-

---

25. 'This [smallholder] credit programme obviously affects the land registration programme since it implies that a given area of land must be registered by the year in which it is planned to bring farms into the project' (p. 130); 'it is clear that registration is a pre-requisite of the range development programme. The acreages which must be registered for this purpose by the beginning of each year are shown in Table 7 . . .' (p. 131).

26. ibid., p. 126; italics added.

requisite to the loan of money for development purposes. Without the certainty of ownership and the clear right of the group to exclude outsiders, which is provided by registration, no agency would be prepared to lend money for range development.[27]

Later, in their report, the mission just extended this argument to the smallholder credit programme as well, in spite of the inconsistency involved: 'Without the security that registration affords, loans (to smallholders) of the duration envisaged . . . would not merit consideration by any financing body.'[28] The mission had got the message; the lenders wanted the land to be registered before they would lend. But they seem to have remained puzzled about the reason – perhaps because it was too obvious. The lenders were not going to disburse £20 million of capital among a peasant population without ensuring that – in a word – it would be as far as possible seen and used as capital, and as far as possible serve to break down precapitalist attitudes and social institutions and replace them with the ideas and incentives of the market.

The 'inner secret' of the drive towards complete individual freehold land tenure was thus not so much its particular merits as its general merits: it flowed logically from the critical decision to accept the general structure of the colonial economy. That structure rested on individual property. The main capital asset of the Africans in Kenya was land. For it to be held ultimately on the basis of some other principle was simply inconsistent with the effective incorporation of the African economy into the wider capitalist structure, which was what the policy of 'channelling future funds to the development of the African areas' (later outlined in Sessional Paper No. 10 of 1965 on African Socialism) meant. This was the felt conviction of the officials in Central Province in the 'forties and 'fifties, of the officials who prepared the loan applications for agriculture in 1964–5, of the commercial banks, and of the World Bank and other aid donors. It also made sense to most of the political leadership, who were or aimed to become landowners; and as the Lawrance Mission noted, to most poor peasants too, since it seemed to give legal protection to their

27. ibid., p. 31. 'Group ranches' were to be created out of land allocated to groups of pastoral families. See H. G. Hedlund, 'The Impact of Group Ranches on a Pastoral Society' (Institute for Development Studies, Nairobi 1971, mimeo); and J. M. Halderman, 'An Analysis of Continued Semi-Nomadism on the Kaputie Masai Group Ranches' (Institute for Development Studies, 1972, mimeo).

28. Lawrance Report, p. 129.

land assets, however small, in an increasingly competitive and insecure world.

The long-term social and economic effects of individualized tenure and the differential provision of credit (which is discussed below) would be far-reaching. In the short run, however, most people with some customary title to land got a new title under registration, and it was only the landless in the overcrowded parts of the former reserves who found themselves worse off, and then only to the extent that the new individual titleholders might be less inclined to afford them customary rights to cultivate small sub-sistence plots. The problem presented by the Kikuyu landless was overcome at first by the Emergency regulations and detention. As the detainees began to be released, it was hoped that increased employment of labourers on the consolidated holdings would mop up the surplus of landless people. But as Sorrenson was the first to point out, the average consolidated holding was incapable of em-ploying a wage-labour force of the scale the officials had counted on.[29] The problem was greatly aggravated by the run-down of the labour force in the white highlands which began in 1960, as some settlers, especially in Uasin Gishu District, ran down their farms and left rather than accept the prospect of an African government. It was at this point that 'settlement schemes' in the white high-lands came to be seen as an urgent necessity, and became fused with the wider problem of financing and administering the transfer of the mixed-farm areas of the white highlands to Africans without damaging the general fabric of the colonial economy.

SETTLEMENT SCHEMES

A great deal has been written about the settlement schemes, which is not surprising in view of their scale in human terms, their finan-cial cost, and their crucial role in effecting the transition to political independence without radical economic change.[30] By

---

29. Sorrenson, *Land Reform*, pp. 223–5.

30. The two major sources to date are the *Report of the Mission on Land Settlement in Kenya* (Nairobi, 1966, mimeo) (the Van Arkadie report), and H. W. Von Haug-witz, op. cit., 1971 (see note 1), which contains a short bibliography. See also W. Nguyo, 'Some Socio-Economic Aspects of Land Settlement in Kenya', University Social Science Council Conference Papers (Kampala, December 1966), and J. W. Harbeson, 'Land Reforms and Politics in Kenya, 1954–70', *Journal of Modern African Studies*, Vol. 9, No. 2, August 1971, pp. 231–52. A forth-coming study by C. Leo is foreshadowed in his 'Neocolonialism and the Adminis-

1970 35,401 families had been settled on the Million Acre Scheme and a further 18,000 on Squatter Settlement Schemes:[31] probably nearly half a million people had their homes on settlement schemes by this time. Excluding the Squatter Schemes, the programme down to the middle of 1969 had cost over £29 m., of which £14 m. was borrowed abroad, a third of all the foreign debt incurred from 1961 to 1969.[32] To the extent that this covered the transfer of land and stock from European to African owners, and was thus entirely unproductive, 'Kenya was agreeing to reduce her future national income in order to facilitate a smooth social transition'.[33]

The first settlement scheme was launched in January 1961. It was to cost £7½ million, provided by Britain, the Commonwealth Development Corporation and the World Bank, and would have settled 1,800 'yeoman' farmers on farms designed to yield net incomes (after loan charges and repayments) of £250 per annum or more; and 6,000 'peasant' farmers on farms designed to yield net incomes of about £100 per annum. This scheme proved unworkable financially. By the time a revised scheme was agreed, late in 1961, the political climate had imposed the necessity of expanding the programme to include an additional 12,000 settlers. These were to be settled on 'smallholder' plots yielding net annual incomes of £25–40. A further expansion was agreed in 1962, while at the same time the 'yeoman' programme was abandoned when only 132 such plots had been settled.[34] The 1962 programme was defined in terms of the acreages to be bought and allocated to 'low density' plots (180,000 acres) and 'high density' plots (987,000 acres), corresponding to the former 'peasant' and 'smallholder' categories. The land purchased lay around the edges of the white highlands, adjacent to each of the surrounding 'African Land Units' – i.e. tribal Reserves.[35] In course of time the

---

tration of Development' (Nairobi 1972, mimeo), and 'The Defence of European Interests at Independence: the case of the Million-Acre Scheme' (Nairobi 1973, mimeo). See also Ministry of Economic Planning and Development, Statistics Division, 'Economic Survey of Settlement Schemes, Preliminary Results, Summary of Data from 1964–65 to 1966/67' (Nairobi 1971, mimeo).

31. Figures from *Economic Survey 1971*, pp. 76–7.

32. Department of Settlement Annual Report 1968/69, p. 13.

33. Van Arkadie Report (see note 30), p. 39.

34. The title of 'yeoman' was replaced by that of 'assisted owner'.

35. For the picture in 1965 see R. S. Odingo, *The Kenya Highlands: Land Use and Agricultural Development* (East African Publishing House, Nairobi 1971), Fig. 85, p. 204.

whole operation became known as the Million Acre Scheme, after the nearly one million acres bought for high-density settlement. By the middle of 1971 roughly 29,000 families had been settled on 'high-density' plots, and 5,000 on larger 'low-density' plots.[36] In 1960 a so-called 'Harambee' (a watchword coined by Kenyatta, meaning, roughly, 'all pull together') Scheme was announced. This was later reduced to a single scheme of about 17,000 acres, accommodating 450 families who were settled in 1969–70, on plots designed to give a net annual income of £40–75, i.e. somewhere in between the target incomes of low- and high-density plots.[37] Meanwhile, in 1965 squatter settlement had also got under way, settling people registered as squatters by a Special Commissioner for Squatters. The 18,000 families settled in this way by 1970 formed yet another tier, this time at the bottom, receiving an average 4·5 hectares each (i.e. an apparent total of roughly 200,000 acres).[38] They were not set any particular income targets, but neither were they provided with any significant loan funds, or technical assistance, and the question of how much they would pay for their plots, and on what terms, was left unsettled, so that in the short run no one was really concerned about the level of cash incomes they achieved.[39]

The total area covered by settlement was thus of the order of 1½ million acres; a fifth of the old white highlands, perhaps 4 per cent of the total area of the country available for agriculture. It was important, but not all that important, in terms of the land resources used. It probably carried rather less than its proper share of the total population, given the quality of the land involved (500,000 people would have been roughly 4 per cent of the estimated 11·2 million total population in 1970). It provided these people with an above-average standard of subsistence and produced cash sales worth at least £2·5 million in 1969–70, or roughly 6 per cent of the total value of production from the 'small farm' sector (i.e. all farms other than the remaining large farms and

36. *Statistical Abstract 1971*, p. 82.

37. *Development Plan 1970–74*, p. 207.

38. ibid., and *Economic Survey 1971*, p. 77.

39. The land used for squatter settlement appears to have been mainly compulsorily acquired by the government from 'mismanaged' (i.e. largely abandoned) European-owned farms, which would explain the lack of haste about determining the settlement terms for purchasing it. The Special Commissioner was another of Mackenzie's innovations. People who could establish that they had no land and were squatting in May 1966 were registered as squatters whom the government undertook to settle: 46,000 were registered.

plantations in the former white highlands).[40] In view of the fact that the settlement schemes were mostly in so-called 'high-potential' areas, marketed production should have been higher, but it was already quite large in relation to the recent date at which the settlers' farms were first established, and it was rising. Output for sale may have been much less than it had been when the land was farmed by Europeans, who were estimated to have marketed £4½–5 million worth of produce from it before settlement.[41] But the difference was more than offset by the expansion of marketed production in the former reserves, and besides, the new settlers were obviously consuming a higher proportion of total output than the former European farmers and their labourers did. In other words, the settlement schemes had succeeded in nine years in converting 1½ million acres to comparatively prosperous 'peasant' agriculture, besides fulfilling what the Van Arkadie mission thought might well be seen as its 'major productive role', namely 'its contribution to the maintenance of a milieu [i.e. a political milieu] in which the rest of the economy could operate effectively.'[42]

There were really only two reasons why settlement schemes continued to attract such special attention as they did throughout the 1960s, apart from the fact that so long as they were incomplete, people still tried all possible ways of being included in them. One was the continued power of the myth of the importance of large-scale mixed farming. This was well captured in a letter from the Director of Agriculture to the Permanent Secretary to the Ministry of Land Settlement (both still Europeans) in June 1963:

---

40. Cash sales through co-operatives are recorded in the *Economic Survey* (1971, p. 76) and total cash sales by the 'small-farm sector' as a whole, in ibid., p. 60. However, not all the marketed output of the settlement schemes goes through the co-operatives, so that the schemes' share in the total is understated. The degree of understatement could be very considerable since the settlers' loan repayments were often deducted from their income from sales through the co-operatives, so that there was a further incentive, in addition to the grave weakness of the co-operatives on the settlement schemes, for the settlers to sell their produce through other channels. The higher 'black market' prices obtainable for some government-controlled crops at various times during the 1960s may also have diverted settlers' sales away from the co-operatives.

41. Van Arkadie Report (see note 30), p. 41. In comparing the value of the schemes' sales with that of the former European-owned farms it must also be remembered that large farms as such enjoyed privileged access to profitable markets (e.g. for maize and, until 1970, milk) which were not enjoyed by the African settlers simply because they were smallholders.

42. ibid., p. 24.

From a purely agricultural point of view we are well aware, and always have been, of the retrograde nature of the present development whereby the economic-sized holdings are being carved up and replaced by small holdings which, although they may in some cases result in increased production, are unlikely to have the same net economic effect on the country. We have, however, been forced into settlement through widespread unemployment and distress and the need to make a beginning in the extraction of that part of the European farming community which wishes to leave Kenya.[43]

From this point of view any drop in marketed production from the settlement scheme represented a 'retrograde' effect, even if gross production had been maintained or even increased. This view seems to have rested partly on the cherished but erroneous belief that the European mixed farmers made a major net contribution to the balance of payments; and partly on unsupported and probably unanalysed assumptions about the disadvantages of distributing incomes in favour of the peasant majority, for instance the assumption that they have a lower propensity to save; and partly on technical suppositions such as that certain crops or animal products cannot be produced 'economically' on smallholdings. Despite contrary evidence these ideas died very hard, especially among those who had acquired large farms.[44] They reinforced the government's decision in 1969 to terminate settlement programmes once the balance of the registered squatters had

---

43. Kenya National Archives, Ministry of Agriculture, 2/352.

44. The Stamp Mission noted that the African large-scale farmers they met 'naturally wished to see preserved the large farm structure which they considered as being more productive and offering greater employment opportunities than the small-scale farms instituted under the settlement schemes'. (*Report of the Mission Appointed to Advise on Proposals for a Further Transfer of European Farmers in Kenya*, 1965, mimeo, p. 38.) In point of fact settlement schemes even in 1967 employed roughly 38,000 men and women as monthly-paid wage-workers on something over one million acres. No separate figures exist for employment in the large-scale mixed farms, as opposed to the remainder of the ex-White Highlands as a whole, but it may be reasonable to suppose that the remaining large-scale mixed farms, covering some 2 million acres, did not employ more than half of the 171,000 workers employed by large-scale agriculture and forestry in 1967, over a total acreage of over 6 million; i.e. roughly 85,000 (a 'conservative estimate' by the Kenyan government in 1963 put the figure at 70,000). The *wage*-employment opportunities created by settlement were thus roughly equal to those of large-scale mixed farming even as early as 1967, and the *total* 'employment opportunities' were evidently far greater. What the large-scale farmers meant was 'opportunities to employ wage labourers under conditions yielding a substantial surplus for the employer'.

been found plots (assuming they were – the government seemed dubious on this point).[45]

But the second reason why the settlement schemes attracted special attention was more important. It was financial. The settlers were not repaying their loans. By 1970 44 per cent of their debt service and repayment charges were in arrears.[46] The total sum outstanding and overdue was £3·1 million. Two years previously it had been only £1·6 million. With interest payable at 6½ per cent on the accumulating arrears, it was clear that a point could soon be reached when the actual payments being made by the settlers taken as a whole would not even cover the annual interest charges, and their total indebtedness would simply climb out of reach of any conceivable ability of the land to repay it. In effect, this would ultimately mean writing off the arrears, if not the original debt. Alternatively, the settlers might in due course come to see the impossibility of ever paying off their debts and start paying less and less each year, rather than more. Either alternative would call in question the basic assumption of the independence bargain, that everything had its price and must be paid for.

In 1965 a mission (the Stamp Mission) was sent to Kenya from London to advise on British aid for further programmes of land transfer. It was horrified by the financial position of the settlement schemes and firmly recommended that there should be no more of them until the Kenya government had undertaken economic surveys to 'reassess the economics of settlement and to initiate measures to avoid any possible catastrophe'. They also recommended that Britain should provide technical assistance to help to determine 'what adjustments in settlement planning and policy are necessary and what measures should be taken to secure the existing loan programmes'. This led to the Van Arkadie mission of 1966. The Van Arkadie mission saw perfectly well that the settlement schemes had been a success, since without them the whole colonial economic structure would very likely have been destroyed. On the other hand they also clearly saw the dilemma presented by the failure of the settlers to repay their loans. There were many reasons for the arrears, but the chief one was that the high-density schemes were a dangerous compromise between what the mission called 'development' schemes and 'social relief'

---

45. See *Economic Survey 1971*, p. 77. The 1970–74 *Plan* projected an expenditure of £3·3 million on squatter settlement (p. 201), but without indicating how it would be allocated as between land purchase, development, and administration.

46. *Economic Survey 1971*, p. 77.

schemes. To get more people on to a given amount of land, the plots had been made so small that even if all went exactly as planned, the settler who paid his debts on time would be left with a net cash income that was simply too small to meet his most essential family expenditure. In many cases, the mission found, even the optimistic target budgets expected the poorest settlers to pay over 70 per cent of their net farming income in debt repayments, and to be left with a sum of £25, from which they could not even afford primary-school fees for their children, let alone secondary-school fees.[47] But if the settlers generally were allowed to default, the whole agrarian credit structure could collapse:

> The danger of a lax attitude would be very great, and a rapid reaction throughout all the settlement schemes to any sign of weakness on the part of the Government would arise, if at any time the pressure was taken off. The effect of a general feeling that Government could be persuaded not to insist on prompt loan repayments would be felt far beyond the boundaries of the settlement schemes . . . the Trustees' . . . attitude toward loan repayment from settlers will inevitably set a pattern for those farmers outside of the schemes who have already undertaken similar loan commitments, or may be encouraged to do so under various development credit programmes.[48]

Faced with this dilemma, the Van Arkadie mission made a number of related proposals. First, the Kenya government's debt to the British government, the Commonwealth Development Corporation and the World Bank should be rescheduled to allow the probable actual rate of repayments by settlers to be accepted without strain by the Kenya government. Second, the settlers' arrears should be made free of interest charges, so that their debt would in effect be rescheduled too. Third, each scheme and each plot should be reviewed to relate the terms of repayment, and if necessary the total level of debt, to what experience showed to be realistic targets of output and reasonable standards of family expenditure. Fourth, in the context of these changes, a much tougher attitude should be taken on evicting persistent defaulters. Down to 1966 only two settlers had been evicted. By 1969, acting under new powers granted in 1965, the authorities had evicted ninety settlers; they evicted seventy-six between 1966 and 1968, and a further fourteen in 1968–9.[49] But down to 1970 this was the only

---

47. Van Arkadie Report (see note 30), pp. 160–61.
48. ibid., p. 162.
49. Department of Settlement Annual Reports, 1967/68 and 1968/69.

way in which the Van Arkadie mission's ideas on this subject seemed to have been implemented. Repayment levels rose in 1968/9 to £820,000, close to the level which the mission thought a reasonable target for that year; but on the basis of only half of the cash sales assumed by the mission. In other words, it seemed as if a tougher policy had produced results by 'squeezing' settlers, many of whom had other sources of income. Meanwhile the interest payable on the arrears alone now amounted to more than a fifth of the settlers' annual level of payments. The situation envisaged by the mission was drawing nearer: 'The existing arrangements cannot fail to lead to a financial crisis for the Kenya Government.'[50]

In the 1970–4 Plan the government reported that it was negotiating with the British government for a rescheduling of the debt. It is interesting to speculate on why this had taken so long. During the three years since the Van Arkadie mission the interest-bearing arrears had risen from under £1 million to over £3 million, a sum equivalent to roughly a third of the settlers' total original debt by that time. It seems clear that there existed in the Kenyan Treasury an extreme dislike of any action which might be taken as a sign of lack of national creditworthiness, and might risk jeopardizing the continued inflow of foreign funds.[51] And the internal rescheduling and writing down of the settlers' debts, however justified, could hardly be carried through in practice without the very risks that the Van Arkadie mission saw as attending the results of inaction: for the fact was that all categories of farmers, large and small, who were in receipt of loan funds were in arrears too, and it is doubtful if a single one who was in arrears did not consider that the terms of his debt were too onerous.

Throughout most of the official discussions of settlement the theme constantly recurs that settlement is particularly expensive and that the settlers were by the same token a privileged group.

---

50. Van Arkadie Report, p. 162.
51. In October 1969 backbenchers pressed a motion in parliament calling on the government to reduce the values of the former European land on which land-purchase loans had been based, and to reduce the rate of interest on the loans. An assistant minister, Martin Shikuku, said he was a settlement farmer with forty acres and could not repay his loans from maize production at present prices. The Assistant Minister for Lands and Settlement replied: 'the present agreement had to be honoured and the Government could not re-negotiate agreements already reached on interest on loans. The Government had an international image to maintain' (*East African Standard*, 4 October 1969). On 31 October, however, with the elections in prospect, the Government accepted a motion calling for a new basis of financing purchase for settlement.

But both of these ideas seem questionable. What was expensive was the price the Europeans demanded and got for their land. By 1969, a total of £12·5 million had been paid to them for land purchase.[52] The British government agreed to pay part of this with a grant of £4·3 million, presumably representing the difference between the price demanded by the Europeans for going quietly or staying and farming properly, and what the land was supposed to be worth to its new purchasers. But this still left £8·2 million to be paid from other funds. It was the essence of the scheme that this should be paid for by the settlers. The high-density settlers contributed some £400,000–500,000 in down payments, and the rest all had to be borrowed. Down to 1968 £7·6 million was lent to the settlers to pay for the land. From this it followed that they had to be provided with stock, fencing, and other improvements to make the land generate income to repay the land loan. These were also to be paid for by the settlers, out of further 'development loans'. To make all this work there obviously had to be a great deal of technical advice and supervision, and in fact the operational cost of the Department of Settlement was £7·1 million down to 1968. Some of this – £1·5 million – was reckoned to be expenditure which would have been incurred however the land had been used, but the extra administrative costs attributable to settlement were covered by an outright grant of £5·4 million made by the British government. In other words, the British government was willing to pay for productive expenditure by means of a grant, in order to ensure that the settlers could pay for unproductive expenditure (the transfer of the land) out of income.

Now let us assume that £10·0 million (the rough total of the two grants actually made) was the maximum amount of grant that Britain could provide. If this had been wholly applied to land purchase, together with the roughly £0·5 million down payments by the high-density settlers, it would have left only £2·0 million to be found by the new settlers for land purchase, an average of about £50 per settler. Even at 6½ per cent interest it is difficult to believe that a loan of this magnitude, to be repaid over thirty years, would have been difficult for most of them to repay without any special credit or supervisory programme. In fact, but for the political issue at stake – the principle that foreign-owned assets must be

---

52. The figures in this paragraph are calculated from the Appendices to the *Department of Settlement Five Year Review and Annual Report, 1969*.

paid for by their new users – the settlers might well just have been put on the land and provided with no more than the normal services given to the rest of the smallholder population. One can even envisage that the £2·0 million of land-purchase money not covered by the total British grant funds might have been paid out of general revenue, since the benefits were really enjoyed by the economy as a whole (not least the remaining European farmers). This might seem to be carrying demystification to absurd lengths; yet the remarkable fact is that in 1970 the British government completely reversed the 1961 formula, and for the last stages of the transfer of mixed farms adopted precisely the approach just described.

But this is to anticipate. It remains true that down to 1968 some 32,000 African settlers on the high- and low-density schemes had been lent some £3·8 million for permanent improvements, stock, and so on, which they in principle owned and could use to generate income.[53] It is difficult to know what to compare this with. In 1966 the Kenya government planned to lend £4·3 million over five years to 30,000 peasant farmers, comprising about 3 per cent of all those outside the settlement schemes.[54] At the other end of the scale, the Agricultural Finance Corporation lent about £2·7 million to 2,200 large-scale farmers for development between 1963 and 1969.[55] This does not take into account commercial-bank lending or government short-term credit for crop finance for large farmers, worth roughly a further £3·5 million in 1966.[56] The Million Acre settlers had thus in this sense been more favoured than most other smallholders down to 1968, much less favoured than large farmers, and no more 'favoured' – in fact almost certainly less – than was necessary to make their land yield the specific incomes required to enable them to pay off the debt of £7·6 million which the government had agreed to burden it with. The 30,000 high-density settlers were supposed to be drawn from the country's most impoverished and underprivileged classes, yet they were being expected to pay the full cost to Kenya of an asset transfer which underwrote the profitability of the rest of the

---

53. ibid., Appendix E.
54. *Development Plan 1966–70*, p. 133.
55. Agricultural Finance Corporation, *Report of the Board*, 1969, p. 14.
56. Bank-lending to agriculture was roughly £6 million in 1966, of which about 20–25 per cent went to mixed farming; and short-term crop finance (Minimum Financial Return credit for maize and wheat) was worth £2·4 million: see *Economic Survey 1971*, p. 27, and AFC *Report*, 1966.

economy. For the next twenty-five to thirty years the surplus which they would generate by their work on the land would go mainly to the former European settlers, not to themselves.[57]

But in 1966 there was a good reason for representing the settlement schemes as expensive and the settlers as privileged. The political uncertainties of 1960–1 were over. The most intransigent of the European farmers had gone. The radical element in Kenya had been removed from positions of influence, and the government was committed to maintain an economic and political climate favourable to expatriate business. There was therefore no reason for the British government to go to special lengths to subsidize the next stage of land transfer. It would lend money for land purchase but not give any. Whoever was put on the land would have to pay for it as before, but without special help. This meant transferring it in the form of intact large farms to Africans rich enough to put up a substantial part of the price themselves, and able to afford to pay interest and repayment charges on the balance because, as the owners, they would get the surplus generated by the workers on the farms.

Thus between 1964 and 1966 a major reversal of policy took place. In August 1964 Kenyatta had announced a new 'Two Million Acre' scheme to resettle 200,000 families on 10–15-acre plots – i.e. the whole of the remaining mixed-farm area.[58] But by the time the 1966–70 Development Plan appeared it said that the 'declared objectives of settlement' had been 'largely attained', and no more settlement was provided for in it. The pressure of the landless had certainly been relieved, of course; the landless of long standing, in particular, no longer represented an immediate political danger. But landlessness was inevitably growing all the time. To say that there would be no more settlement was politically unpopular. Settlement had therefore to be represented as expensive and as conferring privileges on a few at the expense of the many, which the 1966–70 Plan did: one passage in particular deserves quotation, as it neatly combines the myth of the large farm sector (as applied to the mixed farms) with the myth of the expensiveness of settlement, and its threat to the interests of the majority:

---

57. Their payments were of course actually to the Kenya government, which in turn was paying the British government, which in turn had already paid the former Europeans.

58. *EAS*, 13 August 1964.

The economics of settlement are of vital concern to the nation, for two main reasons: firstly, because the former Scheduled Areas were an important source of income, foreign exchange, and employment for the national economy, and these areas must play their part in the national endeavour to accommodate a growing population at an increasing standard of living; and secondly, because by 1968 the Government will have contracted over £16 million of interest-bearing debt to finance the existing schemes, and unless settlement is sufficiently successful from an economic point of view to generate the required annual loan service payment, amounting (by 1970) to roughly £1·4 million, this will pose a heavy burden on the rest of the economy and hold up the development of other sectors.[59]

But by 1970 the pressure of landlessness made a further programme of settlement politically inescapable, and the Kenya government sought a fresh instalment of British aid for a new purchase programme for this purpose. The British government accepted this as inevitable; but to avoid the sort of hostility that had been directed against it on account of the debt burden of the Million Acre settlers, it completely reversed its earlier position and offered £2·5 million as an outright grant for the purchase of the land and such other assets as the Kenya government wished to take over.[60] It is not difficult to see that this reversal reflected a crucial difference between the new situation and that of 1961. Nothing was more certain than that the new settlers would not be given their land free, even though the Kenya government was to get a free grant to buy it with. Kenya's commitment to the international capitalist system was no longer in doubt and there was no reason for the British government to go to elaborate trouble, or to incur any more odium within Kenya, in order to secure it.

The new programme would be called 'settlement' and would involve settling large numbers of people, but unlike the earlier schemes it would actually consist of state-supervised collective farms, with two or three acres allocated to each family for private cultivation. Moreover, the total area involved would be quite modest, about 150,000 acres. In the meantime, however, 1·6 million acres – about three-quarters of the mixed farm areas re-

---

59. *Development Plan 1966–70*, p. 151.

60. The offer also included a grant of £0·25 million for purchasing the farms of designated sick or elderly Europeans which would not otherwise have necessarily been included in the programme, and a further £1·0 million 'soft' loan for ADC/ AFC purchases (see note 71).

maining outside the earlier settlement schemes – had passed into African hands as intact large farms.[61]

AFRICAN LARGE-SCALE FARMERS

This process began in 1960, with the legal end of the 'white' highlands policy, but accelerated dramatically after independence in December 1963; between January 1964 and September 1965 0·46 million acres were acquired by Africans on a 'willing buyer–willing seller' basis, with the Land Bank putting up approximately £0·8 million of the £3·5 million paid for the land, and the Agricultural Finance Corporation (AFC) putting up £0·5 million towards the cost of loose assets (stock, machinery, etc.).[62] Obviously this method of transfer involved mobilizing African savings on a very large scale. Down to 1965, when Exchange Control was imposed, free market sales meant that the European seller could and mostly did export the proceeds of sale.[63] After 1965, this was only possible if the government approved it, which it would normally do only if the transaction involved foreign currency – i.e., if the farms were bought with loan funds supplied from abroad for the purpose. When it became apparent that free market sales might no longer result in the seller being free to take the proceeds abroad,

---

61. Based on summary data collected in the Agricultural Census 1970 for Large Farm Areas, covering the former scheduled areas minus the settlement schemes, a total given in the census as 6·7 million acres. It is unfortunately not possible to reconcile this with the conventional total of 7·6 million acres of 'white highlands', and the total of 1·2 million acres taken by the high- and low-density settlement schemes, but the figure of 1·6 million acres in African hands is based on the local knowledge of officials, working from the land register, and seems to be the most reliable figure available.

62. The data for 1964–5 are from N. Newiger, 'Cooperative Farming in the Former Scheduled Areas of Kenya' (1965, mimeo), which gives a complete analysis of all sales in these areas during this period, except for 28,000 acres sold in lots of less than 200 acres. Loan data are from the *Development Plan 1966–70*, Appendix, Table 6. Some 300,000 acres passed into African hands under various schemes of purchase in addition to the Million Acre Scheme and free market sales, notably the 'compassionate' farms and 'Assisted Owners' schemes.

63. From December 1964 to September 1965 more than half of the acreage sold was transferred from one European to another. This was largely because Europeans who sold their farms under the Million Acre Scheme bought other farms. It is interesting to note that the average price per acre paid under the Million Acre Scheme was £9·2, whereas the average price paid by companies (72 per cent of which were European-owned) for land in 1964–65 was £5·5 per acre and by individuals (70 per cent of whom were Europeans), £6. In 1967, the Kenya government forbade all further sales of agricultural land to non-citizens.

a fresh anticipatory exodus of European farmers began, mainly from the maize-producing district of Uasin Gishu. To prevent a new run-down in the European mixed-farm sector, like that of 1960–3, a fresh initiative involving British finance was required. This led to the 'Mission Appointed to Advise on Proposals for a Further Transfer of European Farms in Kenya', which arrived from London early in 1965.

This mission was led by the Hon. A. Maxwell Stamp, an economist; and among its three other members was the vigorous and candid Mr Swynnerton, the author of the 1955 Plan on which the policy of individualized land tenure was based. The report of the Stamp Mission signalled to the Kenya government the decisive difference between the 1961–3 situation, when the British government was willing to pay a good price to extricate itself from Kenya, provided that the principle of land purchase was accepted, and the situation in 1965. The basic position of the mission was that the Kenya government's proposals (which in their final form called for nearly £35 million of British aid to be spent on land transfer over fifteen years) would 'saddle Kenya with a heavy debt burden and the UK with a heavy aid commitment for little economic advantage, in order to relieve political pressures which should be tackled in other ways.'[64]

Settlement schemes were ruled out as intolerably expensive. Loan funds for free market transfers of intact large farms 'went much further' (i.e., they were lent to people who already had money), but without additional expenditure on training and supervision, and in most cases, additional funds for working capital, they led to drastic declines in output and defaulting on the original debt. In spite of this, the mission expressed a firm preference for this approach because it maintained a market for European farmers wishing to sell and was, all in all, a simple and – to Britain, at least – cheap way of getting them out. The mission considered a third alternative proposed by the Kenya government, namely that the farms should become 'national farms' run by the state, and condemned it in a revealing passage:

> This is not to suggest that a highly socialist organization which enforces very strict control, treats the mis-allocation of government funds as a treasonable offence and uses the technique of forced labour in order to obtain increased productivity at low cost, cannot be a successful way of improving

---

64. Stamp Report, p. 3.

agricultural productivity. All that needs to be said at this stage is that in the developing countries of Africa with their lack of knowledge of the operation of large scale business enterprises, with systems of institutional government still very similar to the European pattern, with the pressures of corruption and the difficulties of controlling it without the constraints of a totalitarian society, then the operation of state-owned farming enterprise can be said prima facie to be a relatively inefficient way of using funds which they have at their disposal . . .

Any such schemes

> should be undertaken, if at all, as an experiment on a small scale. . . . If it can be proved that such national projects can be operated successfully and that they can stand up to rigorous social costing and economic evaluation then of course there is no reason whatever why successful schemes should not be repeated.[65]

The 'of course' was a nice touch, especially when one remembers that of the three alternatives considered by the mission the one which they actually supported most strongly, continued loan funds for free market sales, was the one which was evidently unsuccessful by any criterion (let alone a rigorous one) of social costing or economic evaluation.[66] The mission, however, went on to say that if state-owned farms were to be contemplated, they should be run in partnership with (European) private enterprize.

What the mission really wanted was an absolute minimum of spending on further land-transfer of any kind. It turned a cold and ungrateful eye on the European mixed-farm sector. It considered the claim that it made an important contribution to foreign exchange earnings and found that, as well as it could estimate, the remaining farms in this sector were at best making a marginal contribution, and that the more intensive farms were net consumers of foreign exchange. In addition, the mission pointed out that the effect of the system of protection given to the large-scale mixed farms by the marketing boards and other devices had produced a distorted picture of their economic value to the country. The Kenya government was 'in a sense faced with a possible white

65. ibid., p. 189.
66. The mission had evidence that all those concerned were of the opinion that the government was likely to lose 'a large proportion of the Government money that has been put into these farms', and that the drop in production was far more serious than in the settlement schemes.

elephant in terms of the European mixed farms'.[67] To convert
them to settlement was economically unjustifiable, national farms
would prove inefficient, costly and corrupt, and to transfer them
to African ownership as they stood, without removing their
monopoly protection, was equally undesirable. 'In general', they
concluded,

> the mission is agreed that, were it not for the political press-
> ures it would be better not to have a further programme
> which involves the deliberate transfer, with government
> assistance and subsidy, of European farms to African hands.
> If political pressures make a programme necessary, the smaller
> and slower the buy-out programme . . . the better for Kenya
> – and for the British taxpayer.[68]

The mission welcomed the Kenya government's final proposals,
which involved putting a third of the British aid they were seeking
into land registration and general development in the African
areas. They also thought that the political pressures, both from
Europeans anxious to leave, and from Africans seeking land, were
being exaggerated. They were prepared to support a token programme of settlement ('to demonstrate to the landless and unemployed that land transfer to the peasant sector is continuing'), but
for the rest they recommended cutting the rate of transfer down as
far as possible, to a total of about 85,000 acres a year; part of this
to be financed by loans to free-market buyers, and part to consist
of purchases by the new Agricultural Development Corporation
(ADC), mainly for later transfer to private owners after a period of
supervised tenancy. The ADC would also be able to retain some
of these as national farms for stockbreeding, seed breeding and
other similar purposes, preferably in partnership with private
enterprise.

The Stamp Mission's influence was decisive on the pattern of
land transfer for the rest of the 1960s. This was partly because of
the foreign-exchange problems already referred to – most European farmers would only sell at tolerable prices if they were paid
in convertible currency; once the British government accepted the
Stamp Mission's advice, which it did in November 1965, the
pattern of sales would be bound to take the shape indicated by the
availability of sterling. But it was also because the mission greatly
fortified the position of those officials and politicians who were

67. Stamp Report, p. 263.
68. ibid., p. 10.

already advocating a switch away from settlement towards a policy of transferring large-scale farms intact. The mission itself noted how 'many of the changes which have taken place in the Kenya government proposals during the time the mission was in Kenya could be attributed to the changes in policy which were made after the Kenya government had calculated the total cost and seen the sheer magnitude of the financial implications of previous objectives.'[69] The result could be seen very clearly in the 1966–70 Development Plan, which vigorously developed the mission's own arguments, and especially followed their advice that 'If it can be brought home to Back Bench Politicians that, if they press for faster taking over of European farms, this means less aid for their own constituencies, then their enthusiasm may be modified.'[70]

The result was that during the following five years a further million acres passed into African hands not as small-scale plots but as large-scale farms. About 180,000 acres of this were bought by the ADC, and were then mostly leased to African tenants, who in due course would be converted into 'assisted owners'.[71] The rest was bought on the free market. It is probable that about three-quarters of a million acres of mixed-farm land remained in non-citizen hands at the end of 1970.[72] The next phase of British aid, agreed at the end of 1970, would be likely to produce roughly a further 150,000 acres of 'settlement';[73] by the time this was completed, it seemed likely that a roughly similar amount would also have passed into individual or group ownership by free-market transfers. In the end, about 40 per cent of the European mixed-

---

69. ibid., p. 238.

70. ibid., pp. 11–12.

71. *Agricultural Development Corporation; A Summary of its Activities*, Nairobi Show 1970, p. 5. The ADC was established in 1965 by Act of Parliament primarily to safeguard the breeding of high-quality stock and seed. Its use as an agent for the 'Stamp' Purchase Programme was an afterthought which seriously compromised this objective, as it came to be regarded as existing primarily for that, and political pressures were brought to bear to make it sell farms, some of which were central to its primary role as a breeding agency.

72. Estimates varied. The chairman of the KNFU's Land Transfer committee thought that British farmers alone held about 770,000 acres of mixed farms at the end of 1970 (Minutes, 21 October 1970). A more conservative official estimate put British holdings at about half a million acres in mid-1971. Definitions differed, and the existence of a free market meant that the position was changing constantly.

73. The cost per acre of the land which would be purchased for settlement could not be known in advance of its valuation, but a figure of about £16, including a few permanent improvements, seemed a reasonable guess, yielding a total of about 150,000 acres for £2·5 million.

farm areas would have become settlement schemes, and roughly 60 per cent, or two million acres, African-owned large farms. In other words, the decisive pattern was laid down in the 1960s.[74]

But it would be easy to misinterpret the significance of the new African large-farm sector as a whole. Comparatively few of the farms passed into the outright ownership of individuals. Most of them became the property of groups, ranging from two or three partners to land-purchase 'co-operatives' with several thousand members. One celebrated case, the Nyagacho Chisaro Chikonorwe Co-operative Society, had over 11,000 paid-up members.[75] Starting in 1964, when it became clear to the landless Kikuyu that government settlement programmes were not going to accommodate more than a fraction of them and that in any case the settlers would be obliged to pay for the purchase of the land, people had begun to form 'land-purchase co-operatives' in order to pool enough money for the down payment on a European farm, hoping that a Land Bank loan would be obtained for the balance.[76] By the middle of 1965, 349 of these had been registered.[77] Their aim was to acquire land, not to farm it co-operatively. They formed co-operatives because government officials invariably urged the land-seekers thronging their offices in the Rift Valley to do so, and because it was still the cheapest way of getting the corporate status

---

74. It is difficult to know what to make of the statement made in Parliament on 30 November 1971, by the Assistant Minister for Land and Settlement, Mr G. G. Kariuki, in which he said that the government 'had acquired two thirds of the land owned exclusively by expatriates since uhuru, in 1963', i.e. 2 million out of 3 million hectares. (*East African Standard*, 1 December 1971).

75. By 1970 the position of this organization had become so impossible that a special committee of the cabinet was set up to try and sort out its problems, without success.

76. Two land-purchase co-operatives were registered at the end of 1963. Many of the earliest ones were composed of the employees of particular European farmers in the Rift Valley, with a view to taking over their employers' farms. The Land Bank was merged fully into the AFC in 1969.

77. September 1965, when Dr Newiger completed his study (see note 62), seems to have been the high point of land-purchase co-operatives. His own figures suggest that the volume of new registrations was dropping to zero at this time (p. 30), and in November 1971 the total was smaller than in 1965 (327 compared with 349); some had been liquidated by the Department of Co-operatives, to prevent the further useless loss of their members' funds when they had no hope of ever buying a farm, others had become companies to avoid close control by the Department. On the other hand a total of thirty-three Ranching Co-operatives had been registered since 1965, which reflected the growing interest in ranch land as the scope in the mixed-farm areas narrowed. (Interview with officials of the Co-operative Department, November 1971.)

needed to deal with the sellers and the Land Bank/AFC. But relatively few of these co-operatives succeeded in acquiring land, either because they were poorly organized or led, or because their members were mainly poor and had difficulty in persuading buyers or the lending agencies to do business with them. Gradually limited liability companies, usually with fewer shareholders, became more common; and even more successful in acquiring land were partnerships of a few people, usually already fairly prosperous. Down to mid-1965, 28 per cent of the capital outlay by Africans on the free-market purchase of farms was by co-operatives; 24 per cent was by companies, 33 per cent by partnerships, and only 14 per cent by individuals.[78] But in subsequent years purchases by co-operatives were relatively rare. In Rift Valley Province – comprising the main remaining large-scale mixed farms – in December 1969, out of 1,043 farms owned by Africans, 571 were owned by 'partnerships or companies', 349 by individuals and only 123 by co-operatives.[79] But although co-operatives tended to have the largest numbers of members, companies and even partnerships often had many also; in other words, no matter what organizational form was adopted, very few people could raise the required down-payment of – normally – 20–40 per cent of the purchase price of an average farm of 1,500 acres at £7–8 per acre, without help from friends, kinsmen, or other associates.[80] Even individuals who bought farms might be found on closer inspection to be, in fact, representatives of a group. The so-called African large-scale farms must therefore be looked on as a spectrum extending from enterprises similar to the European capitalist farms they replaced to 'self-help' peasant settlement schemes.

Reliable data on the social and economic character of the resulting large-farm sector are remarkably lacking. What is known is that most of the new farmers immediately 'ran into serious

---

78. Calculated from Newiger, op. cit. (note 62), p. 22.

79. Ministry of Agriculture, *Rift Valley Province Annual Report* (1969, mimeo), p. 111. The figures include 91 African-owned farms in Kericho District, not analysed by type of ownership.

80. Prices given in Newiger, op. cit. (note 62), pp. 74–5. The practice of the Land Bank at this time was to require African applicants for loans to produce 50 per cent of the purchase price, but then to give 60–80 per cent of it as a loan, with a view to leaving the purchasers with enough funds for half of the cost of the loose assets (the other half coming from an AFC 'development' loan) and for working capital. In practice, applicants were thought to borrow in order to satisfy the initial 50 per cent requirement; see H. Ruthenberg, *African Agricultural Production Development Policy in Kenya 1952–1965* (Springer-Verlag, Berlin 1966), p. 93.

trouble'.[81] Output dropped to about a third of former levels, and arrears of debt repayment rose well above the levels reached by the settlement schemes.[82] In 1965 the Chairman of the Central Agricultural Board estimated that 25 per cent of them were 'beyond assistance' and that 'a further 50 per cent could only be saved at considerable expense'.[83] In 1970 a Ministry of Agriculture survey revealed 600 'problem farms', on which output showed no signs of reaching a level at which the debt could be serviced and repaid from income. AFC officials reckoned that in 1971 only two of the farms on which it had lent funds were in principle not 'viable'; meaning that they could not be made sufficiently productive, on any imaginable basis, either to support their so-called 'owners' or to service and repay their loans. But although it was in theory possible that the great majority could do this, the human and technical obstacles in the way were often overwhelming. The 1966–70 Development Plan captured the essence of the situation when it said:

> . . . most of them had to devote nearly all their savings to purchasing their farms, which left them with very little working capital to operate the farms efficiently. A number of farmers, having gone heavily into debt to purchase both farms and loose assets such as machinery and cattle still lacked sufficient working capital to generate loan repayments, and were forced to sell off loose assets in order to meet mortgage payments . . . very few of them had the skills and experience required for the complex task of running a modern mixed farm . . . the Agriculture Department staff was not equipped to work with the farmers, help them prepare farm plans, and advise them on the many operational problems which they encountered.[84]

One has to read the reports of extension and loan officials working in the large-farm areas, or better still visit these farms, in order to understand the diversity and intractability of the problems involved. They were the scene of triumphs as well as tragedies, cooperation and sacrifice as well as exploitation and greed. One of the most successful of the mass-membership organizations was Ndeffo Ltd, a company formed by the Nakuru District Ex-

81. *Development Plan 1966–70*, p. 154.

82. The output estimate is from Ruthenberg, op. cit. (note 80), p. 96. The Stamp Mission were told that on many farms output had fallen to 20 per cent of previous levels.

83. Stamp Report (note 44), p. 206.

84. *Development Plan 1966–70*, p. 155.

Freedom Fighters Organization, which by 1971 had 5,000 members and four farms, providing homes and subsistence for over 2,000 of the members, while maintaining production and meeting its loan obligations promptly.[85] At the other extreme there were some individual notables who took possession of farms as 'telephone' (absentee) farmers, evicted the squatters, dismissed some members of the work force, re-engaged the others at reduced wages, and were still seriously in arrears. But the majority of the large farms which were in multiple ownership of one kind or another gave an impression of disillusionment and demoralization, caused by the contradiction between the peoples' motives – to get individual plots – and their indebtedness, which demanded collective action to repay it. It was not just that the technical know-how to run the farms profitably was lacking, but much more importantly, the initial bond that had brought the new 'settlers' together – the drive to get on to the land – did not afford any basis for discipline or mutual trust or leadership which could be the basis of a collective effort to work the farm back into production and meet its financial obligations.

This led to some extraordinary expedients on the part of the main credit agency, the AFC. The AFC had the power to foreclose and sell up the farms, though politically this was difficult to use;[86] but in any case, there was little certainty that it would find new 'owners' more creditworthy than the existing ones, and in the process it would have to write off the outstanding arrears. The aim was therefore to get the land into commercial production at all costs, if necessary eliminating the resident 'owners' from the operation entirely. In one case, the 'owners' were given the choice of being sold up or of giving a five-year lease of 700 acres – the bulk of the farm – to their neighbour, an African public servant who had a large farm with a pedigree herd and needed more pasture. In another, a European manager was put in complete control, and the farm ploughed, planted, weeded and harvested by an outside contractor. In other cases, a system of share-cropping

85. Interview with Mr Kimunya Kamana, Managing Director of Ndeffo Ltd, 21 October 1971. Ndeffo hit the headlines from time to time by occupying and ploughing farms it was negotiating to buy, apparently as a means of forestalling rival purchasers; see *East African Standard* 29 March 1968 onwards, on Engoshura Farm in particular.

86. Many of the chronic defaulters were politically prominent, and moreover some of the most senior AFC staff were expatriates. Only one large farm had been sold up by the AFC down to September 1971.

was tried, whereby each family on the farm planted five acres of maize and had to deliver ten bags to the collective store for paying the collective debt. There were many other devices, as varied as the character of the farms and the social composition of their 'owners'. To the AFC, the problem appeared one of making the land yield at least the interest due on its debt, representing the cost of the resources committed to it, and of contributing to national income. Officials hoped that in the process, the new farmers would come to be more and more involved in production and eventually take over the responsibility. But a government committee studying the problem in 1971 reported that 'on the majority of group farms, owners have stated that once loans have been repaid, they will subdivide completely (illegally if necessary)'.

In a situation so steeped in ideology it is necessary to stand back and consider some of the elementary facts before trying to see what it all signifies. A clear starting-point is the fact that something like £20 million had been paid to the former owners of the land and loose assets on the 1·6 million acres of large farms in African hands at the end of 1970.[87] How much of this had been exported is anybody's guess. What was not exported had been re-invested in some other sector such as tourism or manufacture, enlarging the foreign stake in profits there.

The price paid for the land was the product of highly peculiar circumstances: the dramatic increases in land values in the first twenty years of the century, for example, due to speculation; the heavy bias of government services towards the white highlands, financed in large part by African taxpayers; the special protection given to the large farm sector by marketing and price control; the political leverage of the European farmers at independence when they were in a position to exercise an element of economic black-mail; and from the mid-1960s onwards, the mounting competition between would-be African purchasers for the remaining free-market farms. Even if one considers the element in the price which represented capital improvements in the land, it must be remembered that these had been made almost entirely out of profits, which themselves were a product, partly of the European farmers' monopolies, and otherwise of the direct exploitation of African

---

87. The 1966–70 Plan calculated that the value of the investment on the 600,000 acres in African ownership at the end of 1965 was 'of the order of £9 millions' (p. 154). On this basis, the investment on 1·6 million acres would be about £24 million.

farm workers, whose real wages had changed little throughout the period of colonial rule.[88]

None the less, something like £20 million had been paid by Africans to the European settlers for these farms. Some of this had been borrowed. Down to March 1970 the AFC had lent a total of £7·75 million to large-scale farmers, but some of this was to Europeans;[89] and even allowing for commercial bank-loans and other sources of credit, Africans must have found not less than a similar sum from their own savings to pay for the 1·6 million acres involved.[90] If anything was owing to anyone for the land, they might be excused for thinking that they had by and large paid it.

All the same, the new large-scale farmers were lent some £3·2 million of public funds for loose assets and new improvements between 1963 and 1969 and, in addition, used several million pounds of short-term crop finance annually. Like the settlement farmers, they were badly in arrears. On a total large-farm debt (for purchase and development) of £7·8 million, the arrears owing to the AFC on 3,220 loans at the end of 1969 were £1·1 million.[91] As much as 10 per cent of the short-term crop finance was not repaid

88. In 1924 N. Leys estimated rural wages at approximately shs 14/- (shs 8/- without rations) per month, which he thought lower than in 1913 in real terms (*Kenya*, pp. 206–7). In 1946 cash wages on mixed farms averaged shs 14/- per month, exclusive of housing and rations (*East African Economic and Statistical Bulletin*, No. 3, March 1949, Table E6). From 1949 to 1954 African wages in 'modern' agriculture (as a whole, usually a bit higher than for mixed farms in particular) rose by 11 per cent per annum; the urban African cost of living rose by 10½ per cent per annum. (*Reported Employment and Wages in Kenya, 1954*, East African Statistical Department, 1954, mimeo, pp. 10–11). Average African cash wages in agriculture in 1956, excluding the value of housing and rations, were shs 40/- per month. It has to be remembered that the cost of living indices do not take into account the cost of education (school fees).

89. These were Land Bank Loans; AFC development loans were available only to citizens. Newiger, op. cit. (note 62), indicates that over £1 million was lent to Europeans for land purchase in 1964–5.

90. It will be recalled that the British government had paid for a third of the purchase price of the Million Acre scheme for a grant. No equivalent subsidy was paid to the purchasers of large-scale farms, although the average price they paid was often close to the price paid for the settlement-scheme land. (The Land Bank report for 1964 gave an average of £8·7 per acre, compared with £9·2 per acre for settlement schemes.)

91. *Tootell Mission on Agricultural Credit, 1970*, sponsored by USAID (mimeo), p. 1. In an earlier memorandum Tootell noted: 'The arrears on most of the government loan programs is [*sic*] fantastic, ranging from 8 per cent to 73 per cent of the amount due.' He referred to an appendix in the draft 1969–74 Development Plan which was later omitted from the published plan. The Plan did say that 62 per cent of the amount due for development-loan repayments on large farms was in arrears in June 1968 (p. 215).

at the end of the year in which it was due.[92] Debtors included some people well able to pay, but hard to press.

The defaulting large farms were a cause of concern, but this concern was not so highly publicized as in the case of the settlement schemes. This may have been partly due to the more diffuse character of the large-farm sector, and the multiplicity of agencies concerned with it. It may also have been due to the political influence of many of the defaulters, who enlisted the support of the Kenya National Farmers' Union and even the Minister of Agriculture in their effort to have their debt burden eased.[93] They were more often described as overburdened than delinquent. But a more fundamental reason than either of these was the fact that the large-farm sector operated in a completely different context of international interest from that of the settlers on settlement schemes in 1961–4.

The British government had only put £3·3 million of interest-bearing loan funds into large-farm transfer; all the aid provided under the Stamp recommendations was interest-free; the aid for purchase for new 'settlement', agreed in 1970, was a grant, and the further £1 million provided at the same time for the AFC and ADC was only at 2 per cent and subject to a seven-year grace period. To a large extent the insolvency of the large-farm sector was thus a purely internal problem, which the government could handle in various ways; the arrears that were building up could have been drastically reduced if the government had not charged interest to the farmers on the interest-free aid which it 'onlent' to them.[94] Moreover, by 1970 the 'large-farm sector' contained a number of ministers and many MPs and senior civil servants. This group of people was not one which the British government, or the government of any other developed capitalist country, wished to

---

92. Interview with Mr H. Lowe, the General Manager of AFC, April 1971.

93. 'New Farmers who have purchased farms are in serious difficulties due to the interest rates and impossible repayment terms which they are unable to comply with. They must be given a 1–2 year moratorium, and loan repayments rephased.' Minutes of KNFU Land Transfer Committee, 21 October 1970. Earlier that year the Minister of Agriculture told them he was determined to alleviate the debt burden of the incoming African large-scale farmers.

94. For instance the £4 million which was lent interest-free by Britain for the Stamp Purchase programme was lent by the Kenya government to the ADC at 5 per cent, yielding a return of £2 million over the period of repayment. The tenants of ADC farms paid a rent of 6½ per cent of the valuation of the farm on entering into the tenancy, and 7½ per cent on loans made to them by the ADC for improvements made to the farms.

antagonize. On the contrary: these were the people whose out-look and interest made possible the continuation of so much of the old economic structure, and their ownership of large farms in the former white highlands reinforced this.

The 'owners' of those 'large farms' which were really collections of smallholdings were also recipients of loan funds. Their position was not very different from that of the settlers on the settlement schemes;[95] they were better off than people without land, and most of them would probably manage to retain a stake in their farms, though in most cases it might be much smaller and less secure than they hoped for. Many would find that the bulk of 'their' land eventually passed into the control, if not the owner-ship, of one or other of the more energetic 'big men' around them, who were in a position to farm the land profitably. The efforts of the AFC to recover its debts from the most acute 'problem' farms pointed clearly in this direction. From among the notables on the large farms there could emerge a core of landowners farm-ing for profit, who might not only stem the tide of 'peasant' en-croachment but in due course turn it back, taking over the mismanaged farms around them.

But for the time being it was not necessarily the 'big men' who ran their large farms efficiently who were most important. What mattered more was the overlap of large-farm ownership and political and social influence. The large-farm owners had a major personal stake in the existing economy. The Stamp Mission noted that they

> tend to identify themselves economically with the large-scale European farmers. Those interviewed by the Mission stressed the help given to them by their European neighbours and were inclined to favour a slow transfer of farms because of the need to retain European expertise. They naturally wished to see preserved the large scale farm structure which they con-sidered as being more productive and offering greater em-ployment opportunities than the small scale farms instituted under the settlement schemes. . . . The Mission was impressed by the broad view taken by these farmers, who were con-cerned, not merely with their own interests, but also with the

---

95. The 34,000 settlers received £3·8 million of developmental loans; the unknown total of large-farm owners – perhaps in all a similar number – received £3·2 million. The main difference was that the distribution among the large-farm owners was much less equal.

national need for increased food production, employment and agricultural exports.[96]

The conviction that what was good for large farmers was good for Kenya was expressed wherever large farmers had influence, which was really everywhere: as civil servants in the ministries, as MPs in parliament, as ministers in the cabinet, as members of Kenyatta's intimate circle at Gatundu. This influence was to have important consequences at the end of the 1960s, when some of the large farmers' indebtedness was becoming critical.

CREDIT

Of course, even if land is collectively owned, the structure of prices may be such that it still requires capital investment which cannot be financed from farming operations. But the impact of farm credit when land is individually owned is very distinctive. For one thing, it costs a great deal to administer many small loans if they are to be used properly. As the Tootell Mission commented:

> Our Mission is aware that officials of the Government were hopeful we would propose a farm credit institution that could extend production-increasing credit in the near future to scores of thousands of Kenya small farmers and to do this at small cost to the government. Unfortunately, no such institution is possible, in Kenya or any place else in the world. Extending such credit, with the educational and supervisory work required for its success, is very expensive. To charge farmers an interest rate that would cover the lending expense, including losses, and the supervisory expense, would be politically impossible . . .[97]

In other words, even if the loan funds themselves were unlimited, they could only be lent to a small minority at a time. This implies an obvious problem of selection. In dealing with the general mass of smallholders, lenders typically look for security for the loan, and ability to use it productively; as the first Plan put it, credit would be going to 'relatively progressive smallholders who

---

96. Stamp Report (note 44), p. 38; '. . . each new class which puts itself in the place of one ruling before it, is compelled, merely in order to carry through its aim, to represent its interest as the common interest of all the members of society . . .'. (Marx and Engels, *The German Ideology*, International Publishers, New York 1947, pp. 40–41.)

97. Tootell Report (see note 91), p. 32.

are by definition already much better off than the rest'. Credit thus tends to widen already existing differences of wealth and opportunity. This is particularly true when the size of a man's landholding is used as a yardstick of his creditworthiness, or when security is seen to consist in his having a non-farm source of income, such as a salary. Both yardsticks operated in the selection of smallholders for credit in Kenya. Other credit programmes, moreover, were by definition for the wealthier farmers.

The following table needs to be treated as a very approximate guide to the orders of magnitude involved, but probably conveys the essence of the situation fairly enough. Roughly 35,000 individuals and roughly 1,200 groups had been lent public funds to buy former European-owned land.

Altogether they had been lent about £12·2 million for this purpose. The so-called 'compassionate case' farm-owners, the Settlement Fund Trustees' 'assisted owners' and about 20 per cent of the AFC purchasers and ADC assisted owners were individuals, i.e. about 500 people who between them were lent roughly £1·6 million, or about £3,000 each on average.

It is also obvious that the great bulk of the development loans – roughly £7·5 million out of £10·5 million – went to the same people who received land-purchase loans. This was even more true of crop finance, nearly all of which went to large farms. Within the roughly £3 million lent to smallholders outside the ex-European areas, it is probable that more than half went to larger farmers in the Central Province. There is also a good deal of duplication in the figures; a successful small farmer who repays his first loan satisfactorily is the most acceptable candidate for a second loan. The government estimated in 1965 that there were roughly one million peasant families, excluding pastoralists; it looks as if a maximum of perhaps 25,000 of them (outside the settlement schemes) had received individual farm loans down to 1970, some of whom probably received several loans, successively or even simultaneously for different purposes.[98]

---

98. This excludes about 20,000 smallholders who received £0·5 million credit in the form of tea stumps or shoots from the Kenya Tea Development Authority down to 1964, and perhaps a similar number and amount since. A considerable proportion of these would be included among the recipients of other, cash, loans. Other sources of credit were available indirectly to smallholders, especially through co-operative societies, though under the system of second payments peasants could often be extending credit to the co-operative, rather than the other way round. In many co-operatives the peasants were also lending, if not giving, considerable cash sums to the 'big men' who ran them through an in-

Table 3.1

Agricultural Loans to Individuals and Groups down to 1970

Purpose of loans

1. *Land purchase*	Numbers of loans	Total value to nearest K£0·1 million
SFT high density (a)	29,000	5·2
SFT low-density (a)	5,000	1·2
SFT compassionate-case farms (a)	123	0·6
SFT assisted owners (a)	132	0·3
SFT co-operative societies (a)	70	0·2
AFC/Land-Bank large farms (b)	1,181	4·6
ADC Stamp purchase farms (c)		0·1
		12·2
2. *Farm development*		
SFT high-density (a)	29,000	2·8
SFT low-density (a)	5,000	1·1
SFT assisted owners (a)	132	0·1
SFT co-operative societies (a)	70	0·3
Government smallholder credit to 1964 (d)	7,850	0·7
Commercial banks – ditto – (e)	10,000	1·0
AFC (1963–9) large farmers	2,203	3·2
AFC small-scale farmers	3,745	0·5
Commercial banks: smallholders 1964–70 (f)	8,000	0·8
		10·5
3. *Short-term annual crop finance*		
GMR/MFR wheat and maize loans, 1969 (g)	4,000	4·0

SFT = Settlement Fund Trustees; GMR = Guaranteed Minimum Return;
MFR = Financial Return

Notes:

(a) Numbers of loans are for 1969; values of outstanding loans for 1968.

(b) £0·8m. of the total was issued as AFC development loans, allocated to land purchase; the balance as Land Bank loans. Of the Land Bank loans £1·4m. was issued to non-citizens for farm purchase between 1961 and 1965.

(c) The total committed under the Stamp Programme was £3·6 million, though a large part of this was for loose assets rather than land.

(d) Under various programmes, prior to the formation of the AFC.

(e) The Lawrance Report disclosed that total commercial bank-lendings to small-holders exceeded government credits down to 1964. Ninety per cent of the commercial bank-loans were to farmers in Central Province, where land registration was completed by 1962–3, after the re-registration of Fort Hall District.

(f) Estimate, based on a 31 per cent recorded increase in total bank advances to agriculture between 1964 and 1970, and on the fact that bank-loans tend to be relatively short-term and so revolve faster.

(g) MFR loans in 1967 were £3·8m. to 2,549 loanees; the figures shown are approximations for 1970.

Sources: Lawrance Report: Department of Settlement Five Year Review and Annual Report, 1967/8, and Annual Report, 1968/9; AFC/Land Bank Reports, 1967 and 1969; Tootell Report; Central Bank of Kenya Economic and Financial Review, Vol. IV, No. 1, July–September 1971; 1966–70 Development Plan; and interviews.

The selective character of farm credit is of course reinforced by the selective provision of many other inputs, most of which are free, and especially extension services. Studies in Nyeri, Kakamega and Kilifi and among Million Acre scheme settlers all indicate clearly how the farmers who had more land and other income got both more credit and more advice.[99] Under the doctrine of applying scarce resources where ('objectively') the returns would be greatest, the differential provision of both credit and technical help benefited a category of landowners whose support the regime needed. It widened existing differences of wealth, income and children's life opportunities. Moreover the first people to get credit were able to build up an advantage that was partly at the expense of anyone who might get it later. This could happen in various ways. For instance, some export crops were subject to quotas; if farmers had not been able to plant coffee by 1964, they were by and large excluded from sharing in this still lucrative crop. The same thing might in future happen to tea. Some fairly inelastic resources were also bid up in price by the first-comers; for instance dairy cattle were being priced out of reach of the sort of credit being made available to new smallholder borrowers at the end of the 1960s. Land itself was also a case in point. Some smallholders would be obliged to subdivide their plots to provide for their adult children, and these plots would thereafter not be likely to be able to get credit. Although there were individual examples to the contrary, it seemed clear that the general effect of credit was to accelerate the emergence of a small profit-oriented class of farmers capable of accumulating capital, and differentiate them progressively from those whose plots were destined either to be sold or to move gradually towards a predominantly food-providing function.

---

formal, not to say illegal, system of cash loans; Hyden cites an official estimate that in 1969 £1·35 million of interest-free loans had been given to 'Committee members, staff of [co-operative] unions, ex-staff, leading politicians and local civil servants' in this way (G. Hyden, *Efficiency Versus Distribution in East African Co-operatives*, East African Literature Bureau, Nairobi 1973, p. 103.)

99. J. Ashcroft and others, 'The Tetu Extension Pilot Project', paper presented to Workshop on Strategies for Improving Rural Development (Nairobi, May–June 1971, mimeo), pp. 20–27; D. K. Leonard, 'The Social Structure of the Agricultural Extension Services in Kakamega District' (Nairobi 1971, mimeo), pp. 8–9; D. Parkin, 'The Monopoly of Ritual: Political Redefinition in a Kenya Rural Trading Centre' (University of Sussex 1972, mimeo), pp. 3–4; C. Leo, 'Neo-colonialism and the Administration of Development: An Interim Report' (Nairobi 1972, mimeo), p. 3; P. Moock, 'The Vihiga SRDP Farm Level Survey; a Preliminary Report and Findings' (Nairobi 1971, mimeo), Tables 12 and 75.

Credit also has secondary effects that are no less significant. A farmer who has taken a loan cannot afford to be sentimental about the operations it helps to finance. The KNFU itself noted: 'Many of the new African farmers [i.e. large-scale farmers] are at present unable to pay the Government Minimum Wage for agricultural workers and in many cases have not paid their labour for months.'[100]

But as the Tootell Mission commented, farm credit 'can be a powerful force for either good or evil' – meaning that credit is also debt, and can lead to arrears, default and even dispossession. At the end of the 1960s it was still too early to assess the significance of rural indebtedness in Kenya. The fact that the debt was mainly owed by the relatively rich to government agencies distinguished Kenya sharply from India and other countries where rural indebtedness means debt owed by the rural poor to private creditors. Debt recovery led in some cases not to eviction but to various kinds of imposed management, share-cropping schemes and so on, with the AFC as a sort of benevolent bailiff. In an important minority of cases, the debtors were influential supporters of the government, so that the ultimate weapon of eviction was generally less likely to be used. On the other hand, its selective use, against prominent people who were in official disfavour, or against a limited number of 'small men' on the settlement schemes who had no currently influential political protector, could serve a double purpose of strengthening the power of the regime over would-be critics or rivals, and at the same time of appeasing the credit institutions and their foreign creditors, on which the regime also depended. The parliamentary 'sifting committee' which authorized the eviction of seventy-six settlers down to 1969 exemplified this balance of considerations in operation at one end of the scale. The threatened foreclosure in 1972 of a small number of prominent large-farm defaulters, who had in various ways recently dropped from favour, illustrated it at the other end.

But the policy of 'squeezing' all the debtors by proceeding against a few vulnerable defaulters did not appeal to the large farmers as a whole. They were the heirs to an elaborately protected and managed sector of the economy, and it was only a matter of time before they used their political influence to try to reduce their debt burden by manipulating the structure of control.

---

100. KNFU, Memorandum on Wheat and Maize (September 1969, mimeo), p. 3.

'LARGE FARMERS' AND POLICY CONTROL

Not all 'big men' had large farms in the ex-white highlands – more politicians had farms in the ex-reserves that were 'large' by local standards; and it is in any case difficult for technical reasons to establish the true pattern of ownership and interest from the public records.[101] It is clear, however, that at independence, and in some cases earlier, it was African 'large farmers' who began to replace Europeans in the apparatus of policy control. In 1965 the Stamp Mission urged a radical reappraisal of the marketing-board structure, in particular, pointing out that these boards had been constituted 'with a strong producer bias and, until the last three or four years, have mainly represented farmers . . . Prices . . . have tended to be biased to the requirements and, to some extent, to the cost of production of the large-scale producer . . .' The mission thought a reorganization urgent, before 'the pressure of political and justifiable discontent in some sectors results either in the removal of the Boards altogether, or in their reorganization merely to the advantage of a different political sector'.[102] The same fears could have been expressed not only about marketing boards, but also about the quasi-public, quasi-private bodies, fully controlled by large farmers, such as the Kenya Co-operative Creameries (KCC), the Kenya Farmers Association (KFA), and the Kenya Coffee Producers' Union (KCPU); but by 1965 it was already too late. The process of Africanization of the large-farm sector was paralleled by the Africanization of all these bodies. The main effect was to widen the concept of the 'large farmer' to include the bigger landowners in the former reserves, whose spokesmen were now inluded in the policy-making structure. Apart from this, it was a case of *plus ça change, plus c'est la même chose*.

Each of these three organizations, which directly represented their producer-members, tended to follow a slightly different pattern from the rest. The KCC, faced with the threat of losing its

---

101. A rough idea of the share of politicians and senior civil servants in the ex-white highlands may be suggested by the pattern among the tenants and assisted owners of the Stamp Purchase farms. Of 109 in African hands in April 1971, 13 were individually owned by a former or current MP, or a civil servant or senior official of a parastatal body, and a further 12 were partnerships or companies involving such people. These are conservative figures as it is probable that other partnerships and companies involved also contained similar people in active roles. On the other hand, the extent of their interest in such cases might be quite small.

102. Stamp Report (note 44), pp. 114–17.

profitable monopoly of the domestic milk market to African small-scale farmers at the end of the 1950s, moved to co-opt two leading spokesmen of African milk producers in 1962, and had handed over control of the board and of management to Africans by 1968. The KFA, reflecting the influence of the European maize, wheat and beef farmers in the Nakuru–Eldoret areas, was much slower to Africanize, and began to transfer effective control only under government pressure in 1970. The marketing boards were more directly under government control. A number of MPs were appointed as board members immediately after independence. This was most striking in the case of the Maize and Produce Board, which handled the most valuable domestic market commodity, and of the Kenya Meat Commission; both of these quickly succumbed to the commercial consequences of over-enthusiastic exploitation and had to be reconstructed in 1967 and 1968 respectively.[103] In the case of the elected KCPU, power was finally transferred to the small African coffee-producers and away from the European planters by an imposed merger with the Kenya Coffee and Marketing Board in 1969.

These differences in timing and degree did not imply big differences in effects. The incoming Africans broadly shared the outlook and the interests of the Europeans they replaced. Some played multiple roles: for instance Peter Sifuma, the owner of a typical large-scale mixed farm in Nakuru District, was President of the KNFU, Vice-Chairman of the AFC, and a member of the board of the ADC. D. Wanguhu, who owned a large farm at Soy, was a council member of the KNFU and a member of the Wheat Board. Charles Murgor, a former Provincial Commissioner turned MP, and owner of a large farm at Turbo, was a Director of KFA and a member of the KMC. Also a number of European farmers who had been active in farm politics before independence remained in the less visible areas of marketing and policy-making and worked closely with the new African policy-makers; examples are J.B. Pollard, a former President of the KNFU, who became Vice-Chairman of the Maize and Produce Board and Chairman

---

103. On the Maize and Produce Board see *Report of the Maize Commission of Inquiry* (Government Printer, Nairobi 1966), which reported with unusual candour on malpractices during the maize shortage of 1964–65. On the Meat Commission, see the reconstructed Commission's report for 1967, which attributed the loss of nearly £350,000 to an ill-conceived, unsound and extravagant incentive-bonus scheme applicable to all workers, and an 'ill-advised price increase to producers', besides premature Africanization of staff and various external factors.

of Uplands Bacon Factory; Sir Wilfred Havelock, who became a member of the AFC board and Chairman of the Coast Province Provincial Agricultural Board; R. O'B. Wilson, who was Chairman of the Central Agricultural Board and became Vice-Chairman of the ADC.

Not surprisingly, the general result was that the protected position of the large-farm sector was left substantially intact. Large subsidies continued to be paid by consumers to large-scale producers of maize and wheat through the price structure, and by all taxpayers to all large-scale farmers through the fertilizer subsidy.[104] In general the privileges of the large-scale producers at the expense of the small-scale producers were reduced, but usually by extending the privilege to some of the larger 'small-scale' producers, not by abolishing privileges as such. Thus the lower limit of size on which the AFC could issue a 'large-scale' development loan was reduced to farms producing over £500 per annum. The lower limit of acreage on which short-term maize- or wheat-crop credit could be obtained was reduced to 15 acres (and this in turn could be put together by up to three separate neighbouring farmers). The number of such loans rose from 1,300 to 4,000 annually between 1964 and 1970.[105] Milk 'quotas', under which large-scale producers capable of maintaining a given minimum of whole-milk supply to the towns during the dry season got a premium price for their milk all year round, were abolished, so that all producers shared equally in the total value of the KCC's sales; but the system of market control was reinforced, with continuing advantage to the larger and more capitalized producers, and at the expense of the poorest urban consumers.[106]

In general, this process of co-optation into the large-farm interest worked fairly smoothly, but there was one persistent problem: a lot of the new large-scale farmers were less efficient. Many of them were also much more seriously indebted than most of their European predecessors, as we have seen. They needed a larger measure of protection in order to survive; and so they adopted the established strategy of bringing political pressure to bear to

---

104. See L. D. Smith, 'Resource Allocation Income Distribution and Agricultural Pricing Policies in Kenya' (University of East Africa, University Social Sciences Council Conference, Nairobi 1969, mimeo), p. 2; and *Report of the Working Party on Agricultural Inputs* (the Havelock Report), (Government Printer, Nairobi 1971), p. 19.

105. AFC *Report*, 1967, and interviews.

106. See below, pp. 110–113.

increase farm-gate prices. The result was that by 1971 they had succeeded in destroying the long-term policy of the government on produce prices. How this happened is a long and complex story, but even a brief outline will indicate its significance for the future underdevelopment of Kenya.

The main crop around which the issue revolved was maize. Originally promoted as an export crop for European farmers, it had subsquently become primarily a crop for domestic consumption. European farmers grew it mainly for sale, while Africans grew it mainly for home consumption. In 1942 Maize Control was established, a government agency with a monopoly of internal purchase and sales. After a drought and 'near famine' in 1943, it was agreed to follow a policy of crop diversification, but of keeping maize production as far as possible related to local demand by means of a fixed producer price. This worked to the great advantage of European growers, who were given a much higher price than small purchasers. It also led in most years to a surplus over domestic requirements, which had to be exported at a loss. But by the early 1960s the development of hybrid strains of maize suitable for Kenya opened up a new possibility, that maize could once again be grown in Kenya cheaply enough to compete in world markets. The producer price could be progressively reduced, initially to keep pace with falling costs of production, so that large surpluses were avoided, and ultimately to arrive at a price at which the surplus crop could be exported without loss, whereupon production could be progressively expanded to take advantage of world markets.[107]

This policy option, which Ministry of Agriculture officials had determined to adopt, was vitiated in 1965 by a fresh drought and famine. The Maize Marketing Board (which had succeeded the Maize Control) and the government failed to act promptly to obtain imports, and considerable profits were made by illegal exports to Uganda (where the free market price was well above that offered by the Board) and by various operations on the internal black market. It was agreed to increase the local maize reserve, and producer prices were temporarily raised again. But from 1966 the policy of price reductions began to be implemented. Then in 1970–1 exactly the same thing happened again. A severe drought

107. For the background see M. Yoshida, 'The Historical Background to Maize Marketing in Kenya, and its Implications for Future Marketing Reorganisation', Economic Development Research Project Paper No. 91 (Makerere University, 1966, mimeo).

in 1970 drastically reduced the African-subsistence crops and led to a huge increase in the demand for marketed maize. The Maize and Produce Board had not maintained the 'carry over' stocks it was supposed to and on this occasion the pressure of demand on the Board was at twice the level reached during the 1965 shortage, partly because more farmers in the Central Province had gone over wholly to dairy production, and were now buyers rather than producers of maize. Once again there was a good deal of illegal export and a flourishing internal black market. In the crisis atmosphere that ensued, the large-farmers succeeded in getting the producer price raised again.

The part played by the Board in these events was in a sense secondary; it made matters worse by failing to maintain the reserve supplies it was instructed to maintain and by being a party to some operations which diverted available supplies into the black market and illegal exports. The government's role was probably more decisive, both in failing to prevent illegal sales and in failing to order imports of maize at an early enough stage.[108]

---

108. The maize crisis of 1970–71 was not made the subject of an enquiry, but the following facts seem clear. First, the Board exported 2·5 million bags in 1968–69, but in 1970 still had not agreed with the government about the financing of the emergency stocks; the 'Cyprus bins' were still empty. The Board expected a large crop in 1969–70 and did not get it. In November 1970 the short rains failed and it became apparent that demand for maize was rising. But no action was taken until March, when the level of demand showed that stocks would be exhausted before the next harvest became available in October. The government at this point refused to order supplies from abroad, agreeing only at the eleventh hour (according to the Minister of Agriculture, in a statement on 9 September, the order was placed on the 7th). Meanwhile an illegal export trade to Somalia and Uganda flourished, with little evidence of police efforts to prevent it. It appeared that a number of 'open licences' had been issued to individuals to buy maize from the Board and direct from farmers, and sell it where they liked. The names of the holders of these licences were never disclosed, and a move by the Board to cancel their licences was reversed by political intervention. The licences were finally withdrawn only in September, when the decision to import had finally been made (*Daily Nation*, 12 September 1971). The licence-holders offered some farmers up to shs 10/- more than the Maize Board price. The Maize Board sold from its stores at shs 40/50 per bag; the black market price was said to be 100/-. Another contributory factor was that the users of maize for feeding stock could buy it at a special price, below the price fixed for sales for human consumption. In the five months August 1969–January 1970 consumption of maize for stock-feed rose 225 per cent over the average of the previous three years! Aldington's comment that 'it does seem likely that a substantial amount of maize designated as stockfeed maize "leaked" into the market for maize for human consumption' was a too tactful understatement. (T. J. Aldington, 'The Animal Feeds Industry in Kenya: A Preliminary Survey', Institute for Development Studies, Nairobi 1970, mimeo, pp. 7–8).

But what really mattered was that the crisis led to an atmosphere which made possible a permanent victory for the spokesmen of the large-farmers, who called for higher producer prices, not lower ones. The KNFU urged that unless prices were raised, there would be further shortages, because many farmers could not produce profitably at the price level set in 1969.

This, of course, was what the policy of price reductions implied. The government had constructed a storage capacity of 1·1 million bags, equivalent to more than half a year's demand in a good year, or enough in a bad year to deal with a much higher demand while maize was being imported. Armed with this facility, and a willingness to import in the years when this was necessary, the government could allow inefficient producers to go out of maize production: with the new seed varieties, an expansion more than sufficient for local sales and substantial exports should be easily attainable at a producer price equal to the export parity price (i.e., the price at which a buyer could ship the maize from Mombasa to markets anywhere in the world and still make a profit). The domestic consumer would no longer be expected to pay, either by a special domestic price or through an export subsidy, for exports which made losses, because the producers were being paid prices above the export parity price. The officials concerned did not intend that there should be a major drop in the producer price. The aim was to reduce producer prices only slightly, letting the economies of scale and improved handling efficiency complete the closing of the gap.[109]

This policy was what the KNFU's campaign for increased producer prices effectively wrecked. It was theoretically possible that at some future date, with their debts substantially repaid, the farmers would agree to a fresh approach. But it did not seem very likely.

---

109. The basis of this was the introduction of bulk handling equipment, which would be a justified investment if policy was directed to production for export; and the abolition of control of domestic marketing, except to provide floor and ceiling prices. The government's working party thought that about 8 shillings per bag could be saved on handling, storage and administration, and that the export parity price at the Board's railway stores in consequence could be raised to about 22–3 shillings, a level not too far below the current producer-price of 25 shillings; if farmers progressively adopted more efficient techniques and the improved seeds, it seemed fairly certain that the gap could be closed. They reckoned without the political realities of the situation. See *Final Report of the Working Party Studying the Maize and Produce Board in Relation to the Expected Crop Production in the 1970s, and in Particular with Regard to the Major Cereal Crops* (Nairobi, November 1969, mimeo).

The government's policy had been formulated by a special working party of officials and outside experts which seems to have foreseen the likelihood of a clash with the farmers, without appreciating its seriousness. The working party were clear that to exploit the possibilities of the new technology so as to give consumers (who were mostly the lowest-paid members of the wage-labour force) the cheapest possible food supply, and ensure that farmers applied resources where the returns were highest, meant a break with the past. Marketing boards, the working party pointed out, 'were set up to protect producers' interests only, at a time when in Europe similar institutions were being set up to protect European farmers. There is no room in modern Kenya to protect one sector of the economy or to give it special privileges . . .'

They went on:

> . . . the time has come to reappraise agricultural pricing policies in general in Kenya so that agriculture makes its optimum contribution to maximising gross national product . . . For maize . . . this means that the *producer price* should be set at the relevant export parity price in the different production areas. At the same time the consumer price should be set at the producer price plus marketing costs incurred in distributing the maize to consumers.[110]

To this the KNFU replied: 'We are frequently being advised by gentlemen sitting in comfortable chairs in Nairobi that farmers must become more efficient and weather the storm. At the same time, no efforts seem to be made in other sectors of the economy to maintain efficiency. In the last resort, increased costs are borne by the farmers.'[111]

It was true that costs had been rising, but then so had yields from the new seeds. The trouble was that so many of the large farmers were not efficient enough to benefit fully from these. Throughout 1969, when maize output had been expanding rapidly for three years, the KNFU constantly emphasized their plight, saying that it was 'impossible for a farmer to make ends meet' under present circumstances. Although the ones said to be most in difficulties were 'small farmers representing more than a quarter of the union's total membership', these were, of course, all large-scale farmers.[112] In 1969, however, the KNFU was still expecting

---

110. ibid., pp. 29 and 38–9.
111. Peter Sifuma, quoted in *East African Standard*, 8 May 1969.
112. ibid.

a large maize surplus and realized that there was no prospect of raising the producer price: 'Taking into account that large quantities of maize will have to be exported to world markets [sc. at a loss, to be covered by a Treasury subsidy], the KNFU sees no alternative but to accept a maize price of shs 25/- per bag . . .'[113] Reducing the debt burden seemed in these circumstances the only way to save many of the African large-scale farmers from bankruptcy. What the KNFU persistently sought throughout this time was relief from loan repayments for all the indebted African farmers, large and small, so that one government official grumbled: 'the big farmers always hid behind the small ones'.

But with the advent of the maize crisis of 1970-1 the situation changed. The shortage could be represented as due not to the drought, but to the lack of a price incentive to plant maize. The KNFU's 1971 memorandum on maize and wheat made no mention of indebtedness, but concentrated entirely on the need for a maize price to the farmer of shs 35/- per bag, to be paid for the 1971 crop which was about to be harvested, as well as for the crop to be planted in 1972.[114]

The government's interministerial Costs and Prices Committee, reflecting the working party's approach, recommended a price of shs 25/- for the 1972 crop. The Cabinet raised this to shs 30/-, and this was announced in August 1971. Two weeks later the President independently authorized a further increase to shs 35/-, applicable to both the 1971 and 1972 planted crops.[115] In December the consumer price of sifted maize meal was raised by 30 per cent. The newspapers received this announcement with acclaim.

The damage that had been done to the long-term growth of internal purchasing power was actually greater than the story of the maize price reveals. The final increase in the price to shs 35/- can only be properly understood in the light of a very similar struggle that was also going on over milk prices. In this case the

---

113. KNFU, *Memorandum on Wheat and Maize* (September 1969, mimeo), p. 3.

114. KNFU, *Memorandum on Maize and Wheat* (September 1971, mimeo).

115. The August announcement was made by the Minister of Finance, acting for the Minister of Agriculture, who was away. These prices were published in the gazette. The subsequent announcement was made as a 'government statement' issued in Mombasa, where the President was on a 'working holiday', in the absence of both these ministers. The *Daily Nation* commented: 'Obviously nothing concerning the maize industry had changed within the two weeks separating these two decisions. The conclusion cannot be escaped that those who make these decisions are ill-equipped to make long range plans.' (14 September 1971). Needless to say, the *Nation* intended this as a compliment to the *President*, adding that the second decision 'treated maize producers with greater fairness'.

principal actor was not the KNFU but the Kenya Co-operative Creameries (KCC); though it would really be truer to say that in both cases, the decisive factor was not the power of any particular organization but the large-farm interest and outlook diffused among both politicians and senior civil servants.[116]

When the chairmanship of the KCC passed in 1967 to Mr D. N. Kuguru, a dairy farmer in Nyeri district in Central Province, the days of the old European-dominated quota system were numbered.[117] Quotas were finally abolished in 1970, and from this time onwards all farmers were paid the same price for any given grade of whole milk supplied to the KCC. At the same time the KCC's monopoly of the sale of milk and milk products was confirmed, and consumer prices continued to be fixed by the government. It was obvious that there would now be a rapid increase of whole-milk supplies to the KCC and, once again, the civil servants urged that the time was ripe to move towards a lower consumer price, with a view to widening the domestic market for whole milk. Hitherto, domestic prices for dairy products had been kept high by tariff protection and the KCC monopoly, offsetting the relatively low returns to butter exports. If milk production was to become a source of income for a mass of smallholders, what was needed was the widest possible expansion of the market. The alternative was the probable production of a surplus by established producers, leading to the familiar pattern of restricted production, subsidized in one way or another, and inevitably benefiting primarily a limited number of established producers.

Another government working party was the scene of the first

---

116. An example of what was involved comes from the reaction of the Provincial Commissioner for Central Province, Mr Nyachae, who attended the conference of District Agricultural Committees in Nairobi in November 1971 and complained bitterly about the KCC's circular in October, in which it effectively reduced the President's increase of June by three-quarters (see below). He said the circular 'said there would be a 20% cut in my milk price . . . this meant that if I sent 100 gallons of milk a day, 20 of these would be paid for at 1/- each. This is a big loss.' Mr Nyachae, in his capacity as PC, was a figure close to the President.

117. Mr Kuguru became an MP in 1969 and was appointed an Assistant Minister for Works. Quotas referred to the quantity of liquid milk which a farmer had demonstrated his ability to supply during the dry season, when cows could be kept in milk only by feeding them with stored foodstuffs. A premium price was paid to the farmer for this quantity of milk throughout the whole year. Other whole milk was paid for at a very much lower rate, and this was what virtually all smallholder producers were getting; most of it was separated, and the price reflected the much lower realization price for butterfat sales, including butter exports.

round of this confrontation. It contained a number of producers' representatives who, according to the working party's own report, 'held that a primary objective of the working party was the development of a justification for requesting a rise in the price of milk to both producers and consumers.'[118] The KCC representatives proposed that consumer prices should in fact be raised by roughly 15 per cent. The civil service members, who by contrast advocated a *lower* consumer price, were defeated by the argument that the price-elasticity of demand for milk was unknown, while 'a majority' of the working party believed that the producer price for whole milk could not be lowered 'in view of the need to increase production and in light of the rising costs of inputs to dairy farmers'.[119] But the abolition of the quota system, which was put into effect while the working party was meeting, meant an increase of about 300 per cent in the milk price realized by smallholders at the existing producer price; so the majority's opposition to a price reduction was really an argument in favour of avoiding any tendency for smallholders to *replace* large-scale producers whose costs were higher. As a compromise, it was agreed to recommend keeping prices more or less as they were. At the 1971 annual conference of the KNFU the Union's president (Peter Sifuma) claimed a share of the credit for this: 'In co-operation with the KDB and the KCC we successfully resisted the idea of reducing the consumer price for milk which would have meant a lower price for the producer . . .'[120]

But the problems of the larger dairy farmers were not disposed of; with milk sales increasing by 14 per cent in 1970–1, they saw an opportunity to increase their incomes and determined to renew the pressure for price increases. On this occasion they went directly to the President, and proposed that producer prices should be raised from the average of 2·80 shillings per gallon achieved in 1970–1 to 3·50 shillings. The President consulted the directors of the KCC, who, he claimed later, made no objection.[121] At the Nakuru Show in June, he announced a new producer price of shs 3/50. The consumer price was increased by 15 per cent immediately afterwards.

All this had implications well beyond the dairy industry. The

118. Final Report of the Dairy Working Party, Ministry of Agriculture, Nairobi, 1970, mimeo, p. 2.

119. ibid., p. 3.

120. *EAS*, 18 March 1971.

121. *EAS*, 3 December 1971.

interministerial Costs and Prices Committee had been bypassed and now fell into abeyance, while marketing boards and the Ministry of Agriculture struggled to mitigate the disruption to production (which a wholesale switch to dairy production would cause) by the only means open to them – a series of *ad hoc* price increases for everything else that was not an exclusively export crop. This probably helps to explain the second increase in the maize price in September. Price increases for beef, pigs and other products followed. The position of the larger farmers was transformed. Their debt burden was apparently to be shifted on to the domestic consumers of farm produce. The remaining European farmers, already the most efficient of the old settlers, and indeed any farmer who had been making a profit before 1971, began to get extremely rich. The KNFU was delighted.[122]

Unfortunately a Presidential *ukase* did not have quite as much magical power as it was commonly credited with. Within three months the KCC was in some danger of bankruptcy and informed its members that it would in effect be cutting the price back to just under shs 3/-.[123] If the new consumer price had not significantly slowed the rate of growth of domestic demand, it had not accelerated it, whereas the new producer price had produced a massive expansion of supplies, some of which could not be disposed of at all, let alone profitably.

At the revised producer price, the KCC evidently expected to be able to break even. Meanwhile the new farmgate prices for other commodities were an accomplished fact. It was very hard to see where the initiative would come from to reinstate the price and production policies that had been put forward by the economists and officials to spread the benefits of new technology to the smallholder and the urban worker. The benefits were instead to be applied to maintaining the position of the least efficient large-scale farmers, who had proved themselves no less capable of dictating the pattern of policy than their European predecessors.

On the other hand, the situation was not quite the same as before. Urban consumers were now more numerous and some of

122. 'Jubilant' was how the KNFU described farmers in a telegram of thanks to the President after the maize price increase (*EAS*, 15 September 1971).

123. The KCC sought to minimize the impression of a departure from the 'President's price' by purporting to maintain it for 80 per cent of supplies, while paying only one shilling per gallon for the rest. The circular in which it explained this was published in the *East African Standard*, 26 November 1971. Mr Kuguru later explained that the KCC had had to exceed its overdraft to meet the payout before its level was cut (*EAS*, 16 December 1971).

them were much more powerful than twenty years previously. It was likely that salaries and wages would rise and that the higher producer prices would be offset by a deterioration in the farmers' terms of trade with the towns. The result could only be inflation. At the end of 1971 the government imposed a temporary price-freeze and set up a committee to advise on all future price-increases. The committee represented all major producer interests except, as usual, small peasants. The Minister of Finance made a major speech to a meeting of farmers and asked them not to seek any further producer price-increases. They must consider, he said, 'where this new spiral of rising prices would lead the country. They must consider who is going to meet the inflation and pay the increased prices . . . they must not deceive themselves that they could pass it on to the urban population as consumers.'[124] The broader truth underlying this remained unspoken. The distribution of income could not be shifted in favour of the rural producers generally except by a system of control over the manufacturing and commercial sectors, which would be incompatible with the high rate of private foreign investment on which the whole economic structure was seen to depend. The large-farmers had probably reached the limit of what they could achieve by price manipulation. For many, it might prove enough to restore their fortunes. For the rest, other expedients would have to be found. There seemed less and less likelihood that they would be allowed to go to the wall.

CONCLUSIONS

From 1964 to 1969 agricultural production rose at an average rate of 4·5 per cent per annum at constant (1964) prices. The volume of output of some commodities, such as tea, sugar-cane, rice, and maize, rose much faster. This was evidence of innovation and technical advance, as well as of Kenya's exceptionally favourable endowments of soil and climate. The rate of growth at least kept pace with the total increase in the population living on the land. All of this was generally interpreted as a story of success. But the question is not whether the policies pursued were a success in terms of the rate of growth or total output, although the strong bias of policy towards the larger farmers very likely produced a slower rate of growth than might otherwise have been achieved.

124. *EAS*, 22 December 1971.

The question is, what significance the agricultural policies of the 1960s had for the long-run character structure of Kenyan society as a whole.

While it still held the initiative the colonial administration arranged for a fairly rapid evacuation of the expatriate mixed-farming sector; this made possible a series of measures which progressively integrated the new peasantry with the foreign-dominated urban sector. One was settlement. Settlement itself was carried out under programmes fully planned and largely implemented before political independence, on terms carefully designed to commit the incoming government to uphold the sanctity of private property at the expense of its former agrarian radicalism. Settlement also reduced the political risks by reducing land hunger in the short run. A second general feature of the new system was the fostering of an intermediate stratum of larger peasant producers, and above them a stratum of potential capitalist farmers. In the former 'white' highlands the low-density settlers corresponded to the former, and some of the new large-scale farmers to the latter. Outside the former white highlands the same process was encouraged by the rapid extension of private land-tenure, which 'froze' the existing distribution of land, to the advantage of the larger landowners, and by the differential provision of loans and technical assistance.

Settlement also played an important indirect role, which complemented the registration of private landholdings. Although most of the high-density settlers, especially in the schemes near Kikuyu country, were landless, some were landowners in the former reserves who sold their former plots to neighbouring landowners rich enough to buy them.[125] The process of settlement thus created some scope for the enlargement of the landholdings of richer peasants, or small 'gentry' farmers in the reserves, while some settlers, including some in the high-density schemes, could also become 'kulaks'.

In these ways the boundaries between the old 'large-farm' sector and the 'African land units', the one expatriate and capitalist, the other African and – at least till the 1950s – not only 'peasant' but 'poor-peasant', were swiftly obliterated. In their place arose a new rural structure, predominantly occupied by Africans, with the foreign-owned plantations and ranches still operating, much less

---

125. This was happening in the bracken zone of Nyeri District and other parts of Kikuyu country in the second half of the 1960s. See C. Leys, 'Politics in Kenya' (note 4), p. 320, note 46, and pp. 322–3.

visibly, though still more profitably, on the side-lines. It contained
a system of gradations of acreage, capitalization, access to credit
and knowhow and political protection which cut across the
distinction between the former white highlands and the rest of the
country, and also the distinction between the settlement schemes
and areas not administered by the Department of Settlement. At
the top were some very large-scale individual landowners, some
of them with farms purchased from Europeans, others with several
hundred acres – not necessarily all in one 'parcel' – in the former
reserves. These men were linked professionally, socially and economically to the foreign capitalist enclave, borrowing from foreign
banks, having accounts with foreign equipment suppliers, holding
directorships in foreign companies. Their farms were mostly run
by salaried managers, in some cases by Europeans. At the bottom
of the scale were the 'peasant' masses, mostly now with freehold
land titles, though with little access to capital, extension services
or other inputs, and – especially among the Kikuyu – a growing
minority of landless labourers and squatters.

For the new system to be successfully consolidated it had to provide all these ingredients: for a majority of the masses, enough
land to prove at least a subsistence and some cash surplus; for the
better educated, salaried or wealthier peasant, room to expand
and innovate; for the urban salariat and politicians, an opportunity to translate political influence into the ownership of capital,
by becoming a large-farm owner. (That this could often be combined with acting as a patron for one's clan, by being the prime
mover in one or more companies or comparatives also purchasing
large farms, was a complication but not a disadvantage, because
it helped to legitimize the new landowning status of the individual too.) The existence of an open 'land frontier', created by
the European farmers' exodus, made all this possible; but it was
equally important that the outgoing colonial administration had
been able to lay down the terms on which this resource would be
used. After the first and in many ways decisive initiative on settlement schemes, the subsequent initiatives on land registration,
large-farm transfer, and the differential use of loan and grant
funds resulted from a complex interaction between governments,
mediated by visiting missions. Just as in Ghana, import licensing
and suppliers' credits have been identified as the key 'mode of
linkage' between foreign private capital and the Ghanaian state,
so the visiting mission, often containing former colonial officials,
could be described as a key mechanism, linking foreign capital

(public and private) to Kenyan agriculture after independence.[126] The independent contribution of the missions differed from case to case; what they had in common was a rather clear awareness, more or less candidly revealed in their reports, of what the 'donors' were prepared to make possible, which was what, broadly speaking, subsequently happened.

---

126. See R. Murray, 'Second Thoughts on Ghana', *New Left Review* No. 42, March–April 1967, p. 36.

CHAPTER 4

Foreign Capital

As a result of the land-transfer programme foreign ownership in agriculture was greatly reduced. But in commerce and industry, by contrast, virtually all the expansion which occurred – a 50 per cent increase of output between 1964 and 1970, and a 100 per cent increase in the annual level of investment – was foreign-owned and controlled. This, of course, was a central feature of the Kenyatta government's economic strategy. At first much of this investment involved capital transferred out of agriculture, especially once exchange control was finally imposed in 1965. But two years later, after an initial period of corporate planning and assessment of the longer-term investment climate, a substantial new inflow of foreign capital began: for the four years 1967 to 1970 the average annual rate of inflow was £10·3 million, a total of £41·3 million.[1]

A good deal of this represented profits earned in Kenya by established foreign companies and re-invested, but during this period a substantial volume of new capital flowed in, mainly belonging to international companies not previously established in Kenya which now moved into manufacturing for the domestic market.[2] Names familiar elsewhere – Union Carbide, Firestone, United Steel, Del Monte, Mitsui, Nomura, Schweppes, Inchcape, Lonrho and many more – now joined others such as Unilever which had been established in Kenya for some time.

In addition to new foreign investment, many local companies, mainly owned by local Europeans, were bought out by foreign-based companies. Lonrho bought very extensive Kenyan interests during these years (including the leading daily paper, the *East African Standard*), as did Inchcape. Steel Brothers bought control of

1. *Economic Survey 1971*, p. 70, and *Statistical Abstract 1970*, p. 40.
2. See Barry Herman, 'Some Basic Data for Analysing the Political Economy of Foreign Investment in Kenya', *Discussion Paper* No. 112, Institute for Development Studies, University of Nairobi, July 1971, mimeo.

Baumann's, a major local trading and industrial holding company. Securicor bought the leading night-guard company. A further notable feature of the period was that long-established European trading companies, such as Baumann, Mitchell Cotts and Mackenzie Dalgety, switched their activities increasingly into manufacturing, as government measures to reserve trade for Africans increasingly took their old business away from them. By the end of the 1960s some foreign companies in service industries, such as insurance, were also beginning to move into manufacturing in anticipation of new measures to transfer these lines of business to Africans.

The only important exceptions to foreign ownership of all this investment were joint ventures between foreign companies and government-owned development corporations. These account for an average of just over 9 per cent of the equity in new foreign investments made during the years 1964–70.[3] However, this affected mainly a few large and questionably profitable enterprises, undertaken towards the end of the decade, which the government considered politically important. At the end of the 1970s Kenya's new industrial sector was still almost entirely foreign-owned.

Yet the net result of the government's policy measures which attracted these new investors and diverted old ones into manufacturing was only to expand manufacturing at the same rate as the economy as a whole. One reason for this was that expanding manufacturing was difficult without a drastic change in the pattern of internal demand.

The other reason was the tacit decision to prefer Western capital, in alliance with an African 'auxiliary bourgeoisie', to an indigenous Asian bourgeoisie as the agency of economic growth. Even in 1971 roughly two-thirds of the non-farm private assets in Kenya were still in Asian hands. Nearly half of their capital was in urban real estate, thanks to their exclusion from farming in the 'white' highlands. But as we have already seen, their movement into manufacturing had begun to accelerate in the 1950s, and it is obvious that their capital resources coupled with their market knowledge and entrepreneurial experience would have enabled them to play a leading role in this field if they had been encouraged to. Official policy was to progressively exclude them from commerce and to encourage them to enter manufacturing.

3. Herman, op. cit. (note 2), p. 19.

Table 4.1

*Approximate Distribution of Private Non-Farm Assets
(but including plantations), 1971*[4]

	K£ million	
	Asian	Non-Asian
Industry or plantations	70	120
Shares in public companies	20	30
Real estate	200	15
Trade	100	25
Cash	35	35
Total	£425m.	£225m.

But political hostility to them led to policies which discouraged them from making any long-term investment in Kenya: difficulties in obtaining citizenship, discrimination against Asians in the trade and transportation sectors even when they held Kenyan citizenship, special regulations to cut down the normally permitted remittance of income overseas if that income came from *rent* (this being the major source of Asians' unearned income), and so on. The result was that the local Asian bourgeoisie was really placed in a special category of foreign investors. They were denied the opportunity for legal exportation of assets or profits (because the capital of non-Kenyan but long-resident Asians did not count as 'foreign' under the terms of the Foreign Investments Protection Act); but they were also made to feel insecure and hence hesitant about investing locally, and inclined to take every opportunity for sending assets abroad by unofficial means.[5] As

4. This estimate was made by a particularly well-informed business consultant in Nairobi. It is certainly very approximate, but various 'harder' figures do roughly correspond to it. For instance a study of the share registers of a sample of the major public companies in Kenya (see below, p. 165) showed that Asians did own roughly two-fifths of the shares in these companies, and the total value of the quoted shares on the Stock Exchange in 1970 was £51 million; pre-tax company incomes for 1967 (the latest available figures in 1971) totalled £37·8 million, which at an average rate of return on net assets of, say, 20 per cent would yield a figure rather under the total company assets implied here, but perhaps would be closer to it if the basis of the income data were not income declared for tax purposes.

5. A study of company savings in the manufacturing sector in 1970 showed that the firms with a majority of shareholders resident in Kenya had a higher tendency to

they were obliged to withdraw their capital from trade, what they could not export they tended to hold in liquid bank deposits.[6] Yet at the same time the government, the United Nations and the Development Finance Corporation of Kenya were all devoting substantial resources to setting up special units to identify and test the feasibility of new industrial projects, and to interest overseas companies in undertaking them.

The contradiction was rendered sharper still by the fact that most Asian firms were family businesses, well suited for small-scale production using relatively labour-intensive techniques, and had shown their ability to enter manufacturing, often with relatively little special protection, in the 1950s; whereas multinational companies generally adopt the capital-intensive technology of the parent firm, adapted to production only on a fairly large scale, with a high level of imported inputs, and requiring relatively high levels of effective protection.[7]

save their earnings than firms with a majority of non-resident shareholders (P. N. Snowden, 'Company Finance in Kenya's Manufacturing Sector', in *Developmental Trends in Kenya*, Centre of African Studies, University of Edinburgh, April 1972, mimeo, p. 17). This suggests that some Asians were effectively being turned into 'domestic' capitalists by the operation of exchange control. But it must be remembered that some of the 'local' firms in the sample were owned by Europeans, not Asians; that 86 per cent of all manufacturing establishments – all the small ones – were excluded from the survey; and that manufacturing probably accounted for only about 15 per cent of all Asian-owned assets. An Asian family manufacturing business worth over £500,000 would only be able to beat exchange control through over-invoicing on a large scale, and would have little option but to reinvest earnings and hope that, in the event of later expropriation, there would be suitable compensation. But such businesses were the exception.

6. Between 1965 and 1971, while demand deposits with the banks rose 72 per cent, or only just faster than national income, time and savings deposits rose 376 per cent, until they were nearly equal to demand deposits. This liquidity was also reflected in a doubling of share prices on the Nairobi Stock Exchange between January 1966 and December 1970.

7. H. Pack, in a study of 'Employment and Productivity in Kenya Manufacturing' (Institute for Development Studies, Nairobi, August 1972, mimeo) states that 'it was typically a subsidiary of a foreign firm which carried out labour-intensive adaptations and was more willing to use older equipment than locally-owned firms which had 'extended their selling operations backward'; and the ILO mission reached similar conclusions as between foreign and locally-owned firms operating in the same sector (*Employment, Incomes and Equality*, ILO, Geneva 1972, pp. 449–51). These studies do suggest that within a given field the multinational companies were able to make better use of cheap labour than locally-owned companies. On the other hand they do not show that if small-scale Asian-owned capital had been more welcome than it was, it would not have developed many more labour-intensive lines than it actually did. Foreign firms predominated in inherently capital-intensive sectors and overall were more capital-intensive than local firms. M. Phelps and B. Wasow confirmed the existence in Kenya of firms whose manufacturing operations cost more in foreign exchange than the imports

The resulting dominance by international firms in manufacturing, and their increasing role in other sectors (for instance in the rapidly expanding hotel industry), when added to their established role in the plantation industry, banking and insurance, oil supplies and other sectors, was soon seen to involve a disconcerting new form of dependency, to which the government responded with a new series of policies. These can be summarized as Africanization of management posts; attempts at government control through regulation, taxation and exchange control; and measures to secure African participation in the equity of foreign firms. These policies met with varying degrees of success; what they did not do, however, was to modify at all significantly the 'development of underdevelopment' which the new forms of foreign investment promoted.

AFRICANIZATION

By 1965 the upper levels of the civil service had been virtually completely Africanized, with the exception of posts in professional or technical fields. Partly to satisfy the demand from the trade unions and from university graduates for comparable prospects of rapid advancement in the private sector, and partly from a growing sense that real economic power lay with the directors of the major foreign companies, official attention turned increasingly towards measures to force the pace of Africanization in them. From 1967 onwards work permits were only issued to non-citizens for jobs which could not be currently filled by Africans, and on condition that the employing firms were making proper efforts to train Africans to fill these posts in the future.

By the end of the 1960s there was no doubt that these pressures were taking effect. Figures are rather unreliable in this field, since they are based on the companies' own classifications, and one way for companies to accommodate the pressures for Africanization is to alter these. This is particularly important in respect of the small number of key senior posts in each company. One study commented:

> The fact of window dressing, otherwise known as 'shadow posts', is not a new invention. One would have thought that this is by now such a transparent screen that no one would

they were substituting for, as Kilby had earlier found in Nigeria (see 'Measuring Protection and its Effects in Kenya', Institute for Development Studies, Nairobi, April 1972, mimeo).

dare hide behind it. But, with little alterations here and there to suit circumstances it is widely used. In many cases it is clothed with changes of job titles whereby the expatriate personnel become either consultants or experts with a hike in remunerations.[8]

This study found that 23 per cent of the posts classified as executive or managerial in US firms operating in Kenya in 1971 were held by indigenous Kenyans (this could include some non-African citizens). Another study of fifty-two large companies, based on FKE records, found that 41 per cent of all management posts in 1971 were held by Africans.[9] Both of these samples were probably biased towards companies with above-average levels of Africanization, so that it was clear that there was a long way to go.[10] It was also obvious that at board-room level, the degree of Africanization depended very much on the character of the company. It was no accident that the first two major foreign companies to appoint Kenyan General Managers were British-American Tobacco and Shell, both of which had been recruiting Kenyan graduates in the late 1950s, profiting from their world-wide experience of the necessity to localize their top management. The smaller the company, and the more of a family business it was, the more reluctant it tended to be to Africanize management posts. Even companies which had gone a long way in Africanizing senior posts were unlikely to relinquish control entirely to Africans. The Financial Director would tend to remain expatriate 'to protect the investment'; in 1971 even in the most Africanized companies two or three of the principal operations managers also tended to be expatriate, with Africans typically occupying senior posts in sales, personnel management and public relations. In the case of some international companies decision-making was in any case often highly centralized, leaving very little discretion to the local management. As one senior African executive remarked: 'Our policies operate within very strict limits. Our budget goes to London, and then to New Jersey . . . take a service station; you

---

8. D. Nzomo, 'Occupational Kenyanisation in the Private Sector', Staff Paper No. 108 (Institute for Development Studies, University of Nairobi, August 1971), p. 15.

9. N. Hunt and L. Whitlock, 'Submission for the Training Review Committee of the Government of Kenya' (Nairobi 1971, mimeo).

10. The Nzomo sample was based only on those companies which agreed to be interviewed. The Hunt–Whitlock sample was based only on large companies (over 150 employees), and ignored those in the original sample (nine out of sixty-seven) which had no African managers.

have to meet a certain minimum return on the investment, whether it is in Greece or in Kenya.'

Foreign control could also be retained by setting up a 'regional' office in Nairobi whose foreign personnel did not need work permits because they were responsible for a much wider area of operations than Kenya alone. Shell was one of the first companies to do this, followed by British-American Tobacco (BAT). It was actually government policy to encourage the establishment of such offices, on the grounds that they could earn foreign currency for Kenya in the form of management fees paid to the regional offices by subsidiaries in other countries in the region.

After talking to a number of the leading foreign companies' senior personnel, however, one became conscious that external control was really less important than the socialization of the new African executives into their roles as foreign-company managers. None of the managers I talked to, African or expatriate, thought that the complete Africanization of top management would entail any significant change in company policies. The Kenyan General Manager of Kenya Breweries (actually not a foreign-owned company) considered that he had pushed for a maximum expansion programme in the national interest, but given the fact that it was a monopoly and the most profitable public company in Kenya, not too much can be read into this. When all is said and done, it is difficult to know just what can be expected from Africanization of management of large companies anyway. There may be some tendency for wage settlements and fringe benefits to become more liberal, and for the style of management to change in some respects, but it can hardly lead to a disregard of profitability or of capital growth, and it is not very likely that the foreign owners will allow local management to determine the fundamental issue of the use of company profits in the long term. In retrospect, what strikes one as significant is that in the course of many discussions no senior African executive mentioned this issue, and in general it was the identity of views of African and expatriate executives that was remarkable, not the differences. Some of the Africans concerned had been fifteen years with their companies, had been on a number of overseas training courses and attachments, and had thoroughly absorbed their companies' management philosophies and styles. The public service had changed little in essentials as a result of being fully Africanized, and there seemed little reason to expect things to be different in the private sector.

CONTROLS

Three main instruments of control over foreign investment existed or were created during the 1960s: taxation, exchange control, and a system of interministerial committees dealing with new investments and protection. In 1971 two new pieces were added to the apparatus: a capital issues committee was set up to control share flotations, and the existing office of Price Controller was supplemented by a new advisory committee on prices as the government began to try to curb inflation by direct controls.

What all these instruments have in common is their very limited effectiveness in face of the sophisticated resources available to the larger international companies, and the ingenuity and complexity of even quite small companies or partnerships which might wish to evade this or that particular control.

This was most striking in relation to taxation. Total income-tax receipts rose from just £13m. in 1961/2 to just over £23m. in 1968/9, so that it appeared that increased levels of taxation imposed under successive post-independence budgets, and rising company and personal incomes, were making a solid contribution to government revenues.[11] But it was obvious that tax collection had become much less effective than it was before independence. A major reason for this was the chronic shortage of tax-assessment staff.[12] This meant that the amount of detailed attention that could be given to each tax file was well below the optimum, at a time when companies were developing new expertise in handling their finances so as to minimize their tax liability, to say nothing of tax evasion. As to the latter, the Investigations Branch had two officers in post, compared with twelve in the first post-independence years. In the years 1955 to 1960 this branch had settled roughly 100 cases annually, bringing in an annual total of well over £1 million of duty and penalty payments from individuals and companies which had understated their incomes.[13] From 1960 to 1969 there was a 70 per cent increase in the number of limited-liability companies and nearly a 100 per cent increase in the number of other enterprises. Yet during these same years the number of cases settled by the Investigations Branch declined

---

11. East African Income Tax Department, *Report* for 1968/69, p. 4.

12. In 1971 there were only 32 Tax Assessors in post out of a total establishment of 54, and 15 trainee assessors out of a total establishment of 25.

13. These data are for all three East African countries. Kenyan income-tax collections generally accounted for 50 per cent of all normal collections in East Africa.

until it reached twenty-one in 1969, and the duty and penalty assessed fell to an average of about £200,000 annually.[14] One has to assume a rather big change in the practice and outlook of the business community not to believe that very large sums of income-tax revenue were in fact being lost in these circumstances.[15] One senior official commented ruefully: 'I wonder how often the cabinet ever discusses income tax – yet income tax is absolutely basic to self-determination.' Perhaps the fact that Africans were replacing Europeans and Asians in jobs and in business during these years had something to do with the apparent indifference of politicians to this question.

No such inhibitions affected the operation of exchange control, which was established in 1965 for all transactions outside East Africa. By the end of the 1960s the two main aims of exchange control with respect to foreign companies were: (a) to ensure that they only remitted abroad capital, or earnings on capital, which had been brought in from abroad in the first place, and (b) to control the extent to which foreign companies employed local funds in their Kenyan operations, by restricting their access to local credit.[16] In spite of certain loopholes, exchange control was probably quite effective in limiting foreign companies' use of local savings to 'gear up' their operations so as to enhance the profits attributable to the foreign equity capital. Some foreign companies certainly complained bitterly about these restrictions.

But given the nature of the international company the case was very different with regard to capital transfers, since they could transfer capital abroad by raising the prices paid to their own plants overseas for inputs imported into Kenya. The ILO mission on Employment which visited Kenya in 1972 reported that 'the exchange control authorities suggest that these practices are prevalent, though they are only occasionally able to prove it'.[17] Another practice which effectively circumvented exchange con-

---

14. East African Income Tax Department, *Report* for 1968/69, p. 7. In November 1972 it was announced that tax collection was to be 'decentralized', and that each East African state 'would have a strong investigations branch to track down offenders'.

15. The practice of 'living off' a small private company was developed into a fine art in Kenya by the end of the 1960s. One garage proprietor remarked: 'My salary is £3,000 but you are a fool if you don't make £10,000.' It appeared to be permissible to charge the running of several private cars, large domestic staffs (including stable hands) and other major items of personal expenditure to business expenses.

16. Central Bank of Kenya, *First Annual Report 1966–67*, pp. 16–18.

17. *Employment, Incomes and Equality*, op. cit. (note 7), p. 454.

trol was the payment of management fees, consultancy fees, and royalties for patents, brand-names and so on. The ILO mission studied a sample of ten foreign manufacturing companies and found that in 1971 such payments constituted 40 per cent of total remittances, and were equal to 67 per cent of dividends. Parts of these payments were 'obviously real payments for real services'; equally obviously, parts of them were not.[18] The 1971 Budget had imposed a special 20 per cent tax on such payments, and it was significant that many companies which had been making all three types of payment preferred to go on making them and pay the tax, rather than scale them down; in other words they were too important a means of remitting funds to be given up even in face of the cost of the new tax. The ILO mission thought it fair to conclude from this that foreign manufacturing companies must also be assumed to be exporting capital by 'transfer pricing', and that it was likely that this practice at least doubled the amount of surplus actually sent out of the country in the form of profits and dividends. Once again, all this was no more than studies in other countries (including Tanzania) had already shown to be typical, or than well-informed local observers knew to be true.[19]

It was possible to envisage a much expanded exchange-control section of the Central Bank attempting to probe such practices, company by company, and at least reducing the grosser forms of such surplus transfers. Certainly the situation was a good deal laxer in this respect in Kenya than in many other underdeveloped countries where the same companies also operated. On the other hand the opportunity to make such remittances was presumably a factor in the rate of inflow of foreign investment; Kenya's position as a 'periphery centre', offering an attractive location for the regional operations of international companies, meant that the government could not easily afford to become too strict about

18. ibid., p. 456.
19. The ILO report's estimate assumed that imports were over-valued by an average of 5 per cent, which the mission thought a very low assumption. A study of the difference between c.i.f. values of Tanzanian imports, and the f.o.b. values of the same goods appearing as exports in the trade statistics of their countries of origin, suggested that the figure of overvaluation for Tanzania was between 10 and 20 per cent (M. Yaffey, 'False Import Valuations', ERB Paper 676, Economic Research Bureau, University College, Dar es Salaam, mimeo, May 1967). The effect of using a 10 per cent assumption for the firms included in the ILO study would have been to yield a probable figure of capital transfer by over-invoicing of about three times the volume of dividend outflows. See also Aart Van der Laar, 'Foreign Business and Capital Export from Developing Countries; the Tanzanian Experience' (Course in Development Studies, University of Dar es Salaam, mimeo, n.d.).

such matters, even if it could muster the technical expertise to police them.

The machinery for vetting new investment proposals and for granting protection perhaps suffered more from initial inexperience than from inherent weakness. As in other African countries, some of the early agreements reached with foreign investors were unnecessarily generous, granting excessive levels of protection, permitting management fees to be paid on joint ventures with the Kenya government regardless of whether the management provided produced profits, and so on. A good deal of experience had been gained by the end of the 1960s which made it less likely that these forms of 'crude private neo-imperialism' would be allowed in the 1970s.[20] What would remain would be only the less crude forms which are inherent in the operation of private capital in the capitalist periphery.

AFRICANIZING THE EQUITY

Perhaps a growing awareness of the ultimate limitations on the effectiveness of controlling foreign companies which, taken as a whole, disposed of far greater resources and skills than the government, contributed to a revival of interest in public ownership towards the end of the 1960s, especially since it had become clear by then that a certain amount of nationalization – on the basis of full compensation – was now widely accepted by international business and need not jeopardize 'business confidence'.

Initially (that is, in the mid-1960s, when the rhetoric of KANU's pre-independence programme calling for nationalization of a wide range of key industries had been largely forgotten), the emphasis of official policy had been on inducing large foreign companies to 'go public', and thus enable citizens to become shareholders. In the case of the large transport companies this policy was reinforced by the Transport Licensing Board, which threatened not to approve the annual renewal of licences unless more than 50 per cent of the companies' equity was sold to the public. East African Road Services (a company with a virtual monopoly of the long-distance bus market) complied in two stages, issuing 25 per cent of its shares in 1969 and a further 32·5 per cent in 1971. Meanwhile several other companies had

20. Cf. Sayre P. Schatz, 'Crude Private Neo-Imperialism: A New Pattern in Africa', *Journal of Modern African Studies*, Vol. 7, No. 4 (1969), pp. 677–88.

decided to do the same, and a series of capital issues followed; with the existing state of liquidity the issues were in most cases heavily oversubscribed. It now became apparent that the real effects of this policy were (*a*) to allow foreign companies to disinvest by selling old shares and expatriating the receipts; (*b*) to enlarge Asians' shareholdings, rather than Africans', since Asians possessed so much of the spare cash.

These discoveries came to light most clearly in the case of East African Packaging Industries, a subsidiary of Canadian Overseas Packaging Industries, which offered £200,000-worth of shares to the public in April 1971. The prospectus showed that the previously issued capital had been £100,000 down to March 1971, on which dividends had been paid to the parent company at the rate of 25 per cent, 25 per cent, 100 per cent, 198·5 per cent and 100 per cent in years 1966 to 1970, that is, just under £450,000 in all. On 23 March 1971 the issued share capital was increased to £600,000 by giving the existing 'shareholders' (i.e. Canadian Overseas Packaging Industries) a bonus issue of five new shares for each existing one, paid for out of accumulated profits and from the capital reserve 'arising from the valuation of the company's properties'. The following day a special 50 per cent dividend was declared, payable to the 'shareholders on the register at that date'. The parent company thus received a further £300,000 and stood ready to receive three-quarters of all subsequent dividends when the share issue of £200,000 worth of new shares had been taken up. But the new shares were issued at shs. 10·75 per five-shilling share, so the company would receive £430,000 of new capital. The dividend yield on the new shares at the issue price would, the directors thought, be not less than 8·6 per cent.[21] This prospectus must have been read by someone in the Treasury, and at the eleventh hour the company was informed that its share issue 'did not have government support'. Since the company's operations were quite legal the implied threat was not at all clear; eventually the issue was allowed to go ahead, but the affair probably contributed to the decision, announced in the Budget Speech in June 1971, to set up a Capital Issues Committee of Treasury officials, which would not only have to approve all future issues but also all capitalizations of reserves in companies having a substantial foreign interest.[22] Enthusiasm for 'going public' declined.

21. i.e., about 18 per cent to the parent company, which got its £600,000 worth of shares at par.
22. See the Budget Speech of 17 June 1971, giving the government's second thoughts

Something of the same problem was encountered in the limited number of cases where the government itself decided to buy a controlling interest in what it considered a strategic industry owned by a foreign company. The companies in question were East African Oil Refineries (the Mombasa installation previously owned by a consortium of the oil companies); the three main commercial banks (National and Grindlays, which became the Kenya Commercial Bank, and the Standard and Barclays Banks); East African Power and Lighting (a utility registered in London);[23] and the grain-milling industry, which belonged in practice (through a corporate structure evidently designed to be too complex to be expropriated without something approaching a revolution) mainly to a group of European ex-settlers. The purchase of a controlling interest in all but the last of these was quite easily negotiated, but the cost in terms of foreign exchange and alternative uses of government funds was high; the cost to the government of those which were completed by the end of 1971 was about £10 million, while the additional cost of acquiring a majority interest in Kenya National Mills would probably be a further £2 million.[24] There was also some talk about the need to control Kenya Breweries, on the grounds that they had a monopoly of a product which had established itself as an article of household consumption. This would cost perhaps a further £5 million (though much less in foreign exchange, as 80 per cent of the Breweries' shares were held in Kenya). The impact of the

on public share issues. The Capital Issues Committee would also 'advise the Minister' on the issue or amendment of foreign-investment protection certificates, applications by foreign companies for local credit in excess of 20 per cent of their foreign equity, and all management and royalty agreements involving external payments of over £25,000 a year (*EAS*, 27 July 1971).

23. The government share of these companies was 50 per cent in the refineries, 60 per cent in Kenya Commercial Bank, 50 per cent in the other banks, and about 51 per cent in EAPL.

24. The figures can be approximately deduced from various statements: the capital assets of the refineries were £6m., the issued share capital of the Union Bank was £5m., and the previous size of National and Grindlay's relative to the two banks which merged into the Union Bank suggests that the value of National and Grindlay's domestic operations might have been of the order of £1·5m. The net assets of East African Power and Lighting in 1969 were £11·7m. The government's offer to London-registered shareholders was worth about £3·7m. The net assets of Kenya National Mills (the main operating company in the millers' group) in 1969 were £4·2m. The government was assisted in its takeover of East African Power and Lighting by the fact that the National Social Security Fund was already in possession of 32 per cent of the shares, bought over the years since its establishment in 1966. The government thus needed to buy only a further 19 per cent.

government's and the public's share purchases in 1971 was clearly seen in the balance-of-payments accounts; £7 million flowed out, cutting net private foreign investment from over £11 million in 1970 to £5 million in 1971.

The government's 1965 policy statement (*African Socialism and Its Application to Planning in Kenya*) had been very conscious of this implication of nationalizing existing assets:

> It should be recognised that if the nation's limited domestic capital is used to buy existing land, livestock, buildings, machinery and equipment, the nation has no more productive assets than before – only their ownership has changed. What may be lost are the new resources that could have been purchased instead . . . and the employment opportunities and added output that these developments would create. Further, the money paid for nationalised resources and the people who managed them before nationalisation would most likely leave the country increasing our foreign exchange and skilled manpower problem.[25]

Instead, it said, the government's efforts would be directed 'towards establishing Africans in a firm position in the monetary sector by ensuring that *a large share of the planned new expansion* is African owned and managed.'[26]

Staking out a government interest in new investments had the additional advantage that the government would have some share in the profitability of enterprises which enjoyed a high level of protection. Moreover, joint ventures with foreign private capital could give the government control over investments without having to finance them fully itself; just as its £11–12-million stake in the oil refineries, the banks, and the electricity industry enabled it to control investments worth perhaps a total of £21 million, even a minority stake in new investments subject to heavy protection could in theory give it a large measure of control.

The main instruments for this policy were the Industrial and Commercial Development Corporation (ICDC), which participated in the equity of foreign companies and also lent money to them, in addition to running small loan schemes for African traders and industrialists; the Development Finance Company of Kenya (DFCK), in which the Kenya government was a 25 per cent partner with the Commonwealth Development Corporation

25. p. 26.
26. p. 30 (italics added).

and the Dutch and West German governments, and which provided mainly loan capital for large-scale new investments by foreigners; and a variety of more specialized institutions, including the Kenya Tourist Development Corporation (KTDC), which invested in the equity of hotels, the State Reinsurance Corporation, and various companies under government control, like Kenya National Properties Limited, the Kenya Wines Agency, the Kenya National Assurance Company, etc.

The activity of all these bodies, together with the government's purchases of control in oil-refining, banking, and power, the activities of the AFC and the ADC in agriculture and the continued expansion of the railways, harbours, posts, and telecommunications systems under the East African Community contributed to make the public sector's share of capital formation rise from about 25 per cent in 1964 to about 33 per cent in 1969. The ICDC had £1·8 million in shares and loans in seventeen mainly foreign companies in 1969–70, with an average shareholding of around 10–20 per cent in the larger ones and 40–50 per cent in the smaller ones. The DFCK had interests worth £2·4 million, two-thirds of it in the form of loans, in twenty-seven foreign companies. The extent of the KTDC's investments in 1970–1 were not known, its administration having fallen on evil days;[27] down to 1967 they amounted only to about £100,000, but the 1970–4 Development Plan indicated that a total of £1·6 million, or some 30 per cent of the total projected investment in hotels, might be made by the government through the KTDC.

Yet it is easy to see that in relation to the total assets of manufacturing and large-scale commercial companies in Kenya – worth something between £150 million and £200 million – these activities had established no more than a toehold for the government in the private sector.[28]

Apart from the purchase of control in 'strategic' industries, moreover, there was also room for doubt as to the significance of some of the government's investments. Some of the ICDC investments were in old businesses which the original Industrial Development Corporation had been set up to rescue during the Emergency, and which were still making a loss, or in later lossmakers like Kenatco.[29] Other investments, both by ICDC and

---

27. The last published report in 1971 was for 1967.
28. There is also some double counting to take into account: £0·5 million of the ICDC's investments represented the government's stake in the DFCK.
29. On Kenatco see below, Chapter 5, p. 161.

the DFCK, were in marginal new ventures which the government wished to encourage for political reasons; for instance large injections of capital were made or committed for sugar-refining and paper-milling in western Kenya, which foreign investors did not expect to be very profitable. When the ICDC wanted to establish itself in profitable businesses, or areas (such as travel agencies) in which it wanted to acquire expertise, it bought shares in existing companies. When foreign investors were confident of the profitability of a new investment within the level of protection offered them, they often tended to prefer to do without government participation.[30] When, however, they foresaw that further protection would be needed, or that whoever first obtained government participation in a still competitive field would tend to get special protection at the expense of the rest, they were eager to secure government participation. Since a very large proportion of the investment in manufacturing was undertaken by international companies to protect their existing share of the Kenya market, and if possible to expand it at the expense of their competitors, it was not surprising that virtually all the proposals for government participation in new investments originated with the private investors, rather than the other way round.

But a more fundamental question remains to be asked: exactly what was the intention and the result of the government's so-called 'partnership' with private foreign investors? Apart from the satisfaction of owning and profiting from a share in the equity in these companies, there were three main areas of influence that were sought: Africanization of staff, investment policy, and pricing policy. The last two could of course only be decisively influenced by means of a controlling interest, since they vitally affected the shareholders' interests, and this is what was achieved in oil-refining, banking, and the electricity industry. Elsewhere, minority shareholdings would sometimes give the government control, but generally not much more than it could exercise over virtually any company operating in Kenya. It is therefore particularly interesting to see what was achieved, or sought, in the 'strategic' industries in which the government took full control.

In the case of the refineries, no outward change was apparent.

---

30. This was specially true of American investors, according to Herman, op. cit. (see note 2). A notable case in point was Cadbury–Schweppes, which undertook a major expansion into food-processing in Nairobi in 1971 without any government participation.

The existing, mainly expatriate top management was retained. It was clear that the government was in a position to know more about the profits of oil distribution, once it controlled the source of supply, and should thus be able to influence that stage of fuel-pricing. However, the distributors still owned the wells and controlled the shipping of oil to the refinery, and it is doubtful if control of the refineries really conferred on the government a significant power to determine the profitability to the oil companies of even the modest Kenya component of their total operations. In the case of the banks there undoubtedly was a significant shift in credit policy, in favour of African borrowers and of borrowers in the rural areas.[31] On the other hand the government was at pains to insist that its control of the commercial banking system was not intended 'to bring about new thinking or practices in commercial banking', and that it expected the banks in which it participated 'to operate on commercial principles'.[32] These principles included acceptance of the 'Summary of Banking Arrangements' which had been laid down in the colonial period and which eliminated competition between the banks in lending rates and charges.[33] The basic limitation on the policy as a whole was most clearly apparent in the case of East African Power and Lighting, where the government offered to buy all the shares registered in London, which comprised the vast majority of them. Only eighty-three shareholders declined the offer, and their shares were then transferred to the Nairobi register. But the question then arose, how far was it incumbent on the government to continue to try to earn profits from power supplies? If it did not, the position of the minority shareholders in all the companies in which it had effective control would be threatened. If it accepted the need to earn profits, however, it followed that it could let 'social rates of return' enter into its thinking about the 'publicly-controlled' sector only to a very limited extent.[34]

---

31. See below, Chapter 5, p. 157.
32. *EAS*, 19 and 20 February 1972.
33. On the 'Summary' see E.-J. Pauw, 'Banking in East Africa', in P. Marlin (ed.), *Financial Aspects of Development in East Africa* (IFO-Institut für Wirtschaftforschung, Munich 1970). The Kenya Commercial Bank did not sign the agreement, but let the other banks know that it would not in fact depart from it.
34. In previous years 1 per cent of the EAPL's gross revenue had been invested in uneconomic schemes in recognition of the company's public-utility responsibilities, but profits net of tax had risen from 9 per cent to 15 per cent on the ordinary capital from 1966 to 1969.

What all this boils down to is that even a majority shareholding, obtained on the basis of – in effect – a take-over bid, conferred in practice only a very marginal power to influence events, because it implicitly accepted and in many ways reinforced the private-enterprise system, which remained overwhelmingly foreign-owned, at least in the urban sector.[35] It represented a new dimension in the evolution of periphery capitalism, not a departure from it.

CONSEQUENCES OF FOREIGN INVESTMENT

To summarize briefly what has been said so far: foreign domination of banking, finance and insurance and of the tourist trade, which was virtually 100 per cent at independence, was only marginally lessened during the subsequent eight years; while the expansion that took place in manufacturing provided an opening for the major trans-national corporations to join the ranks of the existing foreign companies in Kenya. Government participation in new investments became more common, and in some sectors the government bought a controlling interest, but without materially changing the premises of the system or even its detailed operation. Even if it had wished to do so, it could not have done it by the means it adopted; nor did accelerated Africanization of foreign companies' personnel or measures of control seriously limit the freedom of foreign investors to operate as they pleased. Starting from an overwhelming superiority in both capital and expertise, they deployed and redeployed these to their best advantage in a setting where the government remained at bottom heavily dependent on their continued willingness to do so. The question remains, however, how far their operations contributed to underdevelopment in the way general theory suggests. It is convenient to consider this under four heads: the level of profits; the transfer of surplus; the effect on wages and employment, and so on the pattern of demand; and finally the general political and social influence of the foreign-owned sector.

35. Foreign investment (in the strict sense of the term) rose from 35 per cent of capital expenditure in manufacturing in 1966 to 42 per cent in 1968, according to the ILO report already cited (see note 7), pp. 441–2. The ILO study, however, treated as 'local' any company not qualifying for profit export rights under the Foreign Investment Protection Act. In reality most 'local' manufacturing companies were also owned by foreigners – i.e. resident Asians or Europeans.

(a) The level of profits

A 1965 survey of British companies investing in East Africa showed that they generally expected returns well above the rates obtainable in Britain, and all the evidence suggests that in Kenya since independence they should have been able to get them. The following six companies which offered shares to the public between 1969 and 1972 showed their most recent profits as a proportion of their net assets as follows:

Table 4.2

Companies Offering Shares to the Public, 1969–70

	Year	Net assets	Pre-tax profits	Post-tax profits
Bamburi Portland Cement Company	1969	£2·75m.	£0·87m. 32%	£0·75m. 21%
East African Oxygen Company	1969	£0·91m.	£0·26m. 28%	£0·15m. 16%
East African Road Services	1970	£0·36m.	£0·17m. 47%	£0·11m. 29%
National Industrial Credit	1970	£0·44m.	£0·26m. 60%	n.a.
BAT (Kenya)	1970	£3·54m.	£1·28m. 36%	£0·82m. 23%
East African Packaging Industries	1970	£0·92m.	£0·33m. 35%	£0·19m. 21%

The record of the thirty-six public companies quoted on the Nairobi Stock Exchange taken as a whole was somewhat lower, with an average post-tax return of 13·4 per cent for 1969;[36] but most of the foreign companies investing in Kenya (as subsidiaries or associate companies of multinational corporations) were private companies, and private companies generally were well known to make higher profits than public companies. It might be thought that this last point could be due to the fact that most private companies are small companies, and that returns to small amounts of capital tend to be higher than to very large investments. A study by W. J. House, however, showed that the higher the capital requirements, and the more concentrated the industry, the higher the price–cost margin in Kenyan manufacturing, and it was precisely such industries which were dominated by the

---

36. *Stock Exchange Official Yearbook 1971*, p. 6.

large international companies.[37] Additional evidence that foreign
firms had above-average profits was provided by the ILO mission
report in 1972, which found that foreign-owned manufacturing
firms received 73 per cent of total pre-tax profits in 1967, but
produced only 57 per cent of gross output.[38] The mission also
found that the share of profits was above the share of output in
fields where the foreign firm had no competition, but just under
it where there were other firms in the market. The average higher
level of profits of foreign manufacturing companies thus seemed
likely to be related to the element of monopoly in their operations.

But it is somewhat naïve to concentrate too closely on profits
where vertically integrated international companies are concerned, since the profits of the total operation will be taken where
it is most beneficial to the company to show them, and this may
or may not be in the periphery countries where they operate.
There can be no doubt that the operations of foreign companies
in Kenya, and especially from 1965 onwards, had very high rates
of return.

(b) Surplus transfer

There is not much more to be said about this than has been said
already. In the years 1964 to 1970 the officially recorded flows of
private capital were as follows:

Table 4.3

Recorded Inflows (+) and Outflows (−) of Private Capital (K£m.)

	1964	1965	1966	1967	1968	1969	1970
International investment income (profits going abroad)	−9·8	−9·0	−12·5	−14·0	−14·1	−12·6	−6·6
Private transfer payments	−3·1	−1·5	+0·1	−0·7	0·0	+1·0	−0·5
Private foreign investment in Kenya (including reinvestment of local profits)	−5·0	+1·5	+1·0	+8·0	+9·1	+12·6	+11·3

37. William J. House, 'Market Structure and Industry Performance: the Case of
    Kenya', Discussion Paper No. 116 (Department of Economics, University of
    Nairobi 1971, mimeo).
38. op. cit., p. 442.

If the ILO mission was right, and in the manufacturing sector transfer pricing or over-invoicing was between 5 and 10 per cent of the value of imported intermediate goods, we should need to increase the first row of table 4.3 by about £5 million annually over the years from 1967 onwards, if not earlier. These figures would need to be increased still further if there was a significant amount of over-invoicing by firms importing goods outside the manufacturing sector. As we have seen, such firms had a strong incentive to over-invoice, and many of them were in a position to do so through business connections all over the world. Studies carried out in Tanzania suggest that the level of over-invoicing of imports generally was between 10 per cent and 20 per cent at times where there was a strong incentive to get private capital out of the country.[39] As this would apply generally to the Asian community in Kenya from the mid-1960s onwards, it seems reasonable to assume that 10 per cent of imports of consumer goods would also have been concealed capital exports, i.e. a figure of the order of £2 million annually from 1965 to 1970. Similar calculations can be applied to various other items but it is probably not very profitable to pursue them in detail; the forms of capital export already considered, including dividend and interest payments, appear to amount to nearly twice the amount of private foreign investment in the years 1967–70, when private foreign investment ran at a high level, and were equivalent to about a quarter of all capital formation – in other words, enough to make a fairly decisive difference to the chances of an 'autonomous path of capitalist growth'. The net export of private capital over the whole period 1964–70 – that is, the total of the top row of the table shown above, corrected for the effects of transfer pricing and over-invoicing, minus the total of the bottom row – seems likely to have been of the order of £80 million.

(c) Wages and employment

According to the ILO mission, foreign manufacturing firms in Kenya had lower labour costs per employee than locally-owned firms, probably because they used more and better managers and supervisors. In aggregate they were more capital-intensive than

39. See p. 127, note 19 above. In 1972 the Central Bank announced that it had engaged the General Superintendence Company of Geneva to inspect imports destined for Kenya prior to shipment, for 'quality, quantity, and price comparison', and that shipment would be authorized only if the inspection report was 'clean' (*EAS*, 30 November 1972).

local firms, though where both types of firm operated in the same line of production local firms actually seemed to be slightly more capital-intensive than foreign firms. What this means is, again, that foreign firms in the manufacturing sector were better managed than local ones; or rather, better managed than what was in fact a different kind of foreign firm, manufacturing companies owned by locally resident Asians or Europeans. Given the high levels of protection usually provided, even the less efficient firms could still earn a return which satisfied the owners.

More to the point, in fact, is really the actual impact of both kinds of foreign manufacturing investment on employment generally; because given the pattern of demand already established through underdevelopment any firm aiming to produce goods for which there was an existing demand was in practice bound to adopt relatively sophisticated, i.e. capital-intensive, techniques. On this the figures are fairly conclusive. Total employment in the non-agricultural private sector increased by only 2 per cent per annum from 1964 to 1969, whereas total output in the non-agricultural sector, public and private, rose by 9·8 per cent per annum. The wage bill in the enumerated non-farm private sector rose by 7·7 per cent a year;[40] foreign capital was paying rapidly rising wages to a small labour force, expanding much more slowly than the population (with a growth rate of over 3 per cent), and so also tending to reinforce the existing pattern of demand for goods. At the same time the share of wages relative to profits in the national income was declining.[41]

(d) Political and social influence

The 'foreign sector' had its own specialized political institutions, the Federation of Kenya Employers (FKE) (which grouped together a variety of industrial associations, including the plantation sector) and the Kenya Association of Manufacturers, both of which dated from the colonial period.[42] In 1964, following the

---

40. *Report of the Commission of Enquiry (Public Service Structure and Remuneration Commission) 1970–71* (the Ndegwa Commission), p. 27.

41. ibid., p. 38.

42. The KAM began in 1959 as the Association for the Promotion of Industries in East Africa, and was specially concerned with the preservation of the East African common market. In 1963 it became the Association of East African Industries, and became more concerned with supporting its members' requests for increased protection in face of the contraction of the common market during the 1960s. It became the Kenya Association of Manufacturers in 1969. It never achieved the status of the KFE, which rested on its important role in industrial relations.

example of companies with West African interests, an East Africa and Mauritius Association was formed to maintain offices in Nairobi and London and provide intelligence and liaison services for the head offices of foreign companies. By 1971 some 150 overseas companies, two-thirds of them British, subscribed to the Association and received its bi-monthly confidential newsletter. The Nairobi representative acted as a sort of specialized diplomat on behalf of the member companies, making it a point to be on familiar terms with all relevant government ministers and senior officials, effecting introductions for visiting company chairmen, making representations on behalf of companies with tax or work-permit problems, and so forth. But it would be a mistake to attach too much political significance to the Association. It was a manifestation of the fact that international companies are what they are, and have developed their own diplomatic service, transcending those of particular governments in the same way that their investments and management also do.

Of these formal institutions, in fact, much the most important was the FKE. As we have seen, it was a prime instrument of the transition from colonial to neo-colonial rule, and its significance increased over the years. It gradually expanded until it included virtually all the large-scale and medium-sized companies in Kenya. In the meantime its presidency had been Africanized, and by 1970 eleven members of its 28-man Management Board were Africans. Every one of these, however, was a senior executive of either a foreign company or a public corporation or state-owned company.[43] The senior staff of the FKE as well as a majority of its Management Board remained expatriate. The FKE thus represented the bureaucracy of the larger foreign companies and the state-owned commercial corporations. Its president had free access to the Minister of Labour and any other Minister concerned with economic problems, and a regular monthly meeting was held between him (together with the FKE's Executive Officer) and the Permanent Secretary to the Ministry of Labour.

This relationship was very important in ensuring that industrial relations developed in accordance with the needs of foreign capital. This meant a situation in which relatively high wages

---

43. The employers of the African members were: Lonrho, East African Power and Lighting (then still largely controlled by the Balfour Beattie group), East African Airways, Cargo Handling Services, Gailey and Roberts, the *Daily Nation* newspaper (owned by the Aga Khan), the Kenya Planters' Co-operative Union, the Maize and Produce Board, East African External Telecommunications.

could be paid in the most capital-intensive and monopolistic sectors serving the domestic market, and low wages in the rest of the economy. To avoid concerted action between unions in different sectors of the economy, and generally to prevent militancy in the lowest-paid fields, a large measure of government control was necessary. The FKE had succeeded in ensuring that no powerful 'omnibus' union was formed, covering more than one industry, disposing of large funds, and inclined to political action.[44] After independence, it began to urge the government to go further and to take power to control strikes, which it did by passing the Trade Disputes Act of 1965. This measure, like the Trade Unions (Amendment) Act of 1964, which had given the government extensive powers to regulate the internal affairs of unions, was directed in part against those trade-unionists who supported Oginga Odinga and other 'radical' leaders within KANU, who later formed the Kenya People's Union.[45] It prohibited strikes in essential services and sympathetic strikes, and closely controlled the machinery through which any strike could be made legal, empowering the government to declare a strike illegal if in its opinion the machinery for negotiation had not been exhausted. In practice, this meant that employers were able to prolong their consideration of wage claims for not merely months, but in some cases years, confident that the government would be very reluctant to legalize a serious strike merely on the grounds that the machinery was working slowly, if its procedures had not been completed; and in consequence, a large proportion of disputes quickly came to be referred to the Industrial Court, either by agreement between unions and employers or at the direction of the government. Strike action fell dramatically and large-scale strikes were virtually eliminated by the government's repeated indication of its willingness to declare them illegal when they seemed imminent.

As the political confrontation in parliament developed, the corresponding confrontation between pro-government and radical trade-union leaders within the trade-union movement provided a further chance for intervention, and in 1966 a government-

---

44. Based on FKE records; see also A. Amsden, *International Firms and Labour in Kenya* (Cass, London 1971), pp. 66–71.

45. See R. Sandbrook, 'The State and the Development of Trade Unionism', in G. Hyden, R. Jackson and J. Okumu (eds), *Development Administration: The Kenyan Experience* (Oxford University Press, Nairobi 1970), pp. 252–95.

Table 4.4

Industrial Disputes in Kenya

	1964	1965	1966	1967	1968	1969	1970
No. of disputes	267	200	155	138	93	124	84
Man-days lost	167,767	345,855	127,632	109,128	47,979	87,516	49,517

Source: Statistical Abstract 1971, p. 208.

controlled Central Organization of Trade Unions (COTU) was set up, whose chief officers had to be confirmed and could be dismissed by the President. It followed that COTU leaders would have to support the government.

The FKE also devoted some efforts to preserving the important differential that existed between urban and rural wage-levels. It was one thing for companies like Kenya Breweries and other manufacturers producing for the domestic market to pay wages increasing by over 5 per cent a year. It was quite a different matter for the coffee, tea, and sisal estates, producing for world markets. The FKE, having originally fought to prevent the formation of an overall agricultural workers' union, and having found that the natural weakness of organization in the agricultural field made this barely necessary, was well aware that the working of the Industrial Court would inevitably throw into relief the embarrassing differential that existed between urban and plantation wages, so much greater than that between urban and plantation profits. A test case arose in 1965 when the tea-estate workers brought a substantial wage demand before the Industrial Court. The FKE argued on behalf of the employers that instead there should be a wage increase of only 2½ per cent in the first year of a new three-year agreement, followed by further increases of 1¼ per cent in each of the following two years, in return for an undertaking to take on a further 10,000 workers during this period. 'The Industrial Court accepted this and low agricultural wages – below those in either Uganda or Tanzania – are the result', as the Executive Officer of the Federation later put it.[46] In effect the formula was: expanded wage-employment in rural

46. Interview, July 1971. According to the Ndegwa Report average wages per month in the 'modern' agriculture, forestry and fisheries sector were 121 shillings in 1969, compared with 549 shillings in the non-agricultural private sector. This represented 14·4 per cent and 65·2 per cent of GDP per worker respectively.

areas, based on very low wages, as a means of expanding foreign-exchange earnings, to finance an expanded industrial sector based on high wages. This was acceptable to the Court, the employers, and the government; and the tea workers were not strong enough to win against such a well-rationalized alliance.

A further demonstration of the political power of the foreign sector came with the Tripartite Agreement of 1970–1, when both government and private-sector employers agreed to an immediate 10 per cent increase in their labour forces in return for a one-year wage standstill and a ban on industrial action by the trade unions. This agreement, which repeated an earlier one of 1964, is discussed further in Chapter 7. What interests us here is the chance it offered to give a further twist to the screw holding down the political power of the trade unions. As a condition of their acceptance of the agreement (which, as the FKE later recognized, 'hurt the trade unions much more than it hurt us; in fact we did very well out of it'), the FKE demanded a wage and salary policy which would limit the annual increase in the wage-bill as a whole to about $2\frac{1}{2}$ per cent per annum. In principle the government had already accepted this argument in the 1970–4 Development Plan, but the implementation of the policy was likely to entail industrial unrest and, as a preliminary, fresh powers to curtail industrial action were needed.[47] These were now embodied in a new Trade Disputes (Amendment) Bill, pushed through parliament against the strenuous opposition of the Secretary-General of COTU, Denis Akumu, in 1971; after token support for his position from backbenchers, it was passed by the usual obedient majority. Whether, in spite of the powers contained in the Act, the government would feel able to reduce wage increases to about $2\frac{1}{2}$ per cent a year – barely more than the rate of inflation – was another question. What was clear was that the FKE's forcefully expressed views, echoed by civil servants both local and expatriate, had added a new and perhaps lasting element to the economic strategy of neo-colonialism in Kenya: the menace of unemployment was to be dealt with by a long-term downward pressure on wages generally.[48]

---

47. *Development Plan*, pp. 130–32.

48. The FKE's memorandum to the Ndegwa Commission summed up the Federation's views as follows: 'A national wages and salaries policy is an essential element in maintaining economic stability and in accelerating economic development. It will help to stimulate production in industry and most important will promote wider opportunities for paid employment. Perhaps the greatest problem facing Kenya

But in the longer run the informal presence of the foreign sector in Nairobi was probably at least as significant as its formal institutional apparatus. Its expatriate personnel constituted a reference group for the higher African bureaucracy, setting the pace in housing and levels of personal consumption. There were also many specific ties linking African politicians and bureaucrats to foreign companies: directorships, shareholdings, and all sorts of business connections. A notable development of the 1960s was the growth of satellite firms around some of the major companies, sometimes financed from company funds. Some were agencies and distributorships, whose general importance is discussed in the following chapter; for instance, Bata, BAT, the oil companies and several other major firms transferred their distribution networks largely to African dealers after independence, and many of these dealers became men of political consequence in their areas. Oil companies gave business to tanker fleets operated by various political notables. Mitchell Cotts gave their ship-chandling business to a new African firm in Mombasa, whose proprietors in due course achieved political prominence, and gave some of their legal business to the law firm of another leading politician. Mackenzie Dalgety financed Kenya Merchants Limited, with a board of directors of prominent Kenyans, to take over the distribution of its farm supplies outside Nairobi. Nothing in any of these transactions was out of the normal line of business.[49] But the

now and in the immediate future is that of increasing unemployment particularly among educated young people, therefore it must be borne in mind that any general increase in the level of wages beyond that justified by increased production and/or increases in the cost of living would result in a reduction in the existing level of employment.' The Commission broadly endorsed this view and actually went so far as to call for constant real wages; see below, p. 233.

49. A particularly amiable example of the 'satellite' business phenomenon was the formation of Kenya Oil, a petrol-distributing company, under the general aegis of Caltex. Caltex were persuaded by a local English businessman in 1959 that the strategy of the future for foreign companies in Kenya would be to set up associated public companies which Kenyans could invest in but which would distribute the sponsoring company's product. The proposer, Mr R. S. Alexander, became chairman with two 'management shares' which outvoted all the ordinary shares (to prevent other oil companies buying control). In 1971 the issued ordinary share capital was £128,880, of which Europeans held 62·5 per cent, Asians 35·2 per cent and Africans 2·3 per cent. The directors' report for 1969/70 showed that the chairman and the other three directors were paid a total of £2,294; £5,168 was paid to a management company controlled by the chairman for 'management and consultancy fees' provided under an agreement, and a further £1,400 for 'financial and accounting services provided by that company'. The auditors of Kenya Oil were Alexander, MacLennan, Trundell and Co. In 1970 the company paid a dividend of 15 per cent and made a one-in-five bonus issue (there was no capital gains tax in Kenya).

relationships of co-operation and clientage which all large concerns develop around their operations automatically had the effect in Kenyan conditions of cementing the foreign-owned sector and the various elements of the ruling alliance more and more firmly together.

Yet in the end what seems more important than all such specific relationships is the cumulative impact of the foreign presence in the realm of ideology. By the end of the 1960s a quite elaborate version of the private-enterprise creed, adapted to Kenyan circumstances, had been diffused throughout the higher bureaucracy, and among senior KANU politicians. The following extract from a speech to the Kenya Association of Manufacturers by the executive director of the ICDC, Maina Wanjigi, illustrates what was involved:

> We in the Association believe in free enterprise. This is a system of social, economic and political arrangements designed to solve the basic economic problem with greatest efficiency.
>
> I am convinced that unless the African who forms more than 95% of Kenya's population feels that he is part and parcel of our industrial and commercial economy, just as he has begun to feel in the agricultural sector of our economy, it could be difficult to create a stable economy. . . . It is vital that our industry be identified as truly local by the ordinary man in the street. He must be made to feel that it is truly his industry. I feel sure that if anybody can do this, it is those of you who are represented in this Association. I would go further and say that you have a duty, you have a responsibility, to assist in the Africanisation of commerce and industry if for nothing else, at least for the preservation of the institution and value of what I explained earlier as [the] free enterprise system. Those who value the free enterprise system have at times had to make great sacrifices for its preservation. African Socialism does not conflict with the free enterprise system but it does require that property be used in the mutual interest of society and its members. No one is being requested to hand out free shares in his industry for the sake of Africanisation, neither is anybody being requested to risk blindly by placing his investments in the hands of poor and incompetent management in the interest of Africanisation. Indeed if this were done it would be contrary to the spirit of development.
>
> All of us here can assist in the task of Africanisation by various ways, for example:

(a) Conversion of private companies to public companies with a view to offering substantial shareholdings to Africans.

(b) The manufacturers could gradually and firmly build African distributors and wholesalers.

(c) The existing distributors and wholesalers could assist the Africans to share in the market rather than try to prevent their entry into the market.

(d) By inviting African partners and participants in the new ventures you are planning to establish.

(e) By giving the African management opportunity in your organisation and also providing him with management training opportunities.[50]

Not the least interesting aspect of this speech is the almost explicit recognition that what is needed is to persuade 'the man in the street' to accept the existing economic system by promoting the growth of the African petty-bourgeoisie and admitting African graduates into lucrative positions in management.

CONCLUSION

The logic of the pre-independence settlement was that Kenya should attract large amounts of new private capital from abroad into the non-farm sectors of the economy. This was the more important, in that there was also a tacit decision not to allow the resident Asian commercial bourgeoisie to exchange their commercial dominance for dominance in manufacturing. The result was an almost wholly foreign-owned and controlled growth of manufacturing and certain other major fields such as tourism, led mainly by newly established multinational companies. Measures to escape from this new form of external dominance through Africanizing senior posts in the foreign-owned private sector, through measures of taxation, exchange- and price-control, and so on, and through various systems of share purchase, did not really have many of the desired effects. Controls could at best have a very limited effect (even if the resources could be found to administer them efficiently) without contradicting the government's policy of maximizing the inflow of foreign capital. As the ILO mission pointed out in 1972, the acceleration of foreign investment on which the development plans for 1970–4 were

---

50. Record of KAM Annual General Meeting, 30 March 1967.

based was already very unlikely to be achieved; and 'It would be especially unlikely if steps were taken to ensure that it did not create more of the protected, high-profit, capital-intensive industries that bear some responsibility for the present complex of connected exchange and employment problems.'[51]

As for Africanization, both of jobs and shareholding, although these were conceived of as measures for controlling the power of foreign capital, it was clear that they worked primarily to identify the government and the higher civil service more closely with the operations, interests and values of foreign capital. The results were monopoly profits, high rates of surplus transfer, low increases in employment, and a falling share of wages in national income backed up by tight control over the trade unions.

By the end of the 1960s these results – and especially the low rate of increase of employment and an impending foreign exchange problem which could soon bring the import-substitution boom of the 1960s to an end – had begun to alarm some of the government's economic advisers and other economists working in Kenya. They began to urge a drastic reversal of policy, including severe cuts in the existing levels of effective protection and much closer scrutiny of all new proposals for foreign capital investment. Some looked towards a new growth-path based on manufactured exports: 'If the current trend towards protectionism is not reversed, there can be little doubt that Kenya will increasingly get into a situation of export lethargy, chronic balance of payments disequilibrium and eventually declining industrialization and growth.'[52] Others, like the ILO mission, were doubtful if the multinational corporations established in Kenya could be so easily converted into exporters, and advocated massive measures of income redistribution to expand the domestic market. The trouble with this kind of thinking – which will be considered again in Chapter 8 – was that it assumed that government policy was more independent of the interests it was being urged to manipulate than was in fact the case. By the end of the 1960s the nexus between the government and foreign capital was an extremely close one, and was reinforced by the interests of an African petty-bourgeoisie which had been establishing itself inside the system of state protection as an auxiliary of foreign capital.

---

51. op. cit., p. 280.
52. P. N. Hopcraft, 'Outward Looking Industrialisation: The Promotion of Manu-factured Exports from Kenya' (Institute for Development Studies, Nairobi, September 1972, mimeo), p. 15.

CHAPTER 5

African Capitalism

The contradiction between the regime's economic nationalism and its dependence on foreign capital led to the efforts described in the previous chapter to control and 'Africanize' foreign companies. But in a capitalist system the owners of capital can be controlled only within fairly narrow limits, even when they are not foreign. When they are foreign, control is possible only to the extent that there is competition between different foreign capitals for the markets or resources of the 'host' country. The Kenya government had some leverage as a result of the country's strategic position, tourist attractions and carefully pro-Western foreign policy, but this meant that the logic of its dependence on foreign capital could at most be made more palatable, not that it could be escaped.

Foreign dominance of the private non-agricultural sector of the economy was virtually complete at independence; seven years later in 1970, as a result of the reinvestment of profits and of fresh capital inflows, foreigners still overwhelmingly controlled this sector, which had grown by about 66 per cent in real terms, and accounted for 47 per cent of the monetary economy.[1] Public ownership had barely kept pace with this expansion; it was still about 25 per cent of the total non-agricultural 'enterprise' sector. The rest of this sector – the non-farm private sector proper – was still almost wholly owned and controlled by foreigners. For instance in the service sector, which included retail trade, where the most serious efforts were being made to install Africans in business, in 1966 roughly 58 per cent of the turnover was accounted for by firms wholly or mainly owned by non-citizens, while a substantial proportion of the remaining 42 per cent was accounted for by firms owned by non-African citizens, both European and Asian. The 'service' sector was also expanding rapidly with the

---

1. *Statistical Abstract*, 1971, pp. 35 and 38.

increase of tourism. The scale of capital required for much of the tourist trade, however, and the sophisticated linkages between different parts of the service sector which are involved in it, meant that virtually the whole of the expansion in this field was undertaken by non-Africans, increasingly by foreign-owned companies.

The contradiction between economic nationalism and dependence on foreign capital was expressed in the intense pressure put on the government by small African businessmen – traders, bar-owners, transporters and the like – to assist them to break into the more profitable end of the non-agricultural private sector, and since these were the people on whom the regime most depended for securing popular support, and since most politicians were in business, they were helped. Their rate of capital accumulation was generally low, and they started from very low absolute levels. The provision of capital through loan programmes did not produce quick successes, nor did the provision of free business education, which in any case proved a very elusive object of policy. The only alternative was to give them special protection. This was politically attractive in that in several fields it could be done at the expense of local Asian businessmen and not at the expense of foreign-based investors. Thus the 1966–70 Development Plan warned that unless 'special steps' were taken, the 'existing trading communities' would take the largest share of the expected increase of 6 per cent per annum in trade turnover, and that it might be necessary in some cases 'to consider take-over of existing commercial enterprises by African businessmen, co-operatives or the State'.[2] In practice, however, the shift from special assistance to protection can be seen in every field where the government tried to foster African capitalism – except those fields where it moved directly to the creation of monopoly without more ado. The effect of this was to create a new stratum of the African petty-bourgeoisie, ensconced within the general system of protection and monopoly, in such a way as to serve and complement foreign capital, not to replace it.

In many respects what follows does no more than examine how far Fanon's comment fits the Kenyan experience:

> This native bourgeoisie . . . will realise, with its mouth watering, that it lacks something essential to a bourgeoisie: money. The bourgeoisie of an underdeveloped country is a

2. ibid., p. 270.

bourgeoisie in spirit only. It is not its economic strength, nor the dynamism of leaders, nor the breadth of its ideas that ensures its peculiar quality of bourgeoisie. . . . It is the positions it holds in the new national administration which will give it strength and serenity. If the government gives it enough time and opportunity, this bourgeoisie will manage to put away enough money to stiffen its domination. But it will always reveal itself as incapable of giving birth to an authentic bourgeois society with all the economic and industrial consequences which this entails.[3]

But Fanon's categorical and abstract formulation has been succeeded by very few empirical studies (notable exceptions being the work of Samir Amin in Senegal and Ivory Coast) ;[4] more are needed, especially if we are to understand how the new auxiliary bourgeoisies fit into the wider economic system of which they are a part.

TRADE

Retail trade has always been seen as the first sphere in which African capitalism could be established, because of its geographical extent, the possibility of exploiting customer goodwill towards indigenous traders, and the low capital costs involved. By 1960 a total of 17,000–19,000 licensed traders were estimated to be doing roughly £260 million-worth of business per annum.[5] Of these, twelve to fourteen hundred were petty traders estimated to have a total annual turnover of about £9–12 million. A remainder of 5,000 were surveyed. Of these 3,452 were retailers doing £76 million-worth of business: two-thirds of this was in the hands of the 1,055 traders who had five or more employees; hardly any of these traders were Africans. To put it another way, some 1,200–1,400 traders, mostly African, were doing an average of about £1,000-worth of business a year, and getting less than £200 in profit; another 2,400, including probably a fairly large number of Asians, were doing an average of roughly £10,000-worth of business a year, and getting less than £2,000.

To move Africans out of this marginal position on the unprofitable fringes of commerce two loan schemes were developed. One,

---

3. Frantz Fanon, *The Wretched of the Earth* (Penguin, London 1967), pp. 143–4.

4. Samir Amin, *Le Monde Des Affaires Sénégalais* (Minuit, Paris 1969), and *Le Développement du Capitalisme en Côte d'Ivoire* (Minuit, Paris 1967).

5. *Survey of Distribution 1960* (Ministry of Finance and Economic Planning, Nairobi 1963, mimeo), p. 15.

already established before independence, covered the rural areas and small towns, and was primarily for small traders recently established and anxious to expand. Under this scheme the central government and local authorities had lent some £1·2 million in two- to three-year loans averaging £200–300 each to some 5,000–6,000 traders down to 1971.[6] The other was operated through the Industrial and Commercial Development Corporation. Between 1965 and 1971 it lent about £2·5 million in 1,800 three-year loans, averaging about £1,350 each. However, roughly 85 per cent of this was lent from 1969 to 1971 to finance the enforced take-over by Africans of Asian businesses, which was made possible by new legislation implemented in 1968;[7] lending by itself had not been able to make a bridgehead in the profitable urban core of retail trade.

The Trade Licensing Act of 1967 moved from assistance to protection by means of two different kinds of monopoly; non-citizens were excluded from trading in rural areas and the non-central areas of towns, and from handling a progressively lengthened list of specific goods. In addition the government took powers to progressively withdraw trade licences from non-citizen traders within the areas where they were still legally free to trade. It is not clear what proportion of trade was thus protected against non-citizen competition: by 1970 the list of reserved goods covered most basic foodstuffs and clothing in the wage-earner's household budget, together with various other items such as cigarettes, soft drinks, farming implements, and basic hardware.[8] What is clear is that even this measure of protection did not produce all the desired results. This was partly because it protected Africans against competition from non-citizens, but not from established Asian traders who had become citizens. It was also because Africans competed against each other; as there was no machinery to limit the number of trade licences issued to Africans, many

6. This scheme was known as the Joint Loans Board scheme. Figures from interviews with officials of the Ministry of Commerce and Industry. The total number of loans issued was much larger (over 8,000 between 1965 and 1971 alone) but many borrowers took a second loan when they had repaid the first.

7. J. A. Okelo, 'The Role of Credit', in *Small Scale Enterprise* (Institute of Development Studies, Nairobi 1973, mimeo), p. 80.

8. The total turnover of the KNTC and its distributors (to whom the reserved list applied) in 1969–70 was £25 million. This may be compared with a total turnover of wholesale and retail trade in 1966 of £367 million. Assuming that the total turnover increased from 1966 to 1969 by the same proportion as the contribution of trade GDP (15 per cent) the KNTC share in 1969–70 would be about 6 per cent.

entered into trade who were prepared to operate with minimum turnovers and profits, and so very few could hope to accumulate substantial capital in competition with them. This was very clearly illustrated by the experience of the Kenya National Trading Corporation (KNTC).

The KNTC was a public body set up in 1965 with the apparent intention of taking over a major share of the import–export trade. In fact, it proved to be a means of reserving retail and wholesale trade to individual Africans, as opposed to citizens (who might include Asians). A monopoly of trade in specific commodities could be assigned to the KNTC, which then shared this between its appointed distributors, who were all Africans. Perhaps because of this, the KNTC was never given a legislative basis, but remained an almost fully-owned subsidiary of the ICDC. Following the pattern of other state trading agencies in Africa, the KNTC was originally intended to act as an importer and warehouser of the commodities reserved to it. It began by taking over all sugar imports and distributing them through African agents working on credit. By 1969 it had £800,000 worth of bad debts.[9] It stopped giving credit but also moved away from direct trading, and as new items were added to its list, confined itself merely to approving the applications of its appointed agents for licences to import these items. But as in theory its agents were wholesalers, and not necessarily retailers, they were allowed merely to endorse import-licence applications from retailers – still largely Asian – and take a commission on the value of the order without further effort.[10]

The same applied in due course to various locally-produced goods for which the government 'negotiated' a KNTC monopoly. Cement was a good example. In 1970 domestic sales amounted to about 600,000 tons. Half of this was allocated to the KNTC and its agents, at a commission of 10·50 shillings per ton, worth £150,000 annually. Thus the KNTC here possessed a rather attractive item of patronage. Not surprisingly, the political pressures to appoint distributors built up, until by 1971 there were

9. Speech by Mr Osogo, Minister of Commerce and Industry, reported in *EAS*, 10 February 1970. Okelo (op. cit., see note 7) gives a figure of £1 million.

10. The ICDC Report for 1969/70 stated that the KNTC itself handled some essential items like sugar, salt, edible oil: the bulk of other items were handled, if at all, by KNTC agents. In 1968/69 the volume of such indented import business which did not pass through the KNTC's hands, and most of which barely passed through the hands of its agents, was said to be worth £10 million (ICDC Report for 1968/69), on which the KNTC took a nominal commission of 2 per cent and the distributor 3 per cent; in effect a total tax of £0·5 million.

about 200 of them. Although many never traded, the spread was such that not even the largest of the active traders made a lot of money. In some lines it was clear that the active traders were in fact trading for non-citizens, presumably splitting the commission; unless the commission was paid for a service actually performed, it was difficult to see how this could be avoided. In the case of imported textiles the figures on the growth of competition are even more striking. One of the main lines sold in Nairobi was Nytil cotton fabrics made in Uganda. Before the KNTC assumed exclusive rights in it there were three appointed Nytil agencies in Nairobi. By 1971 there were sixty-seven KNTC-appointed textile distributors in Nairobi. KNTC agents who had begun by making a lot of money when they were few in number now found themselves in severe difficulties.

Various solutions were explored. One was to try to expand the volume of business while keeping the number of agents in any given line of trade constant. In the case of cement, the agents pressurized the government in 1971 to oblige cement manufacturers to allow the other half of domestic consumption also to be handled by the KNTC. In most cases, however, expanding the volume of business could only be done by expanding the range of commodities handled by each agent, with a tendency to increase costs, or (if the KNTC was to continue to turn a blind eye towards distributors who really acted for other, non-African traders) a tendency to defeat the object of establishing Africans in trade (as opposed to merely giving them valuable sinecures). The number of KNTC distributors could be pruned by eliminating those who were not in fact trading, but this was not going to solve the problem; and actually withdrawing business from traders was politically impractical. One could even question whether it would be possible to hold the number of active traders constant, allowing the annual growth of trade to gradually raise their profitability. A KNTC distributor put his finger on the problem when he said: 'The trouble is, when a man [sc. a big man] sends a chit to the General Manager of the KNTC to appoint so-and-so as agent, he [the General Manager] *fears.*'

The ideal which the KNTC agents had in mind was the sole-agency system, employed by some of the large-scale foreign manufacturers of consumer goods in Kenya: for instance Bata (shoes), East African Breweries, BAT (tobacco), Cadbury–Schweppes (soft drinks). With a sole agency for a substantial area and a product for which there was a rapidly rising demand the agents of these firms could make large profits; and the firms had an interest in seeing that they succeeded, frequently lending them much or all of their working capital and monitoring their stock-keeping, accounting, and general performance. Other firms (such as Elliots Bakeries) did not give sole agencies but operated a very tightly programmed system of appointed agents such that the potential share of the market of each one would yield him enough profit, if he worked hard, to graduate from one level in the distributive hierarchy to another more capital-intensive but more profitable one. But this ideal could not be achieved by the KNTC. It depended on the commercial interest and expertise of the manufacturer, selling a distinctive branded product and in most cases with a monopoly or near-monopoly of the market, enabling the supervision costs to be covered in the price structure; and it also depended on the fact that the firms in question were mostly foreign, and so had a degree of immunity from political pressures to expand the number of their agents.

The only way in which the KNTC agents could try to profit from the example of the BAT or Breweries agents was by organizing themselves to restrict competition. Towards the end of the 1960s several efforts in this direction were being made. A notable example was the Kenya Wines and Spirits Distributors' Association. The established importers of wines and spirits were two British companies. To avoid damaging charges of expropriation, and because of the trade's dependence on overseas contacts, the monopoly of imports was assigned to a new company, the Kenya Wines Agency Ltd (KWAL), in which the established importers had 51 per cent of the shares, and the Industrial and Commercial Development Corporation 49 per cent; the KNTC was then appointed sole distributor, which meant that KWAL sold only through Africans appointed by the KNTC.[11] Initially one agent was appointed sole distributor for the whole Nairobi area, a fairly attractive proposition in view of the fact that this area probably accounted for about half of the total sales, worth perhaps £1 million annually.[12] In due course, however, four other dis-

---

11. The new monopoly also promptly increased retail prices by amounts ranging from 5 per cent to 25 per cent.

12. It is not possible to establish the retail value of wines and spirits sales from published data. Some indication is given by the fact that in 1970, 473,000 litres of spirits and 525,000 litres of wine were imported, while gin was also distilled locally. It would be surprising on the basis of these figures if national retail sales of wines and spirits had been worth much less than £2 million annually, even allowing for the fact that a sizeable portion of the imports would have been

tributors were appointed in Nairobi. Even so, the average turnover
of each of them should have provided a reasonable return. But
this left out of account the economic power of the large customers,
especially the large foreign-owned hotels and supermarkets. The
distributors competed for this business with large discounts.
Finally one of them, Ben Mwega, organized the Association to
limit competition of this kind. The KNTC's hardware distributors
also organized themselves in the Kenya Hardware Distributors'
Association, and scored an initial success in getting the remaining
50 per cent of domestic cement sales handed over to them in
1971; but whereas there were five KNTC wine wholesalers in
Nairobi, there were in 1970 thirty-five KNTC hardware distributors in Nairobi alone, so that enforcing restrictive agreements
in that sector would be much harder if not impossible.[13] The
influence of most KNTC distributors was therefore more likely to
be directed to enlarging the list of 'specified goods', while the
influence of African traders generally was aimed at getting hold
of monopolies by other means – either import or export licences or
(as a Chamber of Commerce resolution of 1970 suggested)
agencies to supply government ministries or parastatal bodies.[14]

In short, what African traders wanted could be summed up as
fixed shares of specific markets, public loan funds or publicly-
guaranteed commercial credit, fixed suppliers, and fixed prices.
Without these things, African trading was ground between the
upper millstone of the established non-African trader (or in some
cases, consumer) and the nether millstone of mass competition
from other Africans prepared to operate on minimum turnover.
But the effect of granting the conditions in which African traders
could make profits and begin to accumulate capital was to bind
them tightly to the established foreign suppliers and to the state,
making them into highly dependent clients, not entrepreneurs.
As Samir'Amin put it, in summarizing the situation in Senegal:
'It is not so much that the positions held by the Senegal private
sector are quantitatively modest as the fact that they are

destined for the government and foreign embassies and their staffs, and not for sale
through the trade.
13. In 1970 there were 220 KNTC sub-agents (distributors) for hardware throughout
Kenya, 186 for textiles, 644 for produce and provisions, and 31 for wines and
spirits.
14. Motion No. 6 at the 1970 Annual General Meeting read: 'That this Chamber
urges the Government to revise the present unsatisfactory system of appointing
distributors and, together with the Statutory Boards, to have the courage of its
convictions and treat African businessmen as responsible people.'

qualitatively dependent: still largely dependent on foreign import houses and foreign-owned local manufacturers, still more largely dependent on State support . . .'[15]

Above all, the implication was that African traders learned to make their profits through monopoly, in some cases adding no value whatever to the goods they handled, or even reducing their value.[16] In the most successful – that is to say, the most thoroughly protected – cases, they could best be regarded as being an extension of the parastatal system, receiving a commission on turnover instead of a salary, a new and politically powerful section of the 'auxiliary bourgeoisie' to be provided with a share of the national surplus. This is not to say that in course of time some traders would not succeed in accumulating substantial capital from trade, and be able to move into other areas of commerce or into manufacture. What was more difficult to envisage was that they would want to make any radical change in the protective symbiosis between local and foreign capital in general.[17]

Before leaving the subject of trade, we should consider certain other limitations to it as a seed-bed of African capitalism. These arise from what might be called some of the secondary contradictions in the government's development strategy. One was that the technology of foreign investment demanded a matching technology in many sectors of trade. In the short run this meant that past a certain point, it was not possible to Africanize some of the 'modern' sectors of trade without risking serious constraints on the rate of foreign investment. This set practical limits to the rate at which the government could insert Africans into the lucrative core of retail and wholesale trade in the urban centres. By the middle of 1970 it had already proved impossible to find Africans capable of replacing a number of the Asian concerns which the government had wanted to Africanize. In 1971 the Minister for Commerce and Industry, under heavy political

15. Samir Amin, *Le Monde des Affaires Sénégalais*, op. cit. (see note 4), p. 183.

16. This was evidently the case when the KNTC's 'sub-agents' interposed themselves in the importation and distribution of goods without actually handling them. In 1971 the country also experienced a more or less general cement shortage following the allocation of 100 per cent of sales to the KNTC, though it was clear that production had remained more than equal to domestic demand.

17. Marx expected that the petty bourgeoisie would eventually 'completely disappear as an independent section of modern society, to be replaced, in manufactures, agriculture and commerce, by overlookers, bailiffs and shopmen'. The conditions of periphery capitalism may, however, make possible a relationship between the 'auxiliary bourgeoisie' and foreign capital which combines a degree of autonomy for the former with a *de facto* role as 'shopmen'.

pressure to close down more Asian-owned firms, stated that in Nairobi and Mombasa 262 shops had been given quit notices, but only 63 Africans had applied to take them over.[18] It was recognized that a real (if temporary) constraint had been reached, and that if many of the remaining shops run by non-citizens were Africanized, one of three things would happen: the incoming Africans would convert them to some less difficult line of trade, usually general provisions; the incoming Africans would operate as 'partners' with non-citizens, who would pay them a commission for the privilege of continuing in business; or Asian citizens would take over the businesses, permanently excluding Africans from taking them over. The truth was that the rewards in this sector depended largely on specialized knowhow, and it was difficult to see how Africans were going to acquire it, at least in the medium run; while the needs of foreign commercial and industrial investment required that the efficiency of the more sophisticated trading sectors should not be too greatly affected.

Another constraint became apparent when the Central Bank imposed credit restrictions in 1971 to check a fall in foreign-exchange reserves. At first these covered only the importation of cars and electrical goods. But later the Bank came to see the problem as mainly one of a general increase of demand for imports, due to a huge increase in commercial bank lending which had been stimulated in part by the determination of the newly nationalized Kenya Commercial Bank to expand credit for Africans; an increase of £4·2 million, or 225 per cent, in its lending to citizens between January and September 1971 closely reflected the African traders' demand for credit.[19] Now, operating with few or no reserves they found themselves immediately in difficulties when the Central Bank imposed a general credit squeeze. Within a month the squeeze was replaced by direct bans on a wide range of specified imports. There was no doubt that the

---

18. *EAS*, 14 August 1971; the previous year the Director of Trade and Supplies had stated that 'some specialised businesses' could not be transferred to Africans because none were capable of running them (*EAS*, 27 June 1970). In 1971 he stated that 800 businesses of all kinds had been transferred since 1968 and that 400 of the new owners were 'genuine African traders' (*EAS*, 13 August 1971).

19. Speech (to a Lions luncheon) by the chairman, Mr J. N. Michuki, *EAS*, 19 January 1972. The longer-run cause of the expansion was the banks' liquidity; deposits rose from £95 million in 1968 to £158 million by September 1971. Commercial banks as a whole increased their advances to domestic (as opposed to import or export) trade alone from £10 million to £16·5 million between January 1970 and September 1971, and to private households from £4·3 million to £10·6 million during the same period of twenty-one months.

second move dealt more directly than the first with the immediate problem of falling foreign-exchange reserves. Pressure from the traders, however, undoubtedly played a part in the sudden change of approach. But the import bans produced an equal and opposite reaction from the foreign business community, expressed by the editor of the *East African Standard*:

> How can a country continue buoyant trading in such inhibiting conditions? . . . Nobody having a clear notion of the country's economy, and the way trade is conducted, can doubt that the revision of the banned list of imports must be undertaken as a priority, not only to perpetuate trading but to maintain the existing levels of employment.[20]

Finally there was a built-in conflict between the interests of African traders and the government's industrialization policy, which involved restricting or banning imports so as to protect local manufacture. This conflict was particularly sensitive since manufacturing investment tended to be foreign-owned, whereas the opportunity to import goods under import licence was one of the most secure and lucrative forms of trading open to an African trader. A series of cases, never satisfactorily clarified, testified to the intensity of this conflict. It was usually stated that import licences had been issued 'in error'. These 'errors' were allegedly repeated in one industry after another, from boiled sweets, to radios, to suiting, to tyres, to hinges, to buttons, to car batteries, to rice. The case of rice was one of the more notable. Basmati (long-grain) rice imports in bulk were banned in order to protect local short-grain rice production. Early in 1971, however, import licences for a total of 10,000 tons of basmati rice were rumoured to have been issued. The Mombasa Chamber of Commerce alleged that six licences were issued, five of them after it had protested about the first one and had been told that the 'mistake' would not be repeated. Since the c.i.f. price per pound of basmati rice was one shilling at the time, and the retail price in Kenya about four shillings, the value of the licences to the importers of 10,000 tons would have been close to £3 million.[21]

Government policy was to give industrialization priority in all cases; in practice, a number of manufacturing projects were at least temporarily arrested by competition from imports which were supposed to have been prohibited.[22]

---

20. 3 February 1972.
21. *EAS*, 18 May 1971. I am indebted for this calculation to Dr L. D. Smith.
22. The local manufacturers of hinges and buttons who were said to be going out of

The problems just described were not really serious. They were problems in the manipulation of the system. The terms of the solutions adopted, however, always pointed in the same direction, since the problems stemmed from a common cause, the contradiction between the desire to expand the economy, which was dominated by foreign capital, in ways which called for the inflow of still more foreign capital, and the desire for African ownership of capital. The answer in every case was to create a niche for Africans by creating new areas and forms of monopoly in ways which as far as possible would not deter the foreign investor.

ROAD TRANSPORT

The story of road transport parallels the story of trade remarkably closely. Like retailing, road transport is accessible to the small entrepreneur, in this case because of the low cost of second-hand vehicles, and it was another field in which Africans had established themselves in the rural areas after the second world war and sometimes even earlier. But the road-transport licensing system set up in 1937 to protect the railways was also used effectively to exclude Africans from operating on main roads. With the coming of independence, however, control of road-transport licensing passed into African hands and the situation rapidly changed. The Transport Licensing Act was modified by a regulation which purported to give the Transport Licensing Board power to refuse to issue licences to non-citizens, and acting under this power the Board did in fact greatly extend the area of business available to Africans, both by issuing new licences which allowed the holders to engage in carriage of passengers or other peoples' goods, and by not allowing non-citizen companies to carry their own goods.[23] In this way, for example, the oil companies gave up

business as a result were Africans operating in the Nairobi Industrial Estate (*EAS*, 22 April 1971). David Steele has drawn attention to this in 'The Theory and Practice of the Intermediate Employment Sector in Kenya', Discussion paper No. 7 (Institute of Development Studies, Sussex, January 1972), p. 18: 'There is a tendency for the importers to grow too strong to break. Even the modern expatriate industrial sector frequently has to give way to the citizen-owned importing firms. When the citizen wholesalers do finally build up their local trading networks outside the main high income urban centres, it is too late.'

23. The regulation was invalidated by the High Court in one of the very rare cases where a non-African citizen firm sought the aid of the courts to protect its legal rights. Shah Vershi Devji and Co. had been refused goods carriers' licences by the Board 'to remove imbalances between Kenya's citizens'. The court ruled that not

running their own tanker fleets for most of their long-distance petrol haulage, sometimes financing their own drivers to set up as independent carriers operating the company's former tankers; in general foreign manufacturing and commercial firms were under pressure to give their transport work out to African operators as far as possible. Goods carriers' licences rose only slightly (from 2,501 in 1964 to 2,657 in 1969) but non-citizens were completely replaced by citizen, and almost wholly by African, licence-holders. Passenger-service licences rose by over 50 per cent, from 2,878 to 4,410 over the same period. In addition, however, an unknown number of unlicensed operators, mainly of passenger minibuses and taxis, had also established themselves, while a large number of African holders of 'C' licences (permitting the holder to carry only his own goods) were in fact also operating goods-carrying services on a small scale.

The situation by this time closely resembled that in retail trading, with a very large number of one-vehicle operators, licensed or unlicensed, a small but still substantial number of small-fleet owners, operating with minimum overheads, and a very limited number of large-scale, mainly non-African operators. The pressure from large numbers of small-scale operators was felt even by the largest and most efficient operators; its main effect, however, was to make it extremely hard to expand from a small-scale to a large-scale operator, stepping up from the use of various second-hand buses over short distances to a fleet of new long-distance buses, operating a complex time-table; or to a fleet of lorries with central maintenance facilities, proper cost-accounting, etc.

The notable exceptions to this were cases where an African company got a *de facto* monopoly of some kind. The most notorious was the oligopoly accorded to various prominent people to transport oil from Mombasa to Nairobi in road tankers. Until 1968 competition with the railways from road transport was effectively prohibited by the licensing system, and the railway followed a policy of charging very high rates for transporting goods inland from the coast, to offset its losses on low-rated agricultural exports travelling from up country to the coast (another form of subsidy

---

only did the regulation not entitle the Board to discriminate between citizens on racial grounds, it did not in fact legalize discrimination against non-citizens, since the parent Act's intentions contradicted this (*EAS*, 12 May 1970). By 1969, however, there were no applications for road transport licences from non-Kenyans, apart from tour operators (*EAS*, 26 March 1969).

to the farmers in the old white highlands). Then a combination of circumstances – the completion of a tarmac road between Nairobi and Mombasa in 1967, the completion of the oil pipeline from Dar es Salaam to Ndola in 1968, which put a large number of second-hand tankers on the market cheaply, and pressure from the World Bank to let road competition help to produce a more 'economic' railway rates structure – led to a limited number of licences being issued to oil carriers. At the old railway rates, this was extremely profitable business. Soon the new road surface was breaking up under the strain. The World Bank now put pressure on the government to stop issuing licences, and eventually this was done and the hauliers were required to modify their vehicles to spread the load.[24] By 1971 the structure of railway rates had been altered and there was no longer a monopoly profit to be made, though the railways' lack of tank wagons kept the road hauliers in business at lower rates of profit for the time being.

On the whole, however, even medium-sized African transporters were few in number. The situation was characterized by enormous political pressure to admit more entrants, and in fact by what one official described as a 'subsistence transport sector', in which many lorry- and bus-owners were operating uneconomically, from the point of view of a capitalist, not making provision for depreciation, not paying union rates to drivers, in fact just living off the business rather than accumulating capital from it. To begin with, the sudden access of competition into the transport industry was officially welcomed, and even celebrated in the second Development Plan as providing 'one of the most promising fields for new small businesses'. Kenatco, a government-owned company, was required to give up its growing bus fleet in favour of independent African operators.[25] But by 1969, when the process of Africanization was 90 per cent complete, complaints of

---

24. The ban on overweight wheel-loadings was vigorously opposed by the African Road Transporters Association, whose Vice-Chairman was Peter Kenyatta, the President's brother. The Association succeeded in getting the imposition of the ban imposed gradually, but could not accomplish more in view of the fact that the ban was a *sine qua non* of further World Bank assistance for transport development.

25. Kenatco itself was the result of a 'lame duck' rescue operation by the government of a large and confused co-operative transport company founded in 1964, in which some prominent people had a stake. The creditors were paid off and the original shareholders were given an *ex gratia* shareholding of 10 per cent of the equity of the new company. Although it expanded greatly, it continued to have some severe problems, as indicated by the fact that the 1969–70 ICDC Report stated that no accounts had been received for Kenatco since June 1968. The capital employed by 1971 was £1 million.

'cut-throat competition' began to be voiced.[26] The Transport
Licensing Board announced that it would issue no new licences
for main road routes.[27] In 1971 it again announced that it would
be much stricter in issuing licences after the Ministry of Power
and Communications had told it that the roads were becoming
congested.[28] But as it had in fact issued new licences for main road
routes after the 1969 announcement, it remained to be seen how
far it would resist the pressure in future; and how far the fringe
of unlicensed operators would be effectively curtailed by the
police, since it had not been curtailed in the past.

As in the case of trade, the inexorable pressure of mass competition from below was matched by the pressure of non-African
citizens and large-scale foreign operators at the top. From time to
time there were 'scandals' about Africans who were issued
licences and then hired or sold them to non-Africans.[29] Others
kept within the law by formally hiring their own vehicles to non-
African operators. Others went into partnership with non-citizens.
The two foreign bus companies were required to sell 51 per cent
of their shares to citizens and had their own routes invaded by
large numbers of new African competitors, but they remained
highly profitable compared with the newcomers; these then
sought protection by means of a new system of licensing introduced in 1971 which tied every vehicle to a particular route, so as
to prevent the large-scale operators from putting extra capacity
into the routes at peak times.[30]

26. Mr Gatuguta, MP, Chairman of the Road Transport Licensing Board, *EAS*,
    27 March 1969: 'Unless we protect those already operating these routes, and
    especially the railways, there is bound to be cut-throat competition between the
    operators, whose businesses are bound to become unprofitable.'
27. *EAS*, 14 May 1969.
28. *Daily Nation*, 24 July 1971.
29. These were constantly referred to by the Transport Licensing Board chairman in
    public speeches. The most exciting example occurred when the Minister of Power
    and Communications told parliament in March 1971 that he would produce a
    list of names of people, including MPs and Assistant Ministers, who had obtained
    licences and hired them to Asians and Arabs. Later he refused to name the hirers
    but named four firms to whom licences had been hired (*EAS*, 18 and 25 March 1971).
30. The Kenya Passenger Transport Association protested. The chairman of the
    TLB said: 'We know this opposition is initiated by a foreign controlled company in
    this country. We are confident, however, that the small transporters who are a
    majority in this industry will approve.' (*EAS*, 25 November 1970.) The Kenya
    African Road Transport Association duly made a supporting statement (*DN*,
    8 December 1970) saying the new policy 'would eliminate unnecessary competition'
    and that 'the Kenya Passenger Transport Association was likely to put the small-
    scale transporters out of business because they flooded their buses on routes that
    promise most business'. The Minister agreed.

There was no reason why in the longer run some Africans should not establish themselves as substantial transport operators who would accumulate capital from their business. But the indications again were that the path to success was seen as lying through protection and through exclusive contracts with large users – most of whom tended to be expatriate businesses or the government.

CONSTRUCTION

Another field with low initial capital requirements was building. A special organization, the National Construction Corporation (NCC), was set up in 1968 to provide working capital and technical assistance to African contractors. In 1971 there were 700 contractors registered with it. Of these, no more than fifty were effective.[31] It was clear from the first that to break out of the 'odd-job' end of the construction business, Africans would have to overcome a complex technical and organizational barrier. What was not realized was how complex it was. By 1971 it was apparent that in open competition (with mainly Asian contractors) Africans could not succeed. The government had instead introduced a system of giving the NCC first option on all government building work estimated to cost no more than £20,000 per project. The NCC then negotiated contracts with the Ministry of Works and subcontracted them to African contractors. It also provided them with free technical assistance and either lent them funds or guaranteed their bank loans. The African contractors were entitled to any profit made on their share of the contract; they thus got, in effect, both protection and subsidy. It was very difficult to see what other approach might have succeeded; but it was also obvious that in this field, Africans were being trained from the start to operate within a fully protected market and to operate primarily as clients of the government. Even within this setting there was a succession of failures, followed by 'special case' government assistance. It was difficult to foresee a time when this pattern would be deliberately broken up in favour of a competitive one.

---

31. Interview with the General Manager of the NCC, 13 July 1971.

MANUFACTURING

African entrepreneurs had established themselves in small-scale industrial activity in the rural areas as far back as the 1930s, particularly in fields like maize-milling and sawmilling. After independence there was a steady expansion of this kind of activity, especially in Central Province as people moved farther and farther out of subsistence farming and provided an expanding local market for maize flour, building materials, simple furniture, soap, car repairs, etc. To boost African entrepreneurs into more sophisticated activities, however, with a national rather than a local market, called for new methods. The Industrial and Commercial Development Corporation (ICDC) added to its loan programmes for traders (and its large-scale investments in joint ventures with foreign firms) a programme of loans to African-owned manufacturing companies. By 1971 these loans amounted to some £900,000, averaging about £3,000 each. Losses were not spectacular, but it was clear that many of these projects were in difficulties.[32]

To improve their chances, the government began a programme of industrial estate building, starting with one in Nairobi in 1969, which would provide African entrepreneurs with subsidized rents, free technical and commercial assistance, and 100 per cent bank loans for machinery and equipment. The businessmen had to find only working capital, which in most cases would be borrowed on some other security. The difference between this device and that of the NCC in relation to building contractors was the difficulty of giving manufacturers a monopoly of some part of the market. They were vulnerable to the same competition from imports which foreign manufacturers experienced and which the African trading interest made it hard to exclude completely. They were also vulnerable to competition from local Asian producers setting up with superior know-how and knowledge of the market. In 1971 a draft Bill was in preparation to legalize the giving of monopolies to individual local manufacturers.

SHAREHOLDING

An interesting minor theme in this review of African efforts to acquire a stake in the capitalist economy is the ICDC Investment Company, formed by the ICDC in 1967 with a capital of £100,000

32. The default rate in June 1970 was 10 per cent, according to the 1969–70 Report.

to buy shares in profitable companies and to sell its own shares to African citizens. By 1970 59 per cent of the shares had been bought by some 1,900 Africans, and the share price had risen from shs 5/- to shs 7/95.[33] The share register read like a roll-call of the Kikuyu middle classes, who held over 90 per cent of the shares sold to individuals. What is significant in the end, however, is the extremely modest scale of even this transaction. The average shareholding was worth roughly £50, to a total of about £100,000, or 0·02 per cent of the net assets of the thirty-six companies quoted on the Nairobi Stock Exchange in 1970.

Of course the ICDC Investment Company was not the only way for Africans to acquire a stake in the foreign-controlled sector. They could and did buy shares in public companies directly, often with the help of bank loans. In the case of new share issues by foreign companies prior arrangements were made with the banks to lend up to 80 per cent or 90 per cent of the cost of the shares to individual citizen investors. At the end of the 1960s share prices were rising, and it was common to buy such shares with a bank loan and take the profits by reselling before repayment was due. But even if we regard the shares on the registers as fully owned, these suggested that in 1970 the total direct African shareholding in public companies (apart from the ICDC Investment Co.) was worth not more than £0·75 million.[34] In terms of the total assets of these companies (£51 million), let alone of all companies, it was a trivial sum. On the other hand it represented a stake in the system for a lot of people, and no doubt did something to predispose them to support it. This was certainly the hope of the companies themselves.

CONCLUSION

Of course African capitalists comprised a larger set of strata and activities than those considered in this chapter. In particular,

33. *Nairobi Stock Exchange Official Yearbook 1971*, pp. 50–51.

34. Based on a complete survey of the share registers of twelve of the thirty-six public companies quoted on the Nairobi Stock Exchange in 1970, including all those companies known to have been active in various ways in seeking African shareholders, with the exception of East African Breweries, which had the second-largest issued share-capital of any Kenyan company (£7·5 million) and had no single controlling shareholder, so that its shareholdings were very widely dispersed. In 1970 the Breweries claimed to have 8,000 African shareholders, owning £0·4 million-worth of shares. The total value of the African shareholdings in all the other companies studied was £0·17 million.

there were African large-scale farmers, and smaller-scale but also capitalist farmers in the former reserves, and some of the top stratum of the peasant producers, who were increasingly employing hired labour and increasingly committed to specialized commodity production. The drive for protection and monopoly by these agricultural capitalists or would-be capitalists was, as we have seen, similar to that which has been described above in various non-farm sectors. There was also a great deal of overlap between all these strata; to a large extent the same people constituted each of them, and also comprised the top leadership of KANU, and their leading supporters in the districts.[35]

On the other hand, in concentrating on the efforts of these particular strata to establish themselves as capitalists, we have treated other less successful but much more numerous strata only incidentally. But just as the emergence of a landowning peasantry was a central part of the new agricultural system, the emergence of large numbers of small enterprises, using mainly family labour, in trade, transportation, building, and so on, was also central to the operation of these sectors. The official (quoted above) who referred to a 'subsistence' transport sector was making a point of great general importance, though the word 'peasant' might have been more apt. Out of such strata in every field of activity some fully capitalist enterprises could have been expected to emerge, had it not been for the fact that there was already superimposed on the most important of them a top stratum of highly protected foreign capital. To transcend their 'peasant' status African small businessmen had either to use political power to try to dislodge foreign capital, or to install themselves alongside it within the circle of protection. With a few exceptions the first alternative would only have been possible in conditions of social revolution. They and the government therefore naturally chose the second.

It would be helpful if we could conclude by drawing a quantitative picture of what has been described in this chapter. Unfortunately the available data do not make this possible. The best we can do is roughly as follows. In 1969 there were 6,932 limited-liability companies on the register, of which roughly 900 were African-owned; these, however, included farm companies. There were also over 40,000 other firms registered under business names, of which perhaps 6,000 were African-owned non-farm

---

35. This chapter also says nothing about the stratum of rentiers which developed during the 1960s, especially among civil servants; see Chapter 6 below, pp. 193–5.

undertakings.[36] Some of these would also be included in the 51,000 'non-farm enterprises' which a government survey found in the rural areas in 1969, employing 187,000 people, over half of them self-employed or family workers; of the 51,000, nearly 29,000 were retail shops.[37] For the urban areas there were no published data on the number of African enterprises. But using the ILO mission's estimate of 125,000 people in 'informal' (i.e. non-enumerated) employment in the towns in 1969, and assuming a ratio of employees to enterprises similar to that in the rural areas, we get a figure of about 35,000 African enterprises in the urban 'informal' sector.[38] But the total figure of, perhaps, some 80–85,000 'enterprises' includes a large number of people who were simply self-employed craftsmen, hawkers, etc., working alone and with virtually no capital.

In relation to this kind of picture, we may also set down a summary of those involved in government programmes of assistance to businessmen down to 1971:

Table 5.1

Government Loans to African Business to 1971

	Approximate No. of borrowers	*Approximate value in K£ millions*
Joint Boards loans for traders	6,000	1·2
ICDC small commercial loans	1,800	2·5
ICDC small property loans	538	2·7
ICDC small industrial loans	270	0·9
NCC loans to contractors	50	0·1

But the significance of the social and economic changes to which such data refer can really only be grasped qualitatively for

36. *Annual Reports of the Registrar General*, 1968 and 1969. The number of business names registered annually doubled between 1964 and 1969, and in the last two years, 1968 and 1969, over sixty of these were owned by Africans, a total of 4,218.

37. *Survey of non-agricultural enterprises in the rural areas*, Ministry of Finance and Economic Planning 1969, cited in P. M. Mbithi and F. E. Chege, 'Linkages between agriculture and rural small-scale enterprises', in *Small Scale Enterprise* (op. cit., see note 7), p. 35.

38. *Employment, Incomes and Equality* (op. cit., see Ch. 4, note 7), p. 226.

the time being. The figures do no more than remind us that the economy was still small and externally oriented and that the financial task of inserting individual Africans into the ownership of a significant share of its non-agricultural assets without expropriating the existing owners was beyond the means of the government or anyone else. The real result of African businessmen's political activities and of the government's policies was to foster the emergence of a small protected stratum of African capital-owners, a distinctive kind of 'auxiliary bourgeoisie'.

To assess the significance of this development we would need to know much more about the use these people would actually make of their share of the surplus. It is fairly clear, for instance, that during the 1960s profits from trade were used to finance land-ownership, rather than the other way round as was historically the case in most parts of the world; to the extent that these profits were sometimes very large (in relation to the capital employed), thanks to politically secured monopolies of various kinds, this may have constituted a sort of 'primitive commercial accumulation' for the sake of embarking on capitalist agriculture (mainly in the former white highlands), rather than the reverse. The drive to own land was not exhausted, and it was not easy to foresee a time when it would be. The capital requirements for large-farm owner-ship would rise, but so would the capacity of some Africans to raise capital.

Moreover, Amin's comment on Senegalese businessmen holds good for Kenya:

> Senegalese enterprises do not yet exist; only the entrepreneurs who have created them exist. The premature disappearance of an individual almost always leads to that of the business; there is no assured succession. What guarantees the durability of the business is family tradition and the existence of a social milieu which makes possible the permanence of renewed management even in the absence of succession within the family.[39]

One of the most successful African traders I talked to in Nairobi was thinking of moving into manufacturing because the profits were larger, he thought; but also because 'the way of life is easier': 'When my children leave school they will prefer to work ordinary hours; they will want to play tennis, to go to a club.

39. Samir Amin, op. cit. (note 4).

I don't mind about going to a club, or working to ten o'clock at night. But if you have a factory there are various satisfying jobs for your children . . .'

But whatever economic direction this new stratum of African capitalists might be inclined to take, one thing was clear: they had considerable political power, and were likely to retain it. Although they needed alliances with other forces it was difficult to envisage any regime which would not substantially represent them. Because of this, and because not only the existing foreign capital in Kenya, but more of it, was seen as indispensable to their own interests, they were ready to accommodate themselves to it; but they were in a position to insist on reciprocity. This took many forms, as we have seen. One was to become a partner in a joint concern with foreign capital, helping to provide it with political protection in return for a share in profits.[40] Another was to sign a contract with a foreign-owned company to supply it with goods or services. More common still was to become, in effect, part of a foreign company's distribution network.

They also used their political power to secure a rapid extension of the system of monopoly into the areas of Asian enterprise which it had formerly been in the Europeans' interest to keep competitive. The pattern set by the settlers in the large-farm sector, and by foreign manufacturers in industry, was now followed in trade, construction, transport, tourism, etc.[41] However, as it was now very difficult to close access to these fields to new entrants, there was constant pressure from those already in them for still greater protection; but with increased profitability, the pressure from new entrants for admission into the ranks of the protected enterprises would be renewed.

The effect of these forces thus seemed likely to be the consolidation of a firm alliance between foreign capital and the new African 'auxiliary bourgeoisie', operating under more and more heavily protected conditions.

---

40. The number of new registrations of companies owned by 'mixed communal groups' rose from an annual average of sixteen for the years 1960–63 inclusive, to eighty-four for the years 1964–69 inclusive.

41. In November 1972 a major programme was announced to establish Africans in the tourist industry (*EAS*, 25 November 1972).

CHAPTER 6

Neo-colonial Society

Some of the main elements of Kenyan society as it appeared towards the end of the 1960s have already been indicated. It is now time to try to make them more explicit, and in particular to try to identify the structure of classes.[1]

This structure was, of course, the product of both the colonial and the pre-colonial history of Kenya; neo-colonialism saw no more than a development of certain characteristics already formed in earlier phases, the original forms of which can no longer be reconstructed with any confidence. In particular, the modes of production of the various tribal societies of pre-colonial times had already been modified in various ways by the impact of foreign capital when the earliest written accounts of them were made; and it does not seem necessary for our present purposes to try to discriminate carefully between these various 'transformed forms' of production as they have survived up till the present. In what follows they will be called, generically, 'peasant' modes of production: that is, modes of production characterized by the possession of land (and/or livestock) by households; by the production, on the basis of the labour of the household, of agricul-

---

1. The general perspective adopted in this chapter owes a good deal to Pierre-Phillippe Rey's *Les alliances de classes* (Maspero, Paris 1972), although I do not by any means accept all Rey's formulations in this or his previous work, *Colonialisme, néo-colonialisme et transition au capitalisme* (Maspero, Paris 1971). A short exegesis of the marxist concept of class which I have found helpful in thinking about classes in Africa is Theotonio Dos Santos, 'The Concept of Social Classes', *Science and Society*, Vol. 34, No. 2, 1972, pp. 166–93. Less succinct, but still valuable, is Nicos Poulantzas, 'On Social Classes', *New Left Review*, No. 78, March–April 1973, pp. 27–54. Unfortunately not many of the analyses so far made of particular African class structures have been grounded in a consistent method. Notable exceptions are two studies by Issa G. Shivji: *Tanzania: The Silent Class Struggle* (Tanzania Publishing House, Dar es Salaam 1973), and 'Tanzania: The Class Struggle Continues', Development Studies paper, University of Dar es Salaam, 1973, mimeo.

tural commodities (i.e. marketed produce); but in which land (or in pastoral areas livestock) remains 'natural' capital – i.e. it is seen as an indispensable means of providing successive generations of households with the basic necessities of life, and not merely one thing among many in which capital may be invested for profit.

Of all the ways in which capitalism wrought transformations in the pre-existing modes of production in Kenya the employment of wage labour stands out as the most far-reaching. As we have seen, in some areas – notably in Kikuyu country but also in parts of western Kenya – most adult men were regularly engaged in wage labour as early as the 1920s. By 1969, as Table 6.1 suggests, all forms of paid employment taken together yielded roughly two jobs for every three rural households. In reality, this meant that in some parts of the country a high proportion of households had at least one person in wage or salaried employment, while elsewhere (especially in pastoral areas) relatively few households supplied any member of the wage-labour force. The word 'supplied' here is important. Most wage-earners in the towns, and many on estates and large farms, lived away from their nuclear families during most of the time they were at work, returning home (i.e. to the family homestead) for holidays, or for longer spells between jobs. Even the urban labour force (amounting to between a quarter and a third of the total) was thus also 'involved in' peasant production; although when at work they would frequently be members of a very differently composed *urban* household too (generally including other male wage-workers, besides wives and children on shorter or longer visits), most of their immediate relatives – particularly parents, wives and children – lived on and cultivated land, or tended cattle somewhere in the countryside. The capitalist mode of production and the various 'peasant' modes of production were thus intimately linked.

The general basis of this link was that the 'peasant' modes of production depended on the capitalist mode of production, for markets for their products and for income from wage labour to supplement what could be obtained from peasant production itself. On the other hand, the continued survival of the 'peasant' modes of production subsidized the capitalist mode of production in two main ways. One was that they provided a direct subsidy to wages in the capitalist mode of production: 'competition [for work] permits the capitalist to deduct from the price of labour power that which the family earns from its own little garden or

Table 6.1

African Salaried and Wage Employment and Rural Households in 1969

Salaried and Wage workers		Rural Households	
Salariat	50,000		
Wage workers			
urban – over £300 p.a.	15,000	'Rich'	225,000
urban – £100–£300 p.a.	150,000		
rural – £100–£300 (non-agricultural services, etc)	100,000	'Middle'	250,000
urban – £60–£100 p.a.	95,000		
rural – £60–£100 p.a. (estates and large farms)	180,000	'Poor'	620,000
urban – less than £60 p.a.	45,000		
rural – less than £60 p.a. (non-agricultural businesses)	80,000	'Landless'	300,000
rural – less than £60 p.a. (on smallholdings)	475,000		
Total	1,190,000	Total	1,639,000

Note: A further 220,000 pastoral families were not broken down into wealth brackets and are excluded from the above figures. All these figures should be taken as indicating orders of magnitude only. The employment and earnings figures are based on information given in the ILO report, *Employment, Incomes and Equality* (ILO, Geneva 1972), Chapters 1–3, and a comparison of this with data given in the *Statistical Abstract 1971*, although it is not always easy to reconcile the two. The rural household data are also based on the ILO report's estimates, pp. 33 and 35–8.

field'.[2] The other was that they supplied agricultural commodities at very low prices relative to the prices of the manufactured products sold to the peasants and wage workers.

The 'peasant' modes of production were in a sense transitional: with every year that passed they would tend more and more to become mere aspects of the capitalist mode of production, and their relations of production would become more and more capitalist relations: land was already bought and sold, and people who in earlier years had had rights to it would find these eroded and increasingly extinguished; more and more smallholders

---

2. F. Engels, *The Housing Question*, in K. Marx and F. Engels, *Selected Works* (Foreign Languages Publishing House, Moscow 1962), Vol. I, p. 553.

would employ wage labour, often to offset the loss of family labour due to members of the family being engaged in wage labour in the capitalist mode of production; bride-wealth and other social relations would be more and more commercialized; the lineage and the extended family would give way increasingly to the nuclear family.

On the other hand there was another sense in which the 'peasant' modes of production would be likely to endure indefinitely, so long as the capitalist mode of production remained dominant. They would be required to absorb a continually *increasing* proportion of the adult population, and to continue to make available cheap labour and cheap produce. For this reason it seems useful to continue to keep them in view as constituting modes of production still to some extent distinct from that of capitalism, even though they are so thoroughly subordinated to it, and increasingly permeated by capitalist productive relationships.

The bearing of this discussion on the analysis of classes is essentially that in these conditions, the class character of the masses, involved in both wage labour and in 'peasant' production, is inevitably complex and ambiguous compared with the rapid and largely unambiguous crystallization of an African auxiliary bourgeoisie, and of various petty-bourgeois strata. The main problem is therefore not one of trying to identify a 'true' proletariat, living wholly in the towns and wholly divorced from the land, or of trying to determine the rate at which a 'true' rural proletariat is being created by mechanisms of differentiation in the countryside, although both processes may occur. Given the long-term prospect of a continuing articulation of still distinctive 'peasant' modes of production with the capitalist mode of production, the problem is rather one of exploring the contradictions of both the capitalist and the peasant modes, and the links (or 'convergence', as Rey puts it) between the class struggles occurring in each of them. From this point of view, for example, industrial action by relatively highly-paid workers in Nairobi does not necessarily appear as evidence of the antagonism between their interests and those of the rural masses, but represents one form of the class struggle in which the 'industrial peasant' (to adapt Engels's usage) is engaged; conversely the seemingly obscure struggles in the countryside between rival clans, religious sects and the like, over, say, the location of new 'self-help' schools, often prove to be aspects of long-term struggles between 'big' and 'little' men, those with larger farms or better land and those with smaller or worse – i.e. other forms of class struggle in which the same 'industrial peasantry' (represented in this instance, perhaps, by older members of the family or by women) is also engaged.

This chapter, however, does not attempt to explore the various struggles which will ultimately define the class character of Kenya, but is limited to setting out in more detail the conditions under which the main class categories – the bourgeoisie, the petty-bourgeoisie and the workers and peasants – existed at the end of the 1960s.

BOURGEOISIE AND PETTY-BOURGEOISIE

An Algerian saying quoted by Roger Genoud is worth repeating: 'in Africa, there are more bourgeois-minded people than bour-geois'.[3] The owners of the greater part of the non-agricultural capital lived elsewhere. In Kenya in the 1960s their interests were represented by a substantial bureaucracy employed by the branches of foreign firms, mainly in Nairobi, and mainly them-selves foreigners although, as we have seen, they increasingly included Kenyan Africans. But in Kenya there were also excep-tions to the general rule, in the shape of the Asian business families and resident European businessmen who had not sold out to incoming foreign corporations. These formed two distinct elements within the bourgeoisie. Collaboration and even contact between them was generally slight. This was mainly the product of the racialism practised over several generations by European businessmen, settlers and administrators against the Asians, but also of the different routes by which (largely in consequence of discrimination) the two groups had finally come to participate in the same sectors of the economy, particularly in manufacture; for example, Asians had moved 'upstream' from retail and wholesale trading, whereas Europeans had moved 'downstream' from farm-ing, while other Asians had moved laterally from real-estate ownership, whereas Europeans had moved laterally from finance, insurance, etc. But it also reflected the fact that both the Asians and the Europeans saw that their continued operation depended on securing a niche within an economic structure which would increasingly be divided between the international companies and the African auxiliary bourgeoisie and petty-bourgeoisie. The

---

3. R. Genoud, *Nationalism and Economic Development in Ghana* (Praeger, New York 1969), p. 53.

Europeans' initial movement into the tourist industry in the early 1960s is a case in point. For some time they had a strong position in the hotel industry, and a virtual monopoly of tour operating. Ten years later the airlines and the international hotel companies had begun to dominate the hotel industry, and tour operation was being increasingly reserved for Africans. In general both Asians and Europeans were aware that their role was mainly to carry out those tasks which the big international companies did not wish to undertake, and which Africans were not yet able to. Both strata sought to ally themselves in different ways with those two forces, rather than with each other.

As for the African bourgeois and petty-bourgeois strata, there is little to add here to what has already been said in Chapter 5. The success of the larger traders in getting inside the circle of protection and monopoly would in due course make some of them rich, while the bulk of the commercial petty-bourgeoisie, facing 'peasant' trader competition, rarely made profits on a large enough scale to accumulate substantial amounts of capital. The question was, however, what would be the effect of such capital accumulation as was occurring, whether in the competitive or in the monopolistic sectors of African business activity.

The fact that virtually all African businessmen were also farmers, and the larger ones capitalist farmers, was of considerable importance.

As we have seen, something in the region of £7–8 million had been spent by Africans from their own resources for the purchase of ex-European large-farms, and a large part of this must have come from trade. Virtually all African businessmen with substantial assets owned farms, and most had relatively large acreages.[4] This had several consequences. One was that it aggravated the dispersion of the capital and managerial resources of the petty-bourgeoisie, and reduced their rate of accumulation. A successful African businessman who was interviewed in Nairobi in 1971, for example, was not untypical in owning and managing six small businesses in all, two of them farms (one arable, the other dairy, sixty miles apart from each other), three of them shops (of three different types) and one a commodity-export firm. Unlike many

---

4. P. Marris and A. Somerset, in *The African Businessman* (Routledge, London 1971), pp. 119 and 156, report that 70–80 per cent of ICDC-supported businessmen, and 57 per cent of the market businessmen in their sample, had farms of three acres or more; 37 per cent of ICDC-supported businessmen, and 24 per cent of the market businessmen, also had other business interests.

similar cases, he succeeded in making each of them pay. But besides illustrating the tendency of African businessmen to invest the profits of trade in land, he also illustrated the tendency to stake out 'shares' in a very wide range of different business activities, dispersing knowhow and attention and reducing the likelihood of rapid capital accumulation except through large measures of protection.

The commitment to landownership and farming also deeply affected the consciousness of the African commercial bourgeoisie and petty-bourgeoisie. At the bottom end of the scale of capital, it merged into the consciousness of the peasantry. At the top, it was closer to that of the gentleman mixed-farmer, exemplified by the European settlers. In between, it saw land as still the only valid source of security and as the basis of social status, both in traditional African society and in colonial society. The point seems important. If Asian traders had been allowed to go into farming in the 1940s and 1950s when they began to accumulate capital on a large scale, it is open to question how far they would have gone in breaking into manufacturing production, even at a time when few foreign companies had established local plants. The situation of the more successful African traders in the 1960s was different in both respects; their aspirations towards farming and landowning coincided with a short-term opportunity to expand into the large-farm sector, at the same time that foreign capital, both international and local, was actively seizing every opportunity to establish itself in manufacturing. Consequently for the time being the interests of the African petty-bourgeoisie appeared complementary rather than hostile to those of foreign capital.

This does not mean that the African bourgeoisie and petty-bourgeoisie did not have a good deal of class-consciousness. In fact they expressed this in many ways. Their business associations, directed towards the apparatus of the state, were clearly class organizations. Many African businessmen also remarked on the fact that by the end of the 1960s a growing number of new companies were being formed with boards of directors from different tribes – i.e. based on shared commercial aims and values and an appreciation of each others' talents and assets in this context, rather than on the bonds of language and kinship which predominated in most earlier ventures. Class-consciousness was also expressed in the sort of business philosophies explored by Marris and Somerset, and especially in attitudes towards employees. One of Marris's and Somerset's businessmen told them:

Once when I was away in Nairobi, a trade union official came and incited the workers to strike. About 160 bags of flour were wasted. When I came back, I gave a rise to the workers who lived around the township. Then I went to our country branch, and sacked about ten. The rest agreed to come back to work. After a while, I sacked the workers in the town I'd given a rise to, because there were lots of people wanting work who were prepared to accept less.

Others 'only paid less [than the government rate – i.c. the legal minimum] from necessity.'[5] There is nothing like paying wages to make an employer conscious of his class identity and the need to rationalize it.

The crystallizing class-actuality of these strata was recognized by themselves and everyone else by the use of the term 'businessman'. The accepted fact was that they were a politically dominant stratum; but their aspirations at this time were not focused on capturing economic power, which rested in the hands of foreign companies, but on securing a monopoly of small-scale businesses, and on establishing themselves as a landed gentry. Both of these aspirations diverted them for the time being away from the centre of the stage, where the critical decisions of the 1960s were being made.

In addition to the petty-bourgeois strata already considered was the middle-level salariat, both in the state and parastatal apparatus and in the private sector, comprising roughly all those clerical and more senior office personnel earning over £200 a year and excluding only the highest ranks of the policy-making bureaucracy: perhaps about 50,000 people in all. This salariat was heavily concentrated in towns, especially in Nairobi and Mombasa. In so far as they were part of a salaried work-force they were not strictly a petty-bourgeois stratum even though a majority of them probably owned land, and an increasing proportion were involved during the 1960s in land purchase and in all kinds of small business activity; but on the other hand they were not by any stretch of the imagination proletarian in interest or outlook. What distinguished them in practice was (a) their education, which gave them the special advantages of white-collar employment; (b) the special form of their preoccupation with income and status (i.e. above all with promotions and salary scales); and (c), in the case of the civil-service stratum, their consciousness of

---

5. op. cit. (note 4), pp. 113–14.

being state employees, playing a central role in its routine operations, having access to many of its secrets, sacred and profane; and in consequence being broadly identified with the interests of domestic and foreign capital, which the state existed to serve.

WORKERS AND PEASANTS I. WAGE LABOUR

(a) Urban

In the towns 220,000 Africans were in enumerated employment in 1969, and the ILO mission estimated that there were also about 35,000 employed or self-employed in non-enumerated occupations in Nairobi, and an unknown number, perhaps of the order of 50,000, similarly engaged in other towns.[6] This workforce was distributed over a very wide spectrum of differences of pay and conditions, but the data on the basis of which the various urban wage-labour strata could be properly described do not exist. The following estimates therefore represent an extremely rough guess. (a) There were about 15,000 private-sector workers earning £300 a year or over, mainly employed in a few 'leading' industries such as the breweries and soft drinks, chemicals, oil and petrol, printing, cigarette-making (BAT), and other mainly foreign-owned and highly protected fields; these workers' real incomes rose rapidly throughout the 1960s. (b) The rest of the urban work-force in the enumerated-employment sector (private and public) amounted to perhaps 150,000 workers, substantially unionized and mostly earning about £100–200 per annum. (c) There were about 50,000 enumerated part-time and occasional workers earning £60–100 per annum, and perhaps half of the total non-enumerated wage-force, i.e. about 45,000 people, earned similar incomes. (d) The rest of the non-enumerated labour-force – another 45,000 people, earning less than £60 a year – tailed off into the penumbra of unemployed and occasionally employed people, mainly young men in Nairobi, who were really a queue of job-seekers.

These large differences in the conditions of urban wage employment were reinforced by others, for instance the housing or housing allowances provided by both the government and some private employers for their better-paid workers, and they con-

---

6. This figure excludes about 50,000 civil servants and white-collar company employees who have been considered already as petty-bourgeois strata. See *Employment, Incomes and Equality* (op. cit., Table 6.1, note), pp. 53–4.

stituted a major obstacle to the formation of a broadly-based class-consciousness arising from the conditions of urban work. The earlier success of the government and the FKE in getting unions established on an industry basis also played its part. The union movement as a whole failed to oppose the government's successive measures to curb its power to strike partly because the unions in the leading industries had done exceptionally well from wage negotiations throughout the 1960s, and because most unionized workers had enjoyed steady improvements in real earnings;[7] while on the other hand, the existence in the towns of large numbers of unemployed workers curbed the militancy of the lowest paid workers who had jobs. The presence of an 'industrial reserve army' depressed wage levels in non-enumerated employment and created a sense of insecurity and competition for work throughout the whole urban work-force, at least in the private sector (once in the civil service, a worker's job-security was normally high). So long as the process of underdevelopment kept enumerated employment rising by less than $1\frac{1}{2}$ per cent per annum, while population was rising at over 3 per cent, this would get worse.

Furthermore the penalties for militancy could be severe. Under the Preservation of Public Security Act, passed in 1966, trade-union leaders who supported Odinga's opposition group were among the main victims of preventive detention. Radical organization and propaganda were risky. Probably a good deal of discontent and potential opposition was temporarily contained by this method. Just how passive the urban work-force had become in these years could be gauged by the complete absence of serious political opposition offered to the government's policy of slum clearance, which was put in hand in Nairobi during the last three years of the 1960s. This policy continued a tradition of keeping the city 'clean' (i.e. politically as well as hygienically) which stretched far back into colonial times, and which had more recently been a marked feature of the early anti-Mau Mau measures; now, with Kenyatta's personal backing, several slum quarters were razed and burned on the grounds that they were a health hazard, and illegally constructed, a programme accompanied by periodic drives to round up 'vagrants' and other

---

7. From 1964 to 1969 average wages in enumerated non-agricultural employment rose at an average annual rate of about 5 per cent (Ndegwa Report, op. cit., p. 27). Wage *rates* probably rose more slowly however, average earnings being raised by rapid promotions in the public sector.

undesirable residents and expel them from the city.[8] By the end of
1971 large numbers of former slum-dwellers – some estimates put
them at several thousand – were living in makeshift tents, which
had to be dismantled every morning before the police patrols
made their rounds. There were some rather hesitant expressions of
concern about this by middle-class (and especially expatriate)
observers, but there was no political resistance from those involved, and no public reaction at all from the trade unions.

Yet when all these factors have been taken into account the
pervasive influence of the workers' rural base seems more important still. Since 1954 official policy had theoretically aimed at
'stabilizing' the urban labour force by raising urban wages to a
level capable of supporting workers' families, yet at the end of the
1960s the great majority of urban workers were still essentially
migrant workers, whose families lived in the countryside, producing at least the bulk of their own food needs. Studies of the
urban adult male wage-working population of Nairobi in the
1960s showed that two-thirds of them spent at least a week, and
one-third over a month, in their rural home area each year.[9]
Weisner's study of a matched pair of samples of urban and rural
residents from the same rural location showed that there was no

8. On the historical background see R. Van Zwanenberg, 'History and Theory of
Urban Poverty in Nairobi; the Problem of Slum Development' (Institute for
Development Studies, Nairobi, April 1972, mimeo); on slum clearance at the end
of the 1960s see M. Tribe, 'Some Aspects of Urban Housing Development in
Kenya', in C. Allen and K. J. King (eds.), *Developmental Trends in Kenya* (Centre
of African Studies, University of Edinburgh, April 1972, mimeo). Kenyatta's
attitude, as reported in the minutes of the Nairobi City Council's General Purposes Committee, who had gone to see him to find out if he really meant it, was
rather characteristic:

'He said (1) that it was wrong for people to believe that their salvation lay in
residing in towns or the City of Nairobi; (2) that while the Government and
the City Council had every sympathy with *wananchi* [the citizens], they in
turn had the duty and the obligation to obey the laws of the land and the by-
laws of the City Council . . . The President was concerned at what would happen
should an epidemic break out and said people who built shanties were wealthy
people bent on exploiting the poor. . . . Where shanties were demolished they
should not be allowed to be re-erected. People should be made to move and the
Provincial Commissioner for Nairobi area was instructed to ensure that this was
done. Those affected should be repatriated to their home areas by the P.C. and
genuine cases of landless people should be referred to him so that arrangements
to re-settle them could be made.' (*EAS*, 6 July 1971).

9. See Marc H. Ross, *Politics and Urbanisation: Two Communities in Nairobi*, unpublished Ph.D Dissertation (Northwestern University 1968), p. 70, Table 3.1. The
material on workers and peasants down to 1970 is discussed in more detail in
C. Leys, 'Politics in Kenya: The Development of Peasant Society', op. cit.,
pp. 307–37.

difference between them in respect of the number of years they had spent in towns, and that the only meaningful way to look at these families was to see them as single families with two households, one in town and one in the country.[10] It was specially significant that their social focus – their network of friends, their political information, etc. – was exclusively provided by their rural base, not their urban one. Weisner's study was not of a representative sample of Nairobi workers, but another study, which was, showed that it was only the lowest-paid workers who had little contact with the countryside; the better-paid the worker, the more likely he was to have land, and to invest his earnings in it.[11] The low-paid workers, however, also had their families on the land, since they could not afford to maintain them in town; if they were 'landless', it simply meant that their family lived as dependants of someone with land, either having traditional cultivation rights on kinsmen's land, or providing labour or other services (or cash) in return for land use.

In short it is not possible to escape the conclusion that for most of the urban work-force the relations of production of their small-holdings (however coloured these might be by capitalist production relations) still predominated over those of their urban jobs. This is not to deny the reality of the urban culture of Nairobi, Mombasa or even other towns. But it was a transient culture; even highly-placed civil servants commonly looked on some rural plot as 'home'; four out of five wage-workers wanted to retire to the countryside, and indeed the towns made virtually no provision for any except the comparatively rich to live there when they were old.[12] So long as the rural areas alone provided the ultimate security for the mass of urban workers – if not by providing an adequate plot, at least by providing a home, a patch for growing food and opportunities for casual labour – the development of a proletarian class-consciousness based on the conditions of urban work seemed likely to be delayed and hesitant.

10. Thomas S. Weisner, 'One Family, Two Households: A Rural–Urban Network Model of Urbanism' (University Social Science Council Conference, Nairobi 1969, mimeo).

11. See Ross, op. cit. (note 9).

12. ibid., pp. 45 and 68. The National Security Fund established in 1965 would in due course provide pensions for urban workers on retirement, but not at a level which would allow them to retire in the towns without other sources of income.

(b) Rural

The rural wage-labour force comprised the following distinct strata: (a) roughly 100,000 workers on coffee, tea and sisal estates; (b) roughly 80,000 labourers on large mixed-farms; (c) about 80,000 employees of small rural non-agricultural enterprises (shops, repair shops, grain mills, etc.); (d) about 240,000 regular labourers on smallholdings, including settlement schemes; (e) the 235,000 (more or less) in seasonal or casual employment on smallholdings; (f) an unknown number of squatter labourers who had reappeared mainly on African-owned large farms (sometimes disguised as 'members' of large co-operatives or farm companies).[13] In addition, there were about 100,000 people in enumerated non-agricultural rural employment (i.e. government employees, salesmen, etc.) but many of these were really 'modern sector' employees in rural posts, such as those employed in 'services' in Table 6.2:

Table 6.2

Average Annual Earnings in Rural Areas, 1969

	K£
Enumerated rural workers in 'services'	201
Enumerated workers on estates and large farms	69
Non-agricultural rural employees, not enumerated	56
Regular workers on smallholdings	25
Seasonal workers on smallholdings and squatters	under 25

Source: Employment, Incomes and Equality, pp. 39–40.[14]

Of the other categories, the estate workers were the best paid, and were in addition provided with housing and some other services

---

13. In 1972 F. Furedi found that about 25 per cent of the residents on the African-owned large farms he studied in the Rift Valley possessed no means of support (private communication).

14. The only other group of enumerated rural workers cited by the ILO report as having lower wages than those in 'services' were those in 'commerce' whose annual average wages were given as £118. It seems likely that these were really the enumerated 'tip' of a much larger force of assistants in shops and other small rural businesses, most of whom were not caught in the annual labour enumeration and were paid much less. Incidentally the ILO report's figure of 133,000 enumerated rural workers in non-agricultural employment earning over £200 per year seems suspect and without access to the data on which it was based I have thought it safer to treat 33,000 of them as being in reality part of the urban work force.

by the employers. Yet even their wages were clearly based on the assumption that their families produced their own subsistence from cultivation, and as one moves down the scale of wages this assumption becomes more and more obvious until one finally reaches the casual labourers and the squatters. In fact most of the agricultural work-force was drawn from families who were at best poor peasants, and since none could earn wages which would help any but the most fortunately placed families to save money or pay secondary-school fees, it was reasonable to assume that at any rate in the most crowded districts, many of these families would eventually find themselves more and more dependent on their wages for survival, and would eventually approximate a 'pure' proletarian stratum.

Yet it was also clear that this stratum would be no less dependent on access to land for its survival, in view of the level of wages paid. Wage-workers on the large mixed-farms had in any case always been given plots to cultivate; in 1967 about 84,000 farm workers' families were living on the farms where they were employed, each family cultivating on average about three-quarters of an acre, with one cow to every four families, and one sheep or goat to every three.[15] Workers on smallholdings generally had land nearby, though on the settlement schemes, where the plots were much larger than the average of those in the reserves, the labourers were often also cultivating their own food crops on the plots where they were employed. Consequently, although the various strata of the agricultural labour-force were being increasingly separated from their means of production, the conditions of their wage-employment forced even the most proletarianized of them to depend on growing food crops, and to that extent to identify with the mass of the landholding peasantry. Even the estate workers had proved hard to unionize, as their failure to raise wage-levels partly testified, and elsewhere among the agricultural labour force unions did not exist at all.

WORKERS AND PEASANTS II: PEASANT PRODUCTION

The ILO mission estimated that in 1969 there were 1·7 million rural households in Kenya. The great differences between the different parts of the country make generalizations about these households difficult, as Table 6.3 indicates. Ecological differences

---

15. *Agricultural Censuses, 1965–67, Large Farm Areas*, Nairobi, n.d., Table 31 (b).

were important, but the geographical unevenness of development under colonialism was apparently even more important. Some areas, especially agricultural areas close to Nairobi such as Murang'a, Nyeri and Meru, had benefited from earlier access to profitable crops, schooling and other services than other districts, until they had come to enjoy a cumulative lead in output per head which was unrelated to their ecological advantages over other districts. However, in spite of these wide regional differences, a pattern of vertical stratification could be seen in virtually all parts of the countryside.

The ILO mission categorized the agricultural smallholding population of approximately 1,395,000 households as follows.[16] *First*, 225,000 households (about 16 per cent of the total) who had 'rapidly increased their incomes over the last decade', i.e. rich peasants or kulaks, and a handful of large-scale farm-owners, or capitalist farmers; 'theirs tend to be the holdings where workers are hired on a full-time basis, and also on a seasonal basis to assist with farm work. On a number of these holdings, workers are hired to replace the manual labour of the farmer, and sometimes of other members of the farm family.' *Secondly*, a further group of about 250,000 households (18 per cent) with farm incomes of £60–100 per annum, using seasonal hired labour, often paid for in kind or with exchange labour – i.e. 'middle' peasants, roughly able to balance their outgoings by their farm income. *Thirdly*, 620,000 households (44 per cent) with farm incomes of less than £60 per annum supplemented by providing labour for someone else – a neighbouring rich peasant, a large farm in the Rift Valley, or an employer in town, i.e. poor peasants. *Finally*, about 300,000 land-less households (22 per cent), though nearly all of these would have access to someone else's land, either by gift or in return for some kind of service, for growing foodstuffs for their own consumption. The landless families and the poor-peasant households evidently provided a high proportion of rural wage-workers.

The impression of advancing differentiation given by these figures is reinforced by those for the distribution of land. In 1969 slightly over half of all the smallholdings on the land registers contained only 14·8 per cent of all the registered land, while at the other end of the spectrum, 7 per cent of the registered holdings accounted for 34·9 per cent of the total registered land, and 18·3

16. *Employment, Incomes and Equality*, pp. 33–8 (and see table 6.1); there were also an estimated 220,000 pastoral households.

Table 6.3

Some Economic Variations in Fourteen Districts of Kenya

	Area in sq. miles	Population	Population per sq. mile	High-potential land per head (acres)	Total agricultural exports (£ 000s)	Agricultural exports per head (£)
Kwale	3,197	182,970	57	1·7	331·3	1·8
Taita	5,899	104,506	18	1·0	88·8	0·9
Embu	1,048	130,700	125	1·25	835·0	2·5
Machakos	5,790	636,296	110	0·47	856·2	1·4
Meru	3,763	544,237	145	1·09	2,189·8	4·0
Murang'a	702	399,789	570	0·97	2,483·0	6·2
Nyeri	595	295,118	496	1·34	2,665·2	9·0
Baringo	3,941	150,749	38	2·73	243·1	1·6
Nandi	714	138,092	194	4·19	337·5	2·4
West Pokot	1,960	83,906	43	3·03	42·4	0·5
Kisii	752	610,848	800	0·89	1,900·1	3·2
South Nyanza	2,206	558,359	253	2·50	1,518·3	2·7
Busia	668	199,827	299	2·01	401·5	2·0
Kakamega	1,200	705,083	588	1·14	268·2	0·4

Adapted from J. Heyer, D. Ireri and J. Moris, 'Rural Development in Kenya' (Institute for Development Studies, University College, Nairobi) October 1969, mimeo, pp. 34–5 and 42. High-potential land is defined as having an annual rainfall of 35 inches or more, or 40 inches or more in Coast Province.

186 UNDERDEVELOPMENT IN KENYA

per cent of the holdings accounted for no less than 58·7 per cent of the total.[17]

It is clear from all these figures that there was a broad-based system of stratification. The question is what significance it had in the process of class formation. Shanin's review of the debate on the significance of stratification among the Russian peasantry in the period before collectivization should caution us against drawing conclusions too hastily from such essentially static data as we possess on Kenya.[18] In Russia the principle of subdividing the family plot among married sons had operated continually to redistribute individual rich peasant households down the hierarchy of wealth and income, by breaking them up; the same principle also operated in large parts of Kenya, notwithstanding the legislation on land registration which was designed to prevent subdivision of plots when this would result in individual units below a minimum 'viable' size. To accommodate initially existing land rights the law permitted holdings to be registered in the names of up to five people, but it was rare for multiple owners actually to farm the land in common, and so in practice there were many more 'farm units' than registered holdings. This became even more true as time went on, and registered owners died; to avoid the prohibition on subdivision of very small plots on the deaths of the owners, their heirs took to subdividing unofficially. Even the largest plots in Central Province – i.e. the 2,900 plots of 15 acres or more – were often really multiple small plots, carrying as they did an average of just under fourteen people each, more than twice the average number per plot on the smallest plots (i.e. plots up to 2·5 acres).[19] It is apparent, too, that a high proportion of the largest 'smallholdings' lay in the less developed and less fertile agricultural areas of Kenya, and were not necessarily as productive or potentially productive as many smaller ones, especially those (probably a majority) which lay in Kikuyu country. Consequently not only may the official data tend to exaggerate the inequality of plot sizes which actually existed, but the practice of subdivision may have meant that in Kenya, as in Russia before 1929, there was considerable mobility of households up and down the hierarchy of stratification in the countryside, from one generation to another.

17. ibid., p. 36.
18. T. Shanin, *The Awkward Class* (Clarendon Press, Oxford 1972).
19. Cf. Leys, 'Politics in Kenya', pp. 318–19 for further details on these points.

On the other hand it is true that a brisk market in land built up in the Kikuyu country in the 1960s. By 1970 no less than 10·3 per cent of all holdings in Nyeri had changed hands, in whole or in part, since they were first registered, and it seemed as if a high proportion of these transactions were sales of complete plots.[20] But while information is lacking on the significance of these facts, it is far from clear that they indicated the formation of a new type of capitalist farm, and the corresponding formation of a landless class. For one thing, the areas in which a rich farmer could find plots for sale contiguous with his own, or reasonably near, were very limited in Central Province. The density of population already on the land was simply too high. After registration was completed in Kikuyu country 86 per cent of all holdings were smaller than 7·5 acres, which was then reckoned to be a minimum size for a 'viable' farm, let alone a capitalist enterprise.[21] Secondly, the Land Control Boards tried to prevent the sale of whole plots unless the vendors could satisfy them that they either owned another plot elsewhere or had some non-farm source of livelihood.[22] Thirdly, the prices paid for land in Nyeri, at least, were so high that they suggested that the purchasers were primarily salaried officials or businessmen interested in acquiring country homes, or settling dependants on the land, and not in commercial farming as simply a profitable way of investing capital.[23] Some of the salaried purchasers, moreover, could well have come from poor peasant families (in Kisii District Wilson found that purchasers typically owned less land than vendors).[24] In other words, the degree of individual social mobility present in

---

20. Rodney J. A. Wilson, 'The Economic Implications of Land Registration in Kenya's Smallholder Farming Areas', Staff Paper no. 9 (Institute for Development Studies, Nairobi February 1971, mimeo), p. 4, Table I.

21. *Kenya African Agricultural Sample Census, 1960–61* (Nairobi 1962), p. 19, Text Table 14.

22. Wilson comments on the performance of Land Control Boards in this respect in 'Land Control in Kenya's Smallholder Farming Areas', Staff Paper no. 89 (Institute for Development Studies, Nairobi, January 1971, mimeo), pp. 21–3; my general statement is based partly on conversations with people who had attended Board meetings in densely populated areas.

23. Wilson found that land in many locations of Nyeri was fetching over 5,000 shs (K£250) per acre in 1970 ('The Economic Implications', p. 9).

24. ibid., p. 9; half the buyers studied had income from non-farm sources, while only one out of nineteen sellers did: moreover, the buyers had more sons than the sellers. They were thus in many cases using capital accumulated in trade or salaried employment to enhance their family's position in the peasant economy, and the reasons they gave when asked why they bought land were predominantly to do with providing a living for dependants.

the system at 'this time also makes it difficult to interpret the implications of the market in land.

There were two further aspects of stratification in the country-side which also need to be borne in mind when assessing its implications for the development of class antagonisms.

One was the comparative equality of the bulk of the peasantry (or as it may be better to call them, peasants and workers) in the 'middle' and 'poor' categories. A comparison of the ILO's estimates, given above, with the results of a study carried out by the government in 1963–4 on the peasant households of the most advanced agricultural areas of Kenya (Kiambu, Fort Hall, Embu, Nyeri and Meru) helps to make this point clear.[25] Nineteen per cent of all households were not farming at all (i.e. were wholly dependent on non-farm employment).[26] Of the rest, 10·5 per cent had less than an acre, and 1·6 per cent had twenty acres or more. Seventy-one per cent had from one to six acres, accounting for 60 per cent of the total acreage. In other words, the great majority of households were clustered around the average. The number of really large landowners was very small. The appearance of equality was heightened by the figures of household members in relation to household income. The average number of persons per household in those with incomes under £50 per annum was 3·9, compared with 8·2 in those with incomes from £100 to £125. By the end of the 1960s it was quite possible that these data had begun to alter very substantially, with the reduction in the opportunities for land settlement, population growth, and the lengthening purses of the salariat in relation to poor peasant land-holders in need of cash. Moreover, the data are in any case rather crude. Crucial differences in the life situations of individual families could well arise within the rather broad category of those with farm incomes of less than £50. Even so, the figures remind us that a majority of peasant households in Kikuyu country in the mid-1960s shared a common poverty, which was not yet as abject in relation to their most prosperous neighbours as that of peasants in most of Asia and Latin America.

What is more, the inequality which existed in Kikuyu country had always existed, and in roughly the same form, i.e. there had

---

25. *Economy Survey of Central Province – 1963–64* (Statistics Division, Ministry of Economic Planning and Development, 1968).

26. This relatively high proportion of 'rural households' not 'operating' any farm-land at all is mainly accounted for by residents in peri-urban areas with jobs in urban areas. In Kiambu, a quasi-suburb of Nairobi, the proportion was 40·9 per cent.

always been a few 'big men' and a larger number of landless
dependants (the *ahoi* of traditional Kikuyu society). According to
Leakey,

> The Kikuyu population before the Europeans came was
> divided into two quite distinct divisions: the Landowners
> and the Ahoi, or tenants-at-will. . . . Not even 50% of the
> Kikuyu held land as private property. There were probably
> more than 50% who were Ahoi, hoping for the day when they
> too would become landowners.[27]

Inequality was nothing new; and the traditional culture still
operated to give most of the landless some accepted social status
and a minimum garden plot with which to support life.

Barrington Moore at one point remarks:

> . . . it seems more realistic to assume that large masses of
> people, and especially peasants, simply accept the social sys-
> tem under which they live without concern about any balance
> of benefits and pains, certainly without the least thought of
> whether a better one might be possible, unless and until some-
> thing happens to threaten and destroy their daily routine.[28]

This seems rather too strong, though it may be more plausible
when applied to ancient peasant societies rather than to new ones
like Africa's, already deeply penetrated by modern school
systems, extensively engaged (in many cases) with the towns
through migrant labour, and constantly exposed to the rhetoric
of 'modernization' and 'development'. Yet Moore grasps what is
none the less likely to be as critical in Africa as elsewhere when he
notes that what made the Chinese villagers 'explosive material',
compared either with their forefathers or with their counterparts
in, for instance, India, was that they had in so many cases become
marginal – 'not only in the physical sense of living close to the
edge of starvation, but also in the sociological sense that the
reduction of property meant that the ties connecting them to
the prevailing order had worn thinner and thinner';[29] while on
the other hand, 'the government and the upper classes performed
no function that the peasants regarded as essential for their way of
life'. Hence 'the link between rulers and ruled was weak and
largely artificial, liable to snap under any severe strain'.[30] It is

---

27. L. S. B. Leakey, 'The Economics of Kikuyu Tribal Life', *East African Economics Review*, Vol. 3, No. 1, July 1956, at pp. 165 and 168.

28. *Social Origins of Dictatorship and Democracy* (Beacon Press, Boston 1966), p. 204.

29. ibid., pp. 219–20.

30. ibid., p. 205.

in this respect, above all, that the situation of the peasants and workers in Kenya – and in many other African countries – strikes one as different from that of their counterparts in many other parts of the third world. In any society that is highly unequal there is a 'margin' where people are poor and have such low social status that they are largely excluded from effective membership of the society. In Kenya in 1970 few people were yet in this position, and in addition the rich and powerful people in the cities were not yet seen as a race apart; their own rural origins were mostly very recent, and while the link between them and the poorest peasants was becoming artificial and mystified, it was still quite active and personal.

Finally, in another interesting parallel with Russia immediately after the revolution, there had been a major redistribution of land, not at the expense of the larger peasant landholders, but by taking land from a third group (in this case, from the settler farms of the white highlands, and with more than generous compensation, compared with the seizure of former state land and estates belonging to the Tsar and the aristocracy, which fulfilled the same function in Russia).[31] The effects were twofold. One was that the land hunger of the landless was for the time being assuaged without pitting them against the stratum of larger African landowners. The other was that throughout the 1960s peasant production was in fact expanding, relative to capitalist farming. This expansion took place extensively through mass migration into the settlement schemes and through various different forms of peasant production on many so-called 'large farms' in the Rift Valley; and on a smaller scale, through migration into other areas of low population-density, by the purchase of land from other tribes (for example from the Masai south of Nairobi) or by the illegal clearing of forests (the latter processes were accelerated by the opening up in 1971 of various districts which had been legally closed to inward migration since the days of Mau Mau or even earlier).[32] Peasant production also expanded 'intensively' through the

---

31. Cf. T. Shanin, *The Awkward Class* (see note 18), pp. 224–5.

32. The Outlying Districts Ordinance was passed in 1902 and permitted the authorities to exclude from any District anyone not born there. The Special District (Administration) Act, passed in 1934, went further by enabling the Provincial or District Commissions, *inter alia*, to deport troublemakers, or arrest or restrict whole groups of people, in districts designated 'special'. Nineteen districts were wholly or partly 'closed' under these powers: see Y. P. Ghai and J. P. McAuslan, *Public Law and Political Change in Kenya* (Oxford University Press, Nairobi 1970), p. 418, note 38a.

adoption of better techniques and improved seeds, growing new and more profitable crops (such as tea), getting access to more profitable markets (such as the liquid-milk market), and so on, a process accompanied by higher population densities in the former reserves.

Yet when all these qualifications have been taken into account the fact of a significant measure of inequality and – more significantly – the development of a very extensive system of wage-labour within the peasant modes of production, remains. And it is difficult not to think that a process of gradual polarization was also at work, in spite of a continuing measure of social mobility, in which 'kulak' families were consolidating a position of permanent economic (and political) dominance, while other families were being relegated to permanent pauperization and proletarianization. The Stolypin reforms in Russia before 1914 had not been very extensive and were partly undone after 1917, whereas in Kenya full freehold tenure was pushed through everywhere. Land in Kenya could then be bought; a successful household head was not obliged to partition his plot if he could afford to buy other land for his sons, while an unsuccessful household head (not infrequently a woman) could be obliged to sell some, if not all, of the family plot in order to raise essential cash. There was also the fact that in Kenya the rewards to education in terms of salaried or high-wage employment conferred huge potential advantages on families wealthy enough to pay the substantial school fees necessary to support several children through a full secondary education, so that the difference between a household income which made this possible, and one which did not, could prove critical for the long-run fortunes of the family. Hitherto, access to primary schooling, for which the fees were relatively modest, had probably tended to enhance the upward mobility of poor families. As the rewards to primary schooling declined and virtually vanished, a reverse process was liable to set in. And last but not least, the exploitation of political and state power by wealthier families, leading to the consolidation of unequal access to land, farm credit, extension services, marketing facilities, new crops and much else in the field of peasant production alone (not to mention other areas in which the same households were securing parallel advantages) was also working systematically in the same direction.

In the long run, therefore, it seemed reasonable to expect that the wage-labourers on smallholdings (who in 1969 numbered about half a million) would be drawn more and more from house-holds which were more or less permanently obliged to supply such labour, while the 'rich' and 'middle' peasant households which employed them would be more and more permanent employers of such labour, from one generation to the next. It also seemed likely that salaried employment would gradually come to be increasingly monopolized by the members of the richer peasant families, making for a gradual crystallization of classes embracing the social strata formed in both the capitalist and the peasant modes of production.

In any mode of production the conditions under which surplus value is produced and appropriated are critical for the develop-ment of classes and class antagonisms. The exploitation of wage-labour in both the capitalist and the peasant modes of production was obvious enough. Less obvious were the other forms of surplus appropriation within the peasant modes of production. These included: appropriation at the level of exchange, through adverse rural–urban terms of trade and through monopoly elements in the process of collection, processing and selling peasant-produced commodities for foreign markets;[33] regressive taxes of various kinds, legal and illegal, which in effect transferred surplus from the poorer to the richer families; the similarly regressive burden of the co-operatives' and marketing boards' administrative costs, which supported a substantial part of the salariat by means, in effect, of flat-rate charges on every unit of output from both the capitalist and the peasant sectors of agricultural production; by the strong bias in the provision of services in favour of the richer peasant households as well as of the salariat and small- and large-scale owners of capital in the towns; and so on. These mechanisms, and the varied forms of struggle resulting from them, constitute a badly neglected area of research.

At the same time we should not lose sight of the fact that in the peasant modes of production the majority of households produced very little surplus, owing to their lack of equipment, working capital, know-how, stock and, above all, land. This was why wage-employment had become a necessity for so many of them. The main economic importance of the 'peasant' modes of production was as a source of foreign exchange for the purchase of manu-

---

33. Between 1964 and 1969 the internal terms of trade for farmers as against the urban sector declined by 25 per cent (Ndegwa Report, op. cit., p. 42).

factured imports, and as a source of cheap foodstuffs and of subsidies for wages in the capitalist sector. It was for this reason that they had to be enabled to reproduce themselves. In making economic and social policy the state apparatus had therefore to manage the relationship between the modes of production in such a way that the peasant modes remained 'viable', while offering a minimum of effective competition to the capitalist mode. To achieve this balance was really the most important task of the higher bureaucracy.

THE HIGHER BUREAUCRACY

The significance of the higher bureaucracy has been somewhat obscured in the literature on African underdevelopment, perhaps under the influence of Fanon, who appeared to run together the idea of the higher bureaucracy and that of the bourgeoisie or would-be bourgeoisie when he wrote of a 'bourgeoisie of the civil service'.[34] But the important point about higher echelons of the state apparatus is less their class origins or ambitions than their specific function in relation to the ruling alliance of classes and class-strata. Concentrating on the tendency of state officials to try to acquire property is apt to divert attention from this more important point.[35]

This is not to say that the higher bureaucracy in Kenya, as in other African states, did not do what it could in the 1960s to acquire wealth. As the Ndegwa Commission put it in 1971, unconsciously echoing Senator Plunkitt, 'it is understandable that civil servants should have taken their opportunities like other citizens'.[36] But it is questionable whether the thrust of this activity

34. It must be admitted that Fanon is not wholly clear on this point, and my interpretation may be wrong. But passages like the following seem to imply it: '. . . it remains at the beginning and for a long time afterwards a bourgeoisie of the civil service. It is the positions that it holds in the new national administration which will give it strength and serenity . . . If the government gives it enough time and opportunity, this bourgeoisie will manage to put away enough money to stiffen its domination.' (*The Wretched of the Earth*, p. 144).

35. For an approach to the Kenyan situation along these lines see J. J. Okumu, 'The Socio-Political Setting', in G. Hyden, R. Jackson and J. J. Okumu (eds), *Development Administration; The Kenyan Experience* (Oxford University Press, Nairobi 1970), p. 41.

36. Ndegwa Report, p. 14; cf. Senator Plunkitt: 'There's an honest graft and I'm an example of how it works. I might sum up the whole thing by sayin': "I seen my opportunities and I took 'em" '. *Plunkitt of Tammany Hall*, recorded by William L. Riordan (McClure, Phillips, New York 1905), pp. 3–4.

was to enable the higher bureaucracy to constitute themselves as a 'fraction' of the bourgeoisie. For what the bureaucrat needs is income which can be obtained without leaving his bureau; and although there are always borderline cases the main aim of the bureaucrat must be to draw rent rather than look for profits.

This is why house-ownership was so important for the higher bureaucracy in the 1960s. It suited the salaried official because it did not involve any enterprise. From 1964 onwards there was an intense demand for real estate of all kinds in Nairobi, mainly as a result of the private foreign-investment boom. Property was reckoned at this time to yield 18 per cent per annum after tax, so that the capital outlay could be recovered in just over five years. Foreign missions and companies preferred not to own property, partly for political reasons, and were willing to pay extremely high rents, sometimes in the form of several years' advance payment on a lease. The civil servant, and to only a very slightly lesser extent, the executive of a large foreign company, was regarded as a good risk by the lending institutions, which in any case had the security of the property itself. Credit for house purchase therefore expanded dramatically. Between 1966 and 1970, the Housing Finance Company of Kenya (HFCK) lent £2·3 million for middle-class housing, at a special rate for citizens of $8\frac{1}{2}$ per cent; over 50 per cent of the borrowers were civil servants or officials of parastatal bodies.[37] Other building societies lent perhaps a further £1 million for the same purpose; insurance companies had also lent some £2·6 million to private households by 1968, most of it for house purchase. Lending to private households by the commercial banks rose to nearly £8 million by the end of 1970;[38] it is not known what proportion of this was lent on real estate, but perhaps a substantial part. It was significant that the HFCK found that loans tended to be repaid at a faster rate than expected; this was because borrowers typically let the house, paid off the loan as quickly as possible out of the difference between their repayment commitment and the rent charged, and then took a new loan on a second house. Highly placed officials found that they could get HFCK mortgages of up to 90 per cent of the cost of a house, and in addition borrow some of the remaining 10 per cent from the banks.[39]

---

37. Interview with the General Manager of the HFCK, July 1971.
38. Central Bank of Kenya, *Economic and Financial Review*, Vol. IV, No. 2, October–December 1971, p. 16.
39. Thus the Vice President, defending two Permanent Secretaries against a parlia-

Obviously not all the new rentiers were bureaucrats, and certainly not all bureaucrats, even in the most senior cadres, were rentiers. Farming was also a favoured line of activity for them; there was a precedent established by the colonial administration, which had allowed British administrators to buy farms of up to 50 acres while still serving in Kenya, and it was a sphere in which management could be devolved on to a paid manager, and where loan funds were also available to senior officials. In the nature of the case there are no statistics on the question; but it does seem likely that there was a fairly clear distinction between the private interests of the salariat and those of other 'middle-class' Kenyans in the 1960s, with the salariat predominantly involved in urban real estate and to a much lesser extent in activities calling for enterprise and management.

But in any case, although the evidence is mainly impressionistic, I think that the higher bureaucracy had by this time formed a definite conception of themselves, based on their professional function, and distinct from that of the entrepreneurial bourgeoisie. They did not on the whole see themselves as 'businessmen' or future businessmen. It was clear to them that 'modern' means of production were corporately owned, and that the important question was who controlled and staffed the corporations, and what relationship existed between them and the state. Working with expatriate experts and managers, senior officials and senior African company executives found themselves in effect collaborating in the framing of policies and in taking decisions which day by day defined more and more clearly the relations between the different modes of production in Kenya, and their own increasingly pivotal function in these relations. This is not to say that all the higher bureaucracy shared a single, comprehensive view of their situation, let alone one free from illusions. But there was a lot of recognized common ground, and as time passed their particular experiences gradually fused into a more general collective consciousness.

The decision at the end of the decade to appoint a commission

---

mentary attack for corruption, explained how the houses they had bought, worth £15,000 and £10,000 respectively, were acquired: 'The documents show clearly that the money was obtained from financial institutions to buy properties. They also received credit facilities from commercial banks or deposited their life policies against such credit and also used their personal savings . . . Credit facilities from these financial institutions are available to anyone, provided that the requirements of the financial institutions are met.' (*EAS*, 30 May 1969).

of inquiry into the structure and remuneration of the public service (the Ndegwa Commission) threw some light on all this.

For one thing, it brought out the great importance of the private sector as a 'reference group' for higher civil servants, both as a model of 'efficiency' and as an index of the 'market' rates of pay for administrative talent. The widespread feeling that the public service and the private-sector bureaucracy had fundamentally common tasks and interests was well expressed in the composition of the commission itself, which was drawn predominantly from the private sector, mainly from senior executives of multi-national companies, under the chairmanship of the Governor of the Central Bank.[40] And the submissions made to the commission by civil servants at its hearing were notable for their constant repetition of a single theme, namely that unless civil servants were paid as much as private-sector personnel, they would join the private sector. The Senior Civil Servants' Association summed up all of them when it said: 'If civil servant salaries do not keep in line with those in the private sector, the result will be that the Government will be unable to retain the services of its qualified and experienced staff who would drift away from their posts, and the country as a whole would suffer.'

One submission, however, was concerned with wider issues, and deserves to be quoted for the glimpse it affords of the sort of ideas which animated a minority, but an energetic and powerful one, among the highest ranks of the civil service. Kenya's future, it said, must be seen in part as that of a 'service Centre':

> We are too concerned with Trade Licensing and all that. . . . The Treasury must be staffed by personnel of sufficiently high calibre who can think on broader economic horizons. Commerce and Industry must also have capable officers who are bereft of narrow commercial or industrial interests. . . . The City of Nairobi has now achieved the status of an international centre and its future planned development must be approached in that light. . . . We must not spare our efforts in keeping Nairobi facilities etc. well above those of Johannesburg, our only competitor in this part of the world . . .

---

40. The chairman was a former Head of the civil service, and one of the members was a former Head of the civil service of Tanzania, and now a company director. Two members were senior executives of BAT and Shell. The only non-African was a banker. The remaining two members were drawn from East African Railways and the University of Nairobi.

The writer urged the necessity of providing theatres and concert halls to attract international orchestras and ballet companies:

> By provision of suitable facilities we can force ourselves into the circuit. . . . We should deliberately set out and marshal all our efforts in order to obtain the maximum possible amount of scarce world resources. Nairobi offers all necessary advantages for industry, we can at a stroke convert it into a major industrial centre in the East and Central Africa region.

In this scenario, Kenya was destined for continued and dramatic growth as a regional centre for international capital, and the task of the higher bureaucracy was to plan and facilitate this process, acting partly through general policy, partly through statutory boards, and partly through direct partnership with foreign companies. For this it should be paid something near the 'international market rate'.

Whatever else may be said about this it is not the ideology of 'a greedy little caste, avid and voracious, with the mind of a huckster, only too glad to accept the dividends that the former colonial power hands out to it . . . incapable of great ideas of inventiveness'.[41] This might or might not be fair to the petty-bourgeoisie, but what we have here is a glimpse of something much more self-confident and ambitious, with a clear consciousness of mission: the image of a bureaucratic *corps d'élite* controlling and dramatically expanding the 'modern sector' in partnership with Western capital. The vision is chauvinist ('obtain the maximum possible amount of scarce world resources') and elitist; the peasants and workers, the great mass of the ordinary people, barely figure in the scenario, let alone as its central participants. They are at most the presumed ultimate beneficiaries of the dramatic changes to be wrought at the 'centre' by their educated sons.

This was, to repeat, only one view among many. In the outlook of other senior bureaucrats, as well as of politicians, the peasantry featured more centrally, though nearly always as objects of policy, not subjects, as in the rhetoric of 'rural development', 'African socialism', etc. The higher bureaucracy mediated between the capitalist and peasant modes of production in the political and economic tradition in which it had been trained.

41. Frantz Fanon, *The Wretched of the Earth*, op. cit. (see note 3 to Chapter 5), p. 141.

Few senior officials saw any discrepancy between the aims of official economic policy, their own social and economic position, and the interests of the majority in the countryside and in the towns. They believed that the government they served was, within limits, popularly chosen; at any rate no more popular alternative was available. They also considered that it was genuinely benevolent in intention, if not always in practice; it was not unconcerned about poverty, lack of opportunity, and similar problems, and it permitted civil servants a good deal of freedom in formulating programmes for productive investment and for providing social services.

This apparent harmony of aims, interests and functions was reinforced by the closeness of senior public servants – and Kenyan executives in foreign-owned companies – to their extended families in the countryside, a bond not yet too seriously weakened by social distance. All this did not mean that the Kenyan bureaucracy fulfilled less of a 'comprador' function than in other parts of the third world; it meant only that this was perhaps less apparent, both to them and to the peasants and workers.

'TRIBALISM'

So far nothing has been said about 'tribalism'. It is tempting to leave it that way. The fact that 'tribalism' is still explicitly or implicitly treated by so many observers as a mysterious independent force in African politics strongly suggests its ideological function. In the past people frankly declared that Negroes had smaller brains. Today it is said more cautiously what bedevils the African scene is the Africans' inveterate attachment to 'primordial sentiments'. And since 'tribalism' is such a pervasive phenomenon of political life in most African countries it does call for considerable self-denial on the part of most outside observers not to explain almost anything in terms of it.

However, to avoid misunderstanding, the way 'tribalism' was related to the economic and social structure of Kenya in the 1960s can be briefly indicated.[42] Kenya, like virtually all African states,

---

42. Among Africanists the main point of this section perhaps no longer needs arguing. For recent formulations of it see A. Mafeje, 'The Ideology of "Tribalism" ', *Journal of Modern African Studies*, Vol. 9, No. 2, August 1971, pp. 253–61; also Joan Vincent, *African Elite: The Big Men of a Small Town* (Columbia University Press, New York 1971); and R. L. Sklar, 'Political Science and National Integration' *Journal of Modern African Studies*, Vol. 5, No. 1, May 1967, pp. 1–11.

comprised a number of different tribes, each with a different homeland and language. The word 'tribalism' does not refer to this fact, however, nor to the natural affinity which individuals feel for those to whom they can talk in their mother tongue, nor the pleasure they get from the landscape, customs, food and so forth with which they have been familiar from childhood. It refers to relationships between people from different tribes, and two things are immediately clear about it.

One is that modern 'tribalism' is a creation of colonialism. It has little or nothing to do with pre-colonial relations between tribes. In Kenya by the end of the 1960s, as we shall see later, the main poles of 'tribalism' were the Kikuyu and the Luo. Before colonial rule, however, there was not only no enmity, there was scarcely any relationship at all between Kikuyu and Luo. The traditional 'enemies' of the Kikuyu were the Masai, with whom, however, they also traded and even intermarried.[43] What brought Kikuyu and Luo into relations with each other for the first time was their shared involvement in the colonial economy. The same was true of the relations between the Kikuyu and most other tribes in Kenya other than the kindred Embu and Meru, and to some extent the Kamba. The foundations for modern 'tribalism' were laid when the various tribal modes and relations of production began to be displaced by capitalist ones, giving rise to new forms of insecurity, and obliging people to compete with each other on a national plane for work, land, and ultimately for education and other services seen as necessary for security.

Secondly, 'tribalism' is in the first instance an ideological phenomenon. Essentially it consists in the fact that people identify other exploited people as the source of their insecurity and frustrations, rather than their common exploiters. Of course this does not happen 'spontaneously'. Colonial regimes have played an important part in fostering tribalism by their policy of trying to channel all political and economic dealings between individuals and the state through the medium of 'tribal authorities', and by discriminating in favour of some tribes and against others, especially in their own recruitment policies. And after independence politicians have often played similar roles, putting themselves forward as patrons capable of bringing the maximum benefits to 'their' people, at the expense of other people whose leaders are denounced as 'tribalist' for trying to

---

43. See Marris and Somerset, *The African Businessman* (see note 4), Chapter 2.

do the same; calling for tribal 'unity' and condemning as divisive and almost treasonous anyone who calls attention to the real causes of unemployment, landlessness and insecurity, and who tries to direct popular feeling against those who benefit from it – including themselves.

To put the matter in a nutshell: tribalism is primarily a form of consciousness, like racialism, whereas class is primarily a relation of production, and only under certain historical conditions also a form of consciousness. In neo-colonial Africa class formation and the development of tribalism accompany each other.

To see the mutual relationship of class and tribalism in Kenya more clearly, we have first to recall the way in which the uneven development of capitalism affected the position of the Kikuyu. Already before colonial rule the Kikuyu had been expanding demographically and territorially, and had established themselves as a network of trading communities with complex relations with the Masai to the west and the Kamba to the east. European settlement cut them off from the territories into which they had been expanding westward and forced most of the able-bodied men into wage-labour, reducing the productivity of their homelands to a bare minimum. Kikuyu country was thus the first part of Kenya to experience underdevelopment in its most disruptive form. The other side of the coin, however, was that the Kikuyu were the first to adapt their social structure and their culture to the capitalist mode of production. Besides learning to be wage-labourers, some of the more enterprising Kikuyu also learned to trade with the capitalist sector, in so far as they were allowed to, and their notables quickly learned to turn to commercial advantage the colonial chiefships which they were able to obtain, and laid the foundations of numerous petty-bourgeois family fortunes. As early as 1911 a knowledgeable European observer commented:

> The Kikuyu are excellent workers, and are now to be met with in every part of the dependency, and in almost every trade, while the chiefs have taken to building stone houses in place of their native huts, and riding mules. In my opinion the Kikuyu will ultimately become the most important among the native races of this part of the continent, owing to their greater intelligence, industry and adaptability.[44]

44. John Boyes, *King of the Wa-Kikuyu* (Methuen, London 1911; reprinted by Cass, London 1968), p. 310.

The fact that the Kikuyu developed a proto-nationalist political consciousness in advance of other Kenyan peoples – including the Luo – must also be understood in this light. It is not primarily the loss of land which explains it, however important the issue was in Kikuyu political consciousness and as a focus for all other grievances. The Masai lost more land, and the Giriama lost land which was at least as important to them as the land lost by the Kikuyu was to the Kikuyu, but neither of these peoples produced a nationalist movement. The Kikuyu, on the other hand, were undergoing a profound social transformation from the earliest years of colonial rule, based on an abrupt divorce from their established mode of production, and semi-proletarianization within the capitalist mode, accompanied and accelerated by other factors, not least mission education.

It was these 'positive' features of Kikuyu underdevelopment that provided the basis for Kikuyu nationalism in the 1920s and '30s, and for the spectacular progress of Kikuyu agriculture under the Swynnerton Plan in the late 1950s. Underdevelopment had taken a form which did not wholly destroy the Kikuyu social and economic structure; it transformed and compressed it, like a wound-up coil-spring, which expanded again with tremendous energy when the pressure was finally released at independence. The new opportunities created by the Kenyatta government were not monopolized by Kikuyu, but they were able to take advantage of them out of proportion to their share in the total population. As the most land-hungry people, landless Kikuyu were the chief beneficiaries of the Million Acre Scheme. As the people best able to raise capital, Kikuyu led the way in land purchase, both individually and in land-purchase co-operatives.[45] Kikuyu traders and manufacturers took the lion's share of the ICDC's loans programmes.[46] They were the leading recipients in the first Development Plan's smallholder credit schemes, and thanks to their massive lead in school provision, they also occupied a

---

45. No reliable data exist on the tribes of individual purchasers, but for farm-purchase co-operatives there is Newiger's 1965 survey ('Co-operative Farming in the former Scheduled Areas of Kenya', cited above, p. 85). Out of 162 co-operatives on which he obtained information on the members' tribes 120 were exclusively Kikuyu in composition, and a further 38 consisted of Kikuyu with members of other tribes. The great majority had of course not yet bought farms, and many never would; the point is that the Kikuyu dominated the effort to do so by this means.

46. Marris and Somerset, *The African Businessman* (see note 4), p. 71: 64 per cent of industrial loans and 44 per cent of commercial loans down to April 1966 went to Kikuyu recipients.

disproportionate share of higher-level civil-service jobs.[47] They naturally also predominated in the city of Nairobi, which in so far as it was a home for anyone, was a home city for the Kikuyu; and this also meant that they had an exceptionally large share of private wage-employment, since over 50 per cent of this was con-centrated in Nairobi.[48]

There was also the fact that the small-scale Kikuyu traders, transporters and the like were much more successful than those of other tribes in advancing into the protected state-regulated commercial sector, thanks to their longer experience of trade, their capital accumulated from coffee farming since the late 1950s, and the superior access to government credit, licences, contracts and so on which the position of Kikuyu leaders in the government gave them. As a result, by the end of the 1960s the new African 'auxiliary bourgeoisie' was predominantly Kikuyu in composition. Since African traders tended to offer jobs to people from their own tribe, this further extended the field of wage-employment for Kikuyu as opposed to people from other tribes. Kikuyu shop-keepers also increasingly dominated trade in the Rift Valley townships, which also passed more and more under the control of Kikuyu politicians, while Kikuyu groups and individuals were moving in steadily growing numbers on to the former European farms round about.

In effect, the process of *internal* underdevelopment, which had operated to transfer surplus from Africans in general, and the Kikuyu in particular, to the European settlers in the highlands,

---

47. Chaput and Venys, in 'A Survey of the Kenya Elite', Occasional Paper No. 25 (Syracuse University Program of Eastern African Studies, May 1967, mimeo). In 1962 56 per cent of the Kikuyu primary-school age-group had some schooling, compared with only 38 per cent of the Luo, 34 per cent of the Luhya, and 21 per cent of the Kamba. More important, there were 645 Kikuyu with over thirteen years of education; comparable figures for other groups were Luo, 205; Luhya, 329; Kamba, 214; Kisii, 332 (see Dirk Berg-Schlosser, *The Distribution of Income and Education in Kenya*, IFO Institut für Wirtschaftsforschung, Munich 1970, p. 40). By 1968 things had moved on. In North Tetu Division of Nyeri District in Kikuyu country 125 per cent of the primary-school age-group were in primary schools: i.e, the whole age-group plus a further group who were repeating, usually their final year, in the hope of improving their final marks and getting into a secondary school (Heyer, Ireri and Moris, 'Rural Development in Kenya', p. 78, see table 6.3). The closest figure to this in the Rural Development Survey was from Yatta Division in Machakos (Kamba country), with 89 per cent. Nyeri District also had nearly twice as many passes in the Ordinary Level secondary-school certificate as any of the other thirteen districts surveyed.

48. Moreover, Nairobi accounted for two-thirds of the urban wage-bill, so that the Kikuyu share of the benefits of urban employment was enhanced.

now began to operate in favour of some of those who had been its chief victims. And unlike the settlers, with their largely static enclave of about 3,000 families, the number of Kikuyu with commercial experience and some capital was already many times larger and was expanding rapidly.

This background is necessary for an understanding of the development of 'tribalism' in Kenya. Had the new petty-bourgeois and auxiliary bourgeois strata which developed before and after independence been drawn proportionately from all the tribes, 'tribalism' would surely still have developed also, as the petty-bourgeois elements from the different tribes sought support among the masses in their competition for licences, contracts, and so on, and as their clients sought their assistance in their efforts to find jobs. The form of consciousness which could embrace both these interests, and conceal the real conflict between them, was one which pictured all the people of each tribe as having a common grievance against all the people of other tribes. But in these circumstances 'tribalism' would not have had its most striking characteristic, namely that it was almost wholly a consciousness of being either Kikuyu or not Kikuyu; in the endless charges and accusations, however veiled, that were made more and more openly from the mid-1960s onwards, we do not find Luo (for instance) much concerned with Luhya or with Masai, or vice versa, but virtually exclusively with Kikuyu.

In the light of all this the issue around which 'tribalism' was first openly articulated in the 1960s is not surprising: the distribution of white-collar jobs. The reason for this is also fairly obvious. During the 1960s secondary school enrolments increased sixfold. White-collar employment for Africans also increased rapidly at first, as a result of Africanization, but from about 1965 onwards the dramatic increase from this source was largely over. Manufacturing employment rose very slowly (by only 12,000 jobs from 1964 to 1970) and although total public-sector employment rose by 66,000 over the same period the number of *white-collar* jobs becoming available each year fell further and further below the demand from school leavers. It began to be hard for MPs and local patrons to place their clients in jobs. Accusations of tribalism began to be more and more frequently made in parliament, at first mainly in relation to salaried jobs, but gradually extending to jobs in general. What was at stake was the ability of the educated to make good their claims to be benefactors. They discovered that tribal recruitment-patterns built up under colonial rule meant that large areas of patronage – whole departments and firms – were in effect reserved to the patrons of particular tribes.[49] The adoption of 'tribalism' as an ideology among parliamentarians can be fairly clearly traced in the debates of this time. By the end of the 1960s it had been effectively diffused among the population at large.[50]

As the 1960s progressed politics was increasingly conducted in terms of tribal consciousness. Areas of the country where opposition to the government was strong were threatened and to some extent actually punished with reduced levels of public spending, and loyal areas, including Kikuyu districts, were relatively favoured. 'Tribalism' gradually acquired a new basis in reality as a result, and was certainly itself a very real factor in political and economic life; but this does not make it possible to dispense with a clear view of the way 'tribalism' initially develops out of, and feeds on, the real development of antagonistic classes. The need to keep this point firmly in mind was nowhere better illustrated than in the development of class antagonisms within Kikuyu country, where capitalist relations of production were most widespread, and where class conflict had already come to the surface during the Emergency. In the first three years after independence a major preoccupation of the regime was to conciliate and absorb into the neo-colonial system the 'hard core' of the forest fighters, by means of grants of land, jobs in the Army or National Youth Service, and so on. Subsequently the Kikuyu leaders alternately preached the necessity of forgetting the past

---

49. 'Mr. B. M. Karungaru claimed there was tribalism in East African Airways, the Kenya National Housing Corporation, the Kenya National Trading Corporation, and other bodies. He was asked by the Minister for Power and Communications to substantiate his reference to E.A.A. and replied: "It is a monopoly of Abaluyias".' *EAS*, 30 May 1970. For an extract from a 1966 debate on this theme see C. Gertzel, M. Goldschmidt and D. Rothchild, *Government and Politics in Kenya* (East African Publishing House, Nairobi 1969), pp. 41–51.

50. For an interesting discussion of tribalism by a group of school-leavers see K. J. King's forthcoming, *Jobless in Kenya: The Social Life of the Educated Unemployed*: I am grateful to Dr King for an opportunity to read his study in manuscript. By the end of the 1960s the issue of land in the Rift Valley had also become a focus for 'tribalism', in this case between the Kikuyu and the Kalenjin. As will be seen in the following chapter, this issue had been a major one in the years just before independence, and was perhaps the main basis of the division between the African parties, KANU and KADU. Nothing illustrates better the ideological nature of tribalism than the fact that when the Kalenjin leaders of KADU threw in their lot with the Kikuyu leaders of KANU at the end of 1964 this issue, and the 'tribalism' associated with it, disappeared for several years although the Kikuyu occupation of the Rift Valley proceeded steadily (see Chapter 7, pp. 228–30).

(i.e. the role in the Emergency of those who had collaborated with the colonial forces) and (on the other hand) tried to claim the legitimate succession to the martyred leaders of the forest fighters.[51] (One of the many ironies of the situation was that after 1966 Kenyatta was one of the few senior members of the government who could claim any connection with the forest fighters, and that thanks mainly to the determination of the colonial administration and a colonial judge to implicate him in the 'management' of Mau Mau.)[52]

But laying the ghosts of the 1950s could not exorcise the new spectres which were arising in the 1960s.[53] The Kikuyu bourgeoisie were well aware that many of their special advantages depended on their political dominance within the state apparatus. So long as enough of the Kikuyu masses believed that this was also of prime importance to them, appeals to tribal solidarity would serve the double purpose of reinforcing the Kikuyu leadership's position at the centre, and repelling challenges based on class antagonism within Kikuyu society. At a lower level, following the same logic, local Kikuyu politicians mobilized feeling in Murang'a

---

51. In June 1969 Kibaki, Mungai and two other Kikuyu MPs, Mr Gatuguta and Mr Karunguru, led a remembrance service for those who 'fought and laboured for the freedom of Kenya'. The KPU leader Oneko attacked this as hypocritical, saying that when as an ex-detainee he had in the past tried to organize a 'get-together' of 'old colleagues in the freedom movement' he had been accused of opening old wounds, and was told that people were being asked to forget the past (*D.N*, 23 and 24 June 1969). In October 1972, on the other hand, the speaker of the National Assembly ruled that members should not refer to the fact that anyone had been a Home Guard (i.e. on the government side in the Emergency), saying that this was 'reminding people of things they would rather forget'.

52. The one remaining Cabinet minister who had been detained was Paul Ngei, the Kamba leader. On Kenyatta's actual relation to the organizers of Mau Mau see F. Furedi, 'The African Crowd in Nairobi: Popular Movements and Elite Politics', *Journal of African History*, Vol. XIV, No. 2, 1973, p. 286.

53. The fact that reliable data on stratification in Kikuyu country barely exist, nearly twenty years after the Swynnerton Plan got under way and Kikuyu country became the 'cutting edge' of social and economic change in Kenya, is an interesting comment on the social-science research done in Kenya during this time. Examples of recent work which has begun to repair this omission are: J. Gatanyu Karuga, 'Thresholds in the transformation of a rural economy; some preliminary thoughts on the structure of the Nairobi–Kiambu peri-urban zone: the case of Kiambaa location', paper read at a Workshop on Strategies for Improving Rural Welfare, Nairobi 1971, mimeo; M. P. Cowen, 'Differentiation in a Kenya Location', paper presented to the East African Universities Social Science Council Conference, Nairobi 1972, mimeo; and G. B. Lamb, 'Peasants, Capitalists and Agricultural Development in Kenya', paper presented to the 8th Conference of the East African Universities Social Science Council, Nairobi 1972, mimeo; also his *Peasant Politics: Conflict and Development in Murang'a* (Friedmann, London 1974).

or Nyeri against Kiambu, or in one location or clan against others. This kind of manipulation was naturally subject to delicate rules and took some extremely complex forms, such as the so-called KANU 'A' and KANU 'B' factions (which had area, generational and ideological connotations special to the Kikuyu), the formation of GEMA (the Gikuyu, Embu and Meru Association) in 1971, and so on.[54] What is not difficult to see is that all this was essentially mystification; the conflicts which were articulated and manipulated in these terms could not in fact be resolved by the sort of things which these ideologies appeared to call for, such as reducing the share of Kiambu leaders in ministerial posts, lowering the age of KANU office-bearers, redistributing government services or patronage within Central Province, and so on. The real effect of such conceptions was (a) to assist aspiring politicians to gain admission to the comprador circle by mobilizing local support; and (b) to pre-empt the articulation of ideas directed against the educated, propertied and privileged strata of Kikuyu society.

In this way class antagonisms – between farm labourers and their employers, between customers and shopkeepers, and in general between the mass of extremely poor families and the richer farmers, businessmen and salaried officials – were largely displaced or diverted into tribal or clan forms of consciousness; and the more acute the contradictions between their interests became, the more marked was tribal or clan sentiment likely to become. In Kenyan conditions, tribalism was a natural form of consciousness through which the antagonism between exploiters and exploited was partly expressed and partly concealed.

This does not mean that it was deliberately fostered by the bourgeoisie to divert attention from the consolidation of their interests. The speeches of Kenyatta and many of his ministers make it clear that they believed that they were working in the interests of 'the people'. They really wished that people would stop 'thinking tribally', and were quite sincere in constantly calling on them to do so, at the same time that they were consolidating an economic system in which tribal identity and kinship increasingly provided the individual with his only hope of economic opportunity, or even survival.

---

54. At the divisional and locational level religious allegiances often formed poles of political mobilization, often around competing 'self-help' projects for schools, dispensaries, etc., organized by the Independent Church, the Presbyterian Church, and so on.

CHAPTER 7

The Politics of Neo-colonialism

What kind of politics could be founded on an economic and social system of the kind we have been considering? The harmony of interest between foreign capital, the local auxiliary bourgeoisie and the various politically powerful petty-bourgeois strata was a real one, yet their interests also conflicted, and a government based on an alliance between them had to be capable of arbitrating between them. It also had to be strong enough to master the tensions and conflicts generated among the mass of the people by the process of underdevelopment, including those which were expressed in regional or tribal terms. But being strong in this sense meant that the government was heavily dependent on the civil service, police and armed forces, and on the personal popularity of the President. This dependency could be offset by making concessions first to one element in the ruling alliance and then to another, and also when necessary to elements outside it; this, however, involved a succession of somewhat contradictory measures, and had evident limits.

There is a great deal in this situation which recalls Marx's analysis of French politics in 1850 (in *The Eighteenth Brumaire of Louis Bonaparte*), and it is worth considering why. The basic contradiction in Louis Napoleon's situation, Marx saw, was that the government, the state apparatus, was independent of any single class, yet in practice it could not do without class support, and could not prevent its policies fostering the interests of certain classes, even if it wished to. Yet this enhanced the political power of these classes, and so undermined its own independence of action; therefore it also worked constantly to counteract the political power of the classes whose economic power it was simultaneously building up.

> As the executive authority which has made itself an independent power, Bonaparte feels it to be his mission to safe-

guard 'bourgeois order'. But the strength of this bourgeois order lies in the middle class. He looks on himself, therefore, as the representative of the middle class and issues decrees in this sense. Nevertheless, he is somebody solely due to the fact that he has broken the political power of this middle class and daily breaks it anew. Consequently, he looks on himself as the adversary of the political and literary power of the middle class. But by protecting its material power, he generates its political power anew. The cause must accordingly be kept alive: but the effect, where it manifests itself, must be done away with. But this cannot pass off without slight confusions of cause and effect, since in their interaction both lose their distinguishing features. New decrees that obliterate the border line. As against the bourgeoisie, Bonaparte looks on himself, at the same time, as the representative of the peasants and of the people in general, who wants to make the lower classes of the people happy within the frame of bourgeois society. New decrees that cheat the 'True Socialists' of their statecraft in advance. . .

This contradictory task of the man explains the contradictions of his government, the confused groping about which seeks now to win, now to humiliate first one class and then another . . .[1]

Of course the parallel with Kenya is not exact. The 'middle class' whose interests the Kenyan government wished to defend, yet whose power it had theoretically broken, was largely a foreign one. Its real economic and political power lay abroad. The foreign middle class had to be done with great circumspection, if new foreign capital was not to be frightened away, i.e. it had to be only *ritually* 'humiliated', while practically wooed. Hence the development of a rhetoric of economic nationalism to complement the earlier political nationalism of the ruling élite, coupled in practice with the elaboration of a system of partnership with foreign capital ('new decrees that obliterate the border line') which actually implied a steady expansion of foreign ownership of modern productive assets in Kenya, and thus of the political power of foreign capital. The populist rhetoric of bonapartist government was even more pronounced in Kenya than it had been in France ('African Socialism', 'rural development', and so on), but in very similar fashion the political power of the peasants and urban workers was progressively curtailed and neutralized.

---

1. Marx and Engels, *Selected Works* (Foreign Languages Publishing House, Moscow 1962), Vol. I, pp. 340–41.

As is well known, Marx also considered that a smallholding peasantry constituted a natural basis for centralized, authoritarian government:

> By its very nature, small-holding property forms a suitable basis for an all-powerful and innumerable bureaucracy. It creates a uniform level of relationships and persons over the whole surface of the land. Hence it also permits of uniform action from a supreme centre on all points of this uniform mass . . .

> Finally, it produces an unemployed surplus population for which there is no place either on the land or in the towns, and which accordingly reaches out for state offices as a sort of respectable alms, and provokes the creation of state posts.[2]

The expansion of the bureaucracy was not only an answer to the problem of unemployment, it also provided a power base for the regime, which would help it to stay in power without relying too closely on any particular class or group of classes:

> And an enormous bureaucracy, well-gallooned and well-fed, is the 'idée napolienne' which is most congenial of all to the second Bonaparte. How could it be otherwise, seeing that alongside the actual classes of society he is forced to create an artificial caste, for which the maintenance of his regime becomes a bread-and-butter question?

And so on. It is no accident that Marx's discussion of the situation in France in 1850 is so full of clues to the situation in most of sub-saharan Africa in the 1960s. In spite of obvious fundamental differences the two situations have something fundamental in common: a complex and fluid class structure corresponding to the still incompletely evolved interrelationship of the capitalist and non-capitalist modes of production.

Yet it is remarkable how seldom Marx's analysis has been applied to Africa.[3] Perhaps this is due once again to a slightly uncritical acceptance of Fanon's ideas. Fanon focused his attention primarily on the educated strata who were brought into being under colonialism and who inherited state power at independence. The essence of this 'bourgeoisie of the civil service',

---

2. ibid., p. 338.

3. But it has been applied to Pakistan and Bangladesh by Hamza Alavi in 'The State in Post-Colonial Societies: Pakistan and Bangladesh', *New Left Review* 74, July–August 1972, pp. 59–81.

according to Fanon, is that it is weak, financially and therefore politically. It therefore sets about using the state machinery to make itself rich by inserting itself as a sort of commission agent into the foreign-dominated commercial system. There are never quite enough spoils to go round, and the weakness of the new would-be bourgeoisie reveals itself in all sorts of conflicts, which constantly threaten to engulf the rest of society as individuals seek to enlist ethnic and regional support on behalf of their interests. To avoid this the 'national bourgeoisie' discovers the need for 'a popular leader to whom will fall the dual role of stabilizing the regime and of perpetuating the domination of the bourgeoisie'.[4]

His strength in this role is necessarily in inverse proportion to that of representative or popular government. The institutions of the state are progressively reduced to those of the President and his circle. The party becomes a mere shell, and actually 'an implement of coercion'. The leading posts in the bureaucracy are entrusted to men from the leader's tribe, 'sometimes directly from his own family'.[5] Parliament becomes little more than an adjunct of the Presidency where a legislative veneer is fitted over the wishes of the autocracy in return for high salaries and some licence to ventilate popular sentiments (though not, of course, sentiments critical of the President). Parliamentary elections are reduced merely to a choice between individuals, all of whom are pledged to support the President and his government; elections 'circulate the élite', contribute to the mystification of the voters, and thus help to preserve the élite's freedom to go on enriching itself without interference from below. With the passing of elections, this function is performed by a series of military coups.

Although Fanon's analysis is much more plausible than most conventional interpretations we should not be carried away by it. What it really does is to explain 'strong man' government in post-colonial Africa in terms of the needs of the local petty-bourgeoisie and would-be bourgeoisie (who tend to be conflated with the civil service in Fanon's writing) for such a style of government.[6] This leaves a lot unexplained. For one thing, it does not explain why some such leaders survive while others are displaced. The picture Fanon paints is one of antagonistic contradiction between the 'national bourgeoisie', under the protection

---

4. Frantz Fanon, *The Wretched of the Earth* (see note 3 to Chapter 5), p. 133.

5. ibid., p. 147.

6. See Chapter 6, p. 193.

of the leader, and the exploited masses (primarily peasants), leading in due course to revolutionary confrontation. This has some validity, but in a rather abstract and certainly long-run sense. Since Fanon wrote, the course of African politics has clearly indicated the need for more detailed and more complex models. Secondly, it is like the prevailing bourgeois analyses in one respect: in spite of Fanon's obsession with colonialism, his discussion of post-colonial politics omits the neo-colonial factor almost entirely. Foreign capital figures only as an unanalysed exploiting presence which can be turned to the selfish advantage of the 'national bourgeoisie'. Its evolving interests and institutional forms are left out of account, which is certainly Hamlet without the Prince of Denmark. Third, and not least important, is Fanon's conception of the relation between the leader and the 'national bourgeoisie' itself. The leader is seen as a mere agent of the self-enriching bourgeoisie, 'the general president of that company of profiteers impatient for their returns'.[7]

By contrast, Marx's analysis of bonapartism starts out from the essential fact that in this situation the leader is not the agent of any one class, but enjoys a measure of independence. Marx sees this independence as in the long run rather illusory, partly because the leader cannot in reality be 'the patriarchal benefactor of all classes' as he would like, and finds that he 'cannot give to one class without taking from another'; but even more because the development of the capitalist mode of production was steadily eroding the position of the pre-capitalist classes in France, so that the balancing-act of bonapartism would eventually be bound to give way to the solid weight of bourgeois domination. In the conditions of underdevelopment, however, only the first of these two limitations (the impossibility of benefiting all classes alike) necessarily operates, and the independence of the government therefore seems even more significant. What was for Marx a purely transitional and relatively short-term phenomenon may become, in some circumstances, a generic form of government at the capitalist periphery; and the content of bonapartist rule reflects the complexity of the contradictions involved, as well as the increasing difficulty of integrating them and of relying on class hegemony rather than force.

In other words, Fanon's model has the merit of seeing political

---

7. ibid., p. 133.

212 UNDERDEVELOPMENT IN KENYA

·· life in post-colonial Africa without illusions; what he describes is
a lot closer to reality than accounts which assume that the
political institutions of bourgeois society – parliament, cabinet,
even the popular party – have much bearing on what is going on.
On the other hand his model was formulated in 1961, before the
complexity of the emerging class structure of the African states,
and the changing role of international private capital, were
apparent as they are today. The analysis of Kenyan politics must
try to take these things into account, and also consider the significance of the use actually made by Kenyatta's government of the
measure of autonomy which it enjoyed.

THE BASES OF PARTY CONFLICT

As Chapter 2 has already suggested, the basic political cleavage
in Kenyan politics at independence, which corresponded to the
basic contradiction of colonialism, was between the groups and
social strata which bore the brunt of exploitation – the mass of
unskilled workers and peasant farmers – and those which in one
way or another acquired a material interest in the continuation
of the colonial economy. This was very clearly revealed immediately after independence in the way the opposition between
KANU and KADU was suddenly and painlessly dissolved and
replaced by a much more irreconcileable and lasting opposition
between the 'comprador' leaders˜of both KANU and KADU on
the one hand, and a group of 'radicals' within KANU on the
other.

KANU and KADU were both formed in 1960 when national
political parties were legalized for the first time since the declaration of the Emergency in 1952.[8] KANU was a party of the
'notables' of the Kikuyu (with their closely related neighbours,
the Embu and Meru), the Luo, and the Kamba. KADU was a
grouping of the notables of the Kalenjin peoples of the Rift
Valley and of some of the neighbouring Luhya; of the Masai; of
the Taita; and of the various peoples of the Coast. Although the
latter tribes were less numerous they had more land and livestock,

---

8. For the events summarized in this and subsequent paragraphs see G. Bennett and
C. G. Rosberg, *The Kenyatta Election: Kenya 1960–61* (Oxford University Press,
London 1961), Ch. 2; J. C. Nottingham and C. G. Rosberg, *The Myth of Mau Mau*
(Pall Mall Press, London 1966); and C. J. Gertzel, *The Politics of Independent Kenya*
(Heinemann, London and East African Publishing House, Nairobi 1968).

but less education, and less experience of wage-labour, cash-crop agriculture, or trade, than those whose leaders formed KANU.

Originally the African members of the colonial Legislative Council who formed KANU had intended it to be a single nationwide party. The main reason why Ngala, Towett, Muliro, Moi and the other KADU leaders eventually decided to form a separate party was that they thought they could drive a better bargain for themselves and their supporters in this way. They were also urged by some European politicians to form a separate party with which the Europeans could collaborate, and with which they might even hope to form a coalition government at independence. KADU received substantial European assistance in its early days, and there is no doubt that KADU's subsequent demand for 'regionalism' – the division of the country into regions corresponding to the main tribal groupings and enjoying a substantial measure of constitutionally entrenched self-government – was formulated jointly by the leaders of KADU and some members of the New Kenya Group. This strategy was adopted, however, only when a general election held early in 1961 had shown that KANU had too large an electoral majority for a KADU–NKG coalition government to be feasible.

The British government supported the demand for regionalism, and in 1962 obliged the KANU leaders to accept it as the price of getting a date fixed for a fresh general election. In this election there would be no racially reserved seats, and the KANU leaders therefore hoped to demonstrate their overwhelming electoral support and to capture a large majority of seats in the new parliament; they reasoned that once in power after independence, they would not find it too hard to change even the entrenched regionalist provisions of the constitution. The election was held in May 1963, and KANU won an overwhelming majority of the votes and of the lower-house seats. Independence was formally achieved in December.

A year later, in December 1964, regionalism was abolished. The KADU leaders not only did not resist this, but agreed to disband their party in return for seats in Kenyatta's cabinet. It soon became clear that the KADU politicians were divided from most of the KANU politicians by very little, compared with what divided them both from the 'radicals' within KANU. Within a short space of time the ex-KADU leaders were playing a leading part in a struggle within KANU as a result of which the 'radicals' were removed from positions of authority within the party, and

214 UNDERDEVELOPMENT IN KENYA

ultimately from Parliament. The fact was that the tribes from which the KADU leaders came were those least involved in either wage-labour or cash-crop production; and the KADU leaders had been attractive to the European politicians precisely because of their strong commitment to private property, above all because of the relative abundance of land in their areas, and their fears that KANU might try to take it away, under the pretext of 'national-ization', and distribute it to landless people from other tribes. They discovered, however, that this was not the intention of most KANU politicians. On the contrary, most of these were interested in becoming large landowners and were as anxious as anyone to ensure that landed property, and in fact private property in all its forms, would not be threatened. There *was* a problem about the future of European-held land in the Rift Valley, which the 'KADU tribes' looked on as traditionally theirs; even when it was agreed that it would be for sale and not for distribution by the government, the fact remained that many more Kikuyu indi-viduals and groups than Kalenjin could afford to buy it. But although this was to cause some embarrassment to the ex-KADU leaders, the convergence of interest between themselves and their Kikuyu, Kamba and other colleagues in the cabinet was not threatened.

The conflict between all of these and a minority of 'radicals' in KANU was by contrast a deep one. The two main issues around which the conflict crystallized immediately after independence show why. One was land for the landless: especially former squatters, or labourers on European farms, displaced by settle-ment schemes, and ex-detainees or their dependants who had never had land, or who claimed to have been deprived of their holdings in the process of land consolidation. The other was free education. Taken together, these two issues represented the central question of whether the independence settlement would provide security and equality of opportunity for the masses or not. Free education had been promised in KANU's 1963 election manifesto. Land for the landless was not promised in the mani-festo, which already reflected the critical decisions made about land eighteen months previously, but it was regarded by some as a commitment of honour, and especially by some of the Kikuyu leaders most identified with the forest fighters. These men were well aware of the class nature of much of the struggle on the edge of the forests, and as often as Kenyatta called on people to forgive and forget, they reminded their listeners of the country's debt to the forest fighters and the need to create an equal society worthy of their sacrifices.[9]

A significant group of the 'radicals' came from the trade-union movement. J. D. Kali and Bildad Kaggia had both worked with Kubai in the early 1950s, when a union-based group of Nairobi nationalists had tried to 'take over' KAU. Denis Akumu and O. O. Mak'anyengo were younger men, both from the historically militant and predominantly Luo dockworkers' union. Others reflected the problems of landlessness and insecurity in the countryside. This was certainly true of Kaggia, whose following was among squatters and labourers in the Rift Valley and among the landless and smaller landholders in his home area in Murang'a district, which had been a particularly bad case of malpractice in the process of land-consolidation and registration. More generally, the Kikuyu and Luo, besides being the two largest tribes in Kenya (20·7 per cent and 14·1 per cent respectively of the total African population in 1969) had experienced underdevelopment more extensively and for longer than most other tribes, though in different ways: more or less forced labour, the decimation of those conscripted for the East African campaign, restrictions on commodity production and trade and a growing land shortage in many locations. It was natural for the nationalist movement to be largely led by Kikuyu and Luo, and equally natural for some of these leaders to arrive at a socialist position. Their socialism proved to be 'petty-bourgeois'. But they were not prepared to accept without a struggle what they saw as the progressive surrender of the interests of the poor peasants and labourers to neo-colonial interests. They protested and tried to mobilize opinion, at first in the cabinet and parliament and later, after they had been forced into opposition, in the country at large. Their opposition was based on principle, and the regime finally felt sufficiently threatened by its appeal to the unemployed, the landless, the low-paid, those rendered homeless by slum clearance, and similar categories, to suppress it completely. The relative ease with which this was done, however, owed a lot to the fact that the confrontation did not become acute until the neo-colonial system had been successfully consolidated.

---

9. For a late expression of this see the foreword by Kaggia, Oneko and Kubai to Kariri Njama's *Mau Mau From Within*, with D. L. Barnett (MacGibbon and Kee, London 1966).

CONSOLIDATING THE NEO-COLONIAL RELATIONSHIP

This process flowed logically enough from the critical political and economic decisions taken just prior to independence, but it was reinforced by the fact that from May 1963 onwards the KANU leaders – including Odinga and Oneko, who were both cabinet ministers – were increasingly engaged in the daily management of the still-colonial state. They proved quick students. Odinga tells in his autobiography how as Minister for Home Affairs he exploited the executive power of the central government to emasculate the 'regional' administrations set up under the independence constitution; it makes rather ironic reading in the light of his subsequent experience of official harassment when he was leader of the KPU.[10] In September 1963 the KANU leaders were also involved in a final round of pre-independence talks in London, which implicitly recognized the British government as having a 'special relationship' with the Kenyan government, which entitled it to a major say in what were now clearly post-independence issues. The main subject of the talks – the continued efforts of the KADU leaders, with settler support, to entrench the 'regionalist' constitution – also served to distract attention away from questions of social or economic reconstruction. Odinga later wrote: 'Some of us were, perhaps, slow to realize that the time when accession to independence was progress in itself has passed. Only the political and economic content of that independence can reveal whether it will have real meaning for the mass of the people.'[11]

While their attention was focused on such questions as the method of amending the constitution and the respective powers of the central and regional governments with regard to the police and civil service commissions, the major economic and social issues were being settled in a series of measures designed to alleviate pressures which flowed from the transition crisis of the colonial economy.

Land hunger, as we have seen, was assuaged by settlement schemes based on land purchase with the aid of a massive loan (not unlike the redemption debt of the Russian serfs after 1861). Unemployment was temporarily eased by the so-called Tripartite

---

10. Oginga Odinga, *Not Yet Uhuru* (Heinemann, London 1967), pp. 242–4.
11. ibid., p. 255.

Agreement adopted in February 1964. This was proposed by
Mboya, who as leader of the Kenya Federation of Labour and as
Minister of Labour had close connections and influence with the
employers in the FKE. It provided that all private employers
should increase their work-force by 10 per cent and the central and
local governments by 15 per cent, in return for the unions' agreement to a twelve-month wage standstill and a ban on strikes. In
this way it was thought that 40,000 jobs would be temporarily
provided, mopping up about half of the currently unemployed
labour force. The political implications were clearly spelled out
by Mboya in a speech to the FKE calling for support for the
agreement:

> There is no question that the ultimate solution lies in a
> growing economy. We have the job of creating an atmosphere
> in which economic growth can take place. . . . If we attempt
> to wait until the economy can absorb them, the existence of a
> large body of unemployed will work against the creation of
> stability. The threat to security and political stability is
> obvious. Farmers [*sic*] all know the grave security problem.
> We cannot deal with this effectively unless we can provide
> alternatives in the form of jobs for the many people roaming
> about in the Rift Valley and squatting illegally on land.[12]

In other words it was clear to Mboya that the particular form
taken by unemployment at the time – the threat of land-grabbing,
leading to a fresh loss of confidence among the remaining white
settlers – jeopardized the whole strategy of effecting the transition
to independence with the colonial economy substantially intact,
and of quickly reversing the outflow of capital. His speech recognized this, and offered the settlers a *quid pro quo* ('Steps will be
taken immediately to deal with illegal squatters') if they would
co-operate by shouldering the short-run burden of a 10 per cent
increase in their work-force. To the non-agricultural employers

---

12. Speech to the General Meeting of the FKE, 6 February 1964, mimeo. The (white)
farmers were particularly important because in the short run it was the run-down
of their farms which had created the biggest loss of employment opportunities,
and it was in the Rift Valley that some former Mau Mau fighters were organizing
the Land Freedom Army, drawing mainly on unemployed and landless Kikuyu.
It was also the white farmers, selling at fixed prices, who would find it hardest to
absorb the extra wage-costs involved in the agreement. A leading member of the
FKE in those days later recalled: 'The farmers had to bear the brunt of the agreement; at the general meeting we didn't know if the farming community would
back us. They backed us most loyally; but we did have some anxious moments.'
(G. C. Clarke, interview, June 1971).

Mboya made it clear that it was the price they had to be prepared to pay for continuing to have a special relationship with the government: in effect, he gave them to understand that they had no choice if they wanted to preserve a protected *private* sector as they understood it: 'Government feels that if the agreement is rejected, the Employers Federation is evading its responsibilities and giving up its right in future to be taken into confidence and to be consulted in whatever Government intends to do.'[13]

The employers understood this, and when the agreement was signed Sir Colin Campbell, the FKE President, spelled out their interpretation of the terms of the bargain. The agreement, he said, would cost the Federation's members some £26 million. In addition,

> We hope very much that the Agreement we have signed today will help the Government to attract a massive inflow of foreign capital and I think it worth making the point that the best encouragement for overseas investors is to see existing industries receiving fair treatment. . . . We hope we have today taken a concrete step to support democratic government in this country. This is an aim we must all support . . .[14]

By 'fair treatment' Sir Colin particularly meant government action to curb what he called 'thuggery and intimidation' by trade-union organizers, and political interference in industrial relations. At the end of February the FKE spelled out what it required from government in this respect, calling for an 'initial operation effectively carried out' against squatters, which 'would have a salutary effect throughout the whole rural area', and also threatening that unless there was prompt action to control 'wildcat strikes' in contravention of the Tripartite Agreement, 'the Federation must very shortly take a standpoint to this problem which may well place the solution of the current unemployment problem in jeopardy'. The statement concluded:

> It is our Federation's submission that the country now stands poised between the alternative of mounting chaos or increasing prosperity. The second can in the Federation's view only be achieved if the Government will demonstrate that it is united in its determination effectively to uphold the law.

13. ibid.
14. Speech on 10 February 1964, FKE files, mimeo.

The word 'united' in this statement (which was contained in a 'Memorandum to the Prime Minister [Kenyatta] via the Minister of Labour') was an oblique reference to the efforts of Kaggia, then a junior minister in the government, to arouse opinion within KANU on behalf of former workers or squatters on settler farms who were being evicted when these farms were sub-divided for settlement schemes. In May Kenyatta gave Kaggia an ultimatum to desist from what he called 'a general criticism against the Government's policy of discouraging illegal squatting on private property', and Kaggia resigned;[15] it was the first step in the process through which the radicals were progressively excluded from political power over the coming two years.

The FKE memorandum did not, of course, bring about the ultimatum to Kaggia. All it did was to remind the government, in some respects explicitly, in others more delicately, of the fact that the bargain that was being elaborated with foreign private capital had its logic, and its price. A year later Sir Colin Campbell's annual report stated that 'the Government's hope of getting the economy moving forward again has been realized', and went on to describe his conception of the basic principles on which, by implication, the Federation and the Government were operating, in general terms which are also worth quoting:

> Every day that passes in Kenya gives evidence of the extension of its property-owning democracy and the increased participation by local people in positions of responsibility. We welcome this and seek to encourage the acceleration of this trend. . . . Imported capital is essential if Kenya's great manpower potential is to be fully exploited and I believe it is in the interests of all Kenyans that a tolerant and welcoming attitude continues to be adopted towards those non-nationals who are ready to devote all or part of their working lives to this country. . . . We greatly appreciate the accessibility of the Minister and his officers when matters of urgency arise. . . . It has been truly said that man is a selfish animal and this is as true of the peasant in his field as it is of the tycoon in his skyscraper. This is an essential truth any Government ignores at the peril of the wellbeing of its people. . . . The alternative is the sterile levelling of the communist world which so far as I can judge means only an equality of misery and stagnation for the majority . . .[16]

---

15. Quoted in Odinga, *Not Yet Uhuru* (see note 10), p. 266.
16. 8 March 1965, FKE files, mimeo.

As Professor Gertzel has pointed out, it was just at this time that allegations by the conservatives in KANU that the radicals were 'Communists' began to reach their peak.[17] The FKE President's final allusion indicates the latitude which local foreign business-men felt the bargain struck the previous year had given them.

But this is to run slightly ahead. Land-settlement schemes and the Tripartite Agreement on unemployment dealt with two short-term threats to the resuscitation of the colonial economy. An active policy was also needed to deal with the flight of capital. This could not be halted by the imposition of exchange control without prejudicing the chance of getting a fresh inflow of new capital, which was what was really wanted. So besides the policy of cultivating close relations with existing foreign business interests, a Foreign Investments Protection Act was also passed in 1964, which assured all foreign investors that their assets would not be expropriated and that they could remit their capital and profits freely. This helped to bring about the improvement which did occur over the following year, so that when Exchange Control was finally imposed on local assets in 1965 it could be done without any adverse reaction overseas. Meanwhile the first Development Plan, also published in 1964, emphasized the heavy reliance that was being placed on foreign capital, the maintenance of the large-farm sector, accelerated land-registration, and so on; in other words, it emphasized the strong continuity with the colonial economy which was to characterize development strategy throughout the 1960s.

Thus by the end of 1964, when regionalism had finally been abolished and KADU had merged with KANU, the government had already passed a turning-point which Odinga, Oneko and Kaggia do not seem to have fully recognized at the time. When they did protest they were driven from office and ultimately from parliament. Others, especially among the new generation of Kikuyu politicians whose radicalism was more academic in origin, stopped making radical speeches.

'COMPRADORS' AND SOCIALISTS

By the end of 1965, when Kenyatta finally agreed to have the radicals removed from power, the conflict between them and the

---

17. Cherry Gertzel, *The Politics of Independent Kenya* (Heinemann, London 1970), op. cit., pp. 65–8; see also Odinga, *Not Yet Uhuru* (note 10), pp. 291–6.

majority of the KANU leadership had found a fairly clear ideological expression. The majority represented themselves as 'African socialists' but also as nationalists and pragmatists, who put 'Kenyan' interests first, and described the radicals as paid puppets of foreign Communist governments. The radicals pictured themselves as the defenders of the nationalist movement's original socialist ideals, and their opponents as the tools of foreign capital. Maybe neither side fully believed what they said about their opponents, yet in this they came closer to the truth than in what they said about themselves. Kenyatta and Mboya were not tools of foreign capital, but they were collaborating closely with it, and their 'African socialism' was a formulation of 'comprador' ideology. Odinga and Kaggia were not Communist stooges; their socialism was of the petty-bourgeois variety, and even if they had not been so completely outmanoeuvred it is hard to believe that their thinking would have evolved far beyond a redistributive populist position. But they were aligned towards the socialist countries, and stood outside the increasingly intimate relationship between the rest of the KANU leadership and Western firms, Western experts and Western embassies.[18]

The regime's ideology was embodied in the remarkable policy statement *African Socialism and its Application to Planning in Kenya*, which was introduced by Mboya and passed unanimously by the National Assembly in May 1965.[19] Kenyatta described it as Kenya's economic 'Bible'. It was a pure statement of 'bourgeois socialism' (i.e. focused on 'redressing social grievances in order to ensure the continued existence of bourgeois society'), skilfully adapted to the interests of the comprador elements in a neo-colonial situation. According to people who should know it was largely drafted by an American economist in Mboya's ministry, but it does not really matter who drafted it; in considering the contributions of Western technical-assistance experts to comprador administrations one is regularly reminded of Marx's tart dictum on the relation between ideologists and the classes they represent: 'According to their education and their individual position they may be as far apart as heaven from earth. What makes them

---

18. Odinga's receipts of funds from socialist governments were a constant theme of the attacks made on him by KANU leaders. The sums received by Mboya from capitalist sources were almost certainly much larger, however. See L. Cliffe, 'The Underdevelopment–Intervention Thesis; A Reluctant Case Study' (Institute of Development Studies, Sussex 1973, mimeo).

19. Sessional Paper No. 10 of 1965.

representatives is the fact that in their minds they do not get beyond the limits which those they represent do not get beyond in life...'[20]

The essence of Sessional Paper No. 10 of 1965 was as follows:

1. Traditional African society did not exclude the private ownership of capital, but only required that capital be used in ways 'consonant with the general welfare'.[21]

2. The prime need of Kenya was for rapid economic growth, which could only be secured through a large inflow of private foreign investment.

3. Given that private property must never be expropriated without full compensation, nationalization was undesirable except in certain special circumstances.

4. There never had been, nor were there now, any class divisions between Africans.

5. The emergence of an 'inequitable' distribution of wealth and of future class divisions as a result of growth based on private property would be prevented by (a) the 'vigorous implementation of traditional political democracy', and (b) 'a range of sensitive controls' over the use of privately owned resources, which would rule out 'the use of economic power as a political base'. 'Equitably distributed' incomes did not, however, mean equal incomes; there was an opportunity for Kenya to 'recognize the need for differential incentives'.

6. Foreign firms would be controlled so as to make them Africanize their management and make their shares available 'to Africans who wish [sic] to buy them'.

7. Africans would be established in private enterprise by all possible means, such as loans and extension services.

Some of the 'sensitive controls' which would secure social justice without interfering with the hidden hand of free enterprise were specified in the document. They included:

(a) Limitations on the size of individual landholdings

(b) Marketing Boards to be controlled in the interests of the consumer.

(c) Highly progressive taxation, including a progressive capital gains tax and inheritance tax.

---

20. *Eighteenth Brumaire*, loc. cit. (see note 1), p. 275.

21. The previous sentence said 'used for' the general welfare but the subsequent expression, 'consonant with', is more in keeping with the text as a whole.

The document only committed the government to 'consider' these particular controls, none of which was actually adopted. With greater enthusiasm the document urged that the government *should* 'stimulate wider interest and participation in the stock exchange'; and in heavily emphasizing the undesirability of a general policy of nationalization it did not hesitate to point out that there was already a large African business interest which stood to lose from it: 'If the policy [of nationalization] were applied to an economic activity, such as bus transportation, it would affect everyone, African and otherwise, owning productive resources in the industry.'

The general significance of Sessional Paper No. 10 was perfectly apparent to the American ambassador, who summed it up by saying that it encouraged private investment, and explicitly rejected Marxism; and quoted the American columnist Roscoe Drummond (who was visiting Kenya at the time) as writing in his column that it stood 'about midway between Lyndon Johnson's Great Society and the conservative wing of British Socialism'.[22] A similar verdict, though from a different point of view, had been pronounced many years before on all programmes of this kind: 'Bourgeois Socialism attains adequate expression when, and only when, it becomes a mere figure of speech.[23]

But Sessional Paper No. 10 was a resourceful statement, to which the bare summary given above does less than justice. It claimed to embody not merely the interests of all sections of Kenyan society, but the universal goals of mankind in general. It appealed to nationalist sentiment in order to dismiss as alien and irrelevant any suggestion that socialism in Kenya should be derived from Marxist analysis. It appealed to the deeply entrenched 'property instinct' of an overwhelmingly agrarian population, and to the notion that by relying on controls and not on public ownership, a benevolent and intelligent state machine could not only assure social justice but also, by implication, do so without impinging much on Kenyan business interests as opposed to foreign ones.

Besides Mboya's superior ideological skills the regime also held the initiative; Sessional Paper No. 10 was introduced in April 1965, before the open breach with the radicals, but without prior discussion, so that they were unprepared to dissent from it.

---

22. W. Attwood, *The Reds and the Blacks* (Hutchinson, London 1967), p. 247.

23. Marx–Engels, *Selected Works*, op. cit. (see note 1 above), p. 61.

It took a year for them to articulate a full reply. Before this could happen they had been manoeuvred out of KANU and into opposition by a series of skilful manoeuvres planned and executed largely by Tom Mboya, a personal rival of Odinga's, who now emerged as the compradors' main tactician and ideologist. Odinga, Kaggia and their supporters were progressively removed from positions of influence within parliament and the government, and finally Odinga was publicly humiliated by the abolition of his post of party Vice-President at a highly manipulated party conference at Limuru in March 1966.[24] By the time the Limuru conference met it was obvious that Kenyatta had authorized the exclusion of the 'radicals' from political power, and a group of them anticipated the outcome by forming the KPU. After the conference Odinga resigned from the country's Vice-Presidency and accepted the KPU leadership. His place as Vice-President was taken by the Rift Valley leader Daniel Arap Moi, whose Kalenjin supporters had also been instrumental in carrying through Mboya's tactics at the Limuru conference.

Retrospective legislation was now quickly passed which obliged the twenty-nine MPs who had switched to the KPU to fight by-elections, which became known as the 'Little General Election' of May 1966.[25]

It was for this election that the 'radicals' prepared their first manifesto. KANU's African Socialism, it said, had become a 'meaningless phrase', a mere 'cloak for the practice of total capitalism'; small-scale settlement had been saddled with impossible debts and then brought to a halt, while African large-farmers were substituted for white ones; the idea that large-farm co-operatives should replace the former European farms had been forgotten, and credit for land purchase had been withheld from co-operatives in favour of individuals. In general, the government was

> promoting vigorously the development of a small privileged class of Africans; the rich are getting richer and the poor poorer. Not a single act of nationalisation (with the exception of V.O.K. [the Voice of Kenya broadcasting organisation])

---

24. In place of a national Vice-President of KANU seven provincial Vice-Presidents were elected. Kaggia won the Vice-Presidency for Central Province, but the vote was declared void, new delegates were admitted, and at a second vote he was defeated by Gichuru.

25. Those MPs who had joined KPU mainly because they thought their home areas were neglected tried to switch back to KANU, but were not allowed to.

has been carried out. On the contrary, its development plan will make capitalism in the country even stronger. The control of the economy by foreigners grows every day.

This was substantially true; the question was, what would the KPU propose as an alternative? So long as they hoped for popular support, they had to reckon with the intense commitment of the majority of the landowning peasantry to their land, a commitment made more sensitive by growing land-hunger and insecurity during the years of colonial administration. Consequently they proposed only that land should be taken from the remaining non-Kenyan white settlers and given free to the landless, and that no African-owned land should be expropriated. Hesitantly, the manifesto said that on land taken from Europeans co-operative farming would be 'preferred'. Big landholdings would be reduced in size; 'we do not want a new class of big landlords'.

What the peasants wanted was private property with social justice. If the KPU leaders grasped that this was impossible, perhaps under any conditions, but certainly in conditions of capitalist underdevelopment, they did not dare say it. Even what they did promise – free land for the landless and free primary education for all – could easily be turned against them, as Kenyatta well understood. Who could believe, he asked in speech after speech, that the KPU could give anyone 'free things' without first taking them away from someone else? The KPU's promises meant that private land, buildings and livestock would be confiscated. His famous statement that 'all things belong to someone' correctly summed up the situation which both the British and his own government had been working to create.[26] The KPU were not really prepared to contradict him.

Kenyatta's attack on Kaggia at a mass meeting in Kaggia's constituency, where he reinforced the line taken earlier by other KANU leaders, identifying Kaggia as a renegade who had sided with the Luo to challenge him, reduced Kaggia's previously strong support in the area to only 10 per cent of the votes cast. Only nine KPU MPs survived the polls, seven from Luo and two from Luhya constituencies, so that the KPU's parliamentary representation became an all-western and mainly Luo affair.

---

26. 'Those who speak about getting everything for nothing must mean that I should ... seize by force a lot of land or buildings or livestock . . . which belongs to some of you . . .' (*EAS*, 2 June 1966).

From this time onwards the government used the state machine to harass the KPU, which was painted as unpatriotic, divisive, foreign-financed and influenced, and finally as tribalistic and subversive. Some of its activists were detained without trial under the Preservation of Public Security Act, also passed in 1966. Its branches were refused the registration required under the Societies Act to enable them to operate legally; it was not allowed to hold meetings. In 1968 the first nationwide local-government elections to be held in Kenya were 'won' by the simple expedient of finding 'technical' faults in all but six of the KPU candidates' nomination papers, so that the KANU candidates everywhere were returned unopposed.

In spite of all this the KPU continued to have overwhelming grass-roots support in Nyanza Province, and the suspicion persisted that its support elsewhere might still be considerable. General elections were due by 1970 (the life of parliament had been extended by two years in a constitutional amendment of 1968).

In anticipation of these elections the KPU published a more sophisticated ideological statement, the Wananchi (People's) Declaration (in which it is as easy to detect an expatriate hand as in Sessional Paper No. 10). The most striking thing about this document is that it added virtually nothing to the 1966 manifesto, and for the same reason: it was again aimed at getting support among an electorate still overwhelmingly composed of landowning peasants. The resulting tendency to get the worst of both worlds became even more pronounced. On the issue of *land* it promised to reduce debt, but also the size of landholdings, and to redistribute land to the landless; on the subject of *agriculture*, while remarking that 'co-operative methods are the way to a better use of human resources', it said that under KPU, 'small farmers and other individual farmers, once their holdings have been set at sizes consistent with democracy and socialism, will benefit from the improved network of extension services'. It even sought to reassure the 'small trader' (who was exempted from propͧ measures to replace the 'rich' trader by state or co-operative trading), by saying that

> KPU will take steps to ensure that the African small trader
> does not continue to be starved of credit facilities, expertise
> in business control and support from the manufacturer and
> wholesale supplier; but [the document added] it will not see

him as an isolated middleman, trying to exploit the consumer in a cut-throat free-for-all society.

The Declaration's proposals on agricultural wages were also significant. It called for a minimum wage for estate workers, 'to put a stop to the present extreme exploitation of these workers'. It said nothing about the much lower wages paid to workers on African-owned smallholdings, or in African shops, workshops, maize mills and the like. In short, the socialism of the KPU used, 'in its criticism of the bourgeois regime, the standard of the peasant and petty-bourgeois' (and did indeed end 'in a miserable fit of the blues').

None the less the KPU tapped real frustrations and antagonisms arising from the contradictions of underdevelopment. Landless and unemployed men; squatters threatened with eviction; settlement-scheme farmers threatened with eviction for debt arrears; smallholders prohibited from planting coffee or tea; coffee farmers cheated by the 'big men' on co-operative committees; low-paid labourers on rich peasants' or businessmen's tea plantations; low-paid or even unpaid labourers on African-owned large farms; small farmers or traders who saw government loans monopolized by larger farmers and traders; school-leavers unable to get white-collar jobs; people in areas poorly provided with schools, agricultural services or credit; the list of categories of people who experienced exploitation and were beginning to identify the causes of it was a long one, and could be easily discerned between the lines of the KPU's two manifestos and in the KPU MPs' speeches in parliament. The government's scope for doing anything about this was very limited, since these frustrations sprang from the nature of the neo-colonial economy. What could be done was to adopt a variety of measures which wherever possible would displace antagonisms and co-opt potentially dangerous groups. Some of these measures were quite effective in the short term, although others came up against the fundamental requirements of the neo-colonial structure and had to be abandoned.

In the rural areas the scope for softening or disguising the central contradiction between foreign capital and the mass of poor peasants and landless people was limited by the commitment to preserve capitalist farming. The immediate threat to the neo-colonial settlement from the Kikuyu landless of 1960 had been averted by the Million Acre scheme. By the second half of the 1960s, however, landlessness was again becoming a major problem, no longer presenting an immediate threat to political stability but feeding the kind of opposition which the KPU represented. Some of the pressure was siphoned off in the Squatter and Harambee settlement schemes.[27] More was absorbed by the process of private purchases of large farms by co-operatives or companies, in which landless people generally found a place as the paid work-force on the part of the land to be farmed collectively, or simply as squatters. The final stages of the British-financed buy-out of mixed farms were marked by a significant blurring of the boundary between 'settlement' and large-farm transfer, the President regularly 'handing over' large farms to hundreds of assembled people at well-publicized ceremonies. This served the purpose of keeping hope alive among the constantly renewed ranks of the landless, while formally maintaining the legitimacy of 'large-scale' farming, which was important both to the remaining expatriate farmers and estate-owners, and also to the genuinely capitalist ventures among the African-owned large farms in the former white highlands.

The major difficulty which this policy presented was that it did involve a further large-scale immigration of Kikuyu on to land in the Rift Valley which was regarded by the various Kalenjin tribes as traditionally theirs. At first this problem was muted, but in the second half of the 1960s it began to dawn on everyone that the amount of mixed-farm land still available for purchase in the Rift Valley was limited, and the question was, who would get hold of it? The prices offered to the remaining European farmers by rival groups of would-be purchasers, at least one of which would generally be composed of Kikuyu, began to escalate; and in a number of cases, while the owners delayed coming to terms, one group or the other lost patience and occupied the land, with resulting violent episodes.

The inwardness of the realignment of the alliances within KANU at the 1966 Limuru Conference (which led to Odinga's breakaway) now became apparent. Moi was the main leader of the Kalenjin peoples of the Rift Valley, where most of the mixed farms were in European hands still. The substitution of Moi and the Kalenjin leaders for Odinga and the Lùo leaders as the chief allies of the Kikuyu leaders implied a bargain: the Kalenjin leaders would not resist Kikuyu movement into the Rift Valley,

---

27. See Chapter 3, p. 75.

while the regime would provide the Kalenjin, who lacked capital and organizational experience, with state assistance for their own efforts to compete in the land-purchase market.[28] Moi redoubled his efforts to encourage and help Kalenjin groups to buy farms, incurring the somewhat misguided reproach of being the owner of sixteen farms, since he often lent his name to the companies concerned; he did own a large farm (known as 'Campi Moi' – Moi's Camp) north of Nakuru. The President for his part also acquired a large farm near Nakuru and took increasingly to spending a number of weeks each year at Nakuru, during which he would preside at the ceremonial 'handovers' already mentioned, normally accompanied by Moi. From time to time Moi, in face of Kalenjin resentment of the Kikuyu influx, was obliged to make the bargain almost explicit, for instance in this speech in early 1972:

> The Vice-President warned against undue competition in buying farms in Rift Valley between Kalenjin and Kikuyu tribes who negotiate prices at night. This type of activity was the cause of soaring land prices. . . . 'It is because of lack of unity and cooperation that this trend persists', he said. 'For a long time I have urged Rift Valley people to unite and work together as one family. Apparently my appeal has fallen on deaf ears . . .' The Vice-President described as 'utterly irresponsible and petty politics' acts of certain people who spread rumours that he was against a particular section of the community buying land in the Rift Valley Province . . . As a matter of fact, I have worked shoulder to shoulder with President Kenyatta to provide land to the wananchi [people] in this Province.'[29]

Down to this time, the bargain had worked to maintain the peace. Earlier on, the Nandi (in the south-west corner of the Province, and after the Kipsigis the second largest Kalenjin tribe) had shown how it might break down. In July 1969, with the general election impending, the leading Nandi MP, John Seroney, published the 'Nandi Hills Declaration', which claimed all settler-held land in the area for the Nandi alone. Seroney was

---

28. A further weakness of the Kalenjin was that they did not have such an acute problem of landlessness as the Kikuyu. Kalenjin teachers and the like were keen enough to become shareholders in large farms, but the additional thrust provided by hundreds of landless people anxious to live and work on such farms was not always there.

29. *EAS*, 10 January 1972.

prosecuted for sedition and convicted. On the other hand he was fined and not jailed; the Kikuyu–Kalenjin alliance could not be strained too far.[30] It was an interesting illustration of the way the ideology of 'tribalism' worked in Kenya. The government re-asserted the availability of all European-owned land for purchase by Africans with capital, a large proportion of whom would be likely to be Kikuyu, while attacking Seroney's 'tribalism'.

So long as there was still foreign-owned land to be drawn upon, the problem of landlessness could be at least partly absorbed. The problem of general poverty among the mass of the peasantry could not. It was a direct consequence of the whole process of underdevelopment.

This particular contradiction was partly grasped at quite an early stage by some of those involved in the preparation of the first Development Plan in 1964. They reached the conclusion that the development strategy it implied would not generate enough employment to absorb more than a small fraction of the growth of the labour force, nor could it hope to relieve the poverty of those who would be left dependent on the rural areas. In the belief that a remedy could be found within the framework of existing policy, a conference was held at Kericho in 1966 out of which grew the Special Rural Development Programme, an experimental scheme to try out comprehensive approaches to stimulating increased incomes and job opportunities in fourteen selected divisions (sub-districts) throughout Kenya, with a view to applying the lessons which would be learned more generally. Much publicity was given to the SRDP, and it led to rural development becoming the major theme in the presentation, if not the content, of the 1970–4 Development Plan.

But from first to last the SRDP itself was plagued with trouble, and in 1971, after barely a year of formal operation in only five out of the proposed fourteen experimental areas, it was abandoned, in theory because the next Development Plan, then under dis-cussion, would incorporate the lessons already gained from it, and because rural development was already the central theme of development planning. This was not completely untrue, yet it was clear that the SRDP itself had proved largely abortive. All sorts of particular explanations were advanced and all of them were valid: confusion about objectives; excessively visible expatriate involvement; lack of support from senior civil servants or of

---

30. For the trial proceedings see *EAS* 2–7 October 1969.

political backing from on high; lack of suitably trained field staff; and so on.[31]

What most of these difficulties really reflected, however, was that the programme simply ran counter to the development strategy implied by the regime's overall policies, which were inherently urban-oriented. This contradiction could not simply be ignored; it imposed itself in practice at every juncture. The SRDP was seen as offsetting the urban bias of underdevelopment; but like all programmes for rural development conceived in that spirit, it rested on illusions about the possibility of a harmonious path of rural progress based on general rural equality and social cohesion, when both of these things had already been largely destroyed or were being destroyed as fast as possible by other components of agricultural policy.[32] But in any case the SRDP, or any serious plan for rural development, implied transfers of resources from the better-off to the worse-off, and on a national scale these were seen by those concerned to be – as one of them put it – 'unthinkable'.[33] This was a revealing phrase. The cost of the initial SRDP schemes worked out at about £3 per head of the population in the areas affected over five years, equivalent to roughly £6 million per annum if it had been repeated over the country as a whole. This was certainly a lot of money, but it was not found 'unthinkable' in 1971 to allocate nearly £5 million per annum for increased civil service salaries.

In its early stages the SRDP also ran foul of the Provincial Administration, whose supremacy in the rural areas it appeared to threaten. The problem here was that the Provincial Administration was primarily an agency of political control, not of rural development, since the primary commitment of the government

---

31. There is a large collection of papers on the SRDP, thanks to the work of an evaluation team established for it at the Institute for Development Studies at the University of Nairobi. For a general review see J. R. Nellis, 'The Administration of Rural Development in Kenya', paper presented to the Conference on Comparative Administration (Arusha, September 1971, mimeo).

32. Compare Samir Amin, in 'The Development of Capitalism in Black Africa', *L'Homme et la Société* No. 6, Oct.–Nov.–Dec. 1967, where he refers to 'current policies of rural intervention and cooperative development' as 'practised everywhere according to paternalistic formulas which are a bit naïve, and resulting undoubtedly from the utopian wish to see the entirety of the countryside progress without any inequality and at a steady sustained rhythm . . .'

33. R. Chambers, 'The Special Rural Development Programme: Planning and Replication', SRDP Research and Evaluation Unit Evaluation Report No. 2 (December 1970, mimeo), p. 3.

was not the development of the rural areas generally but, as in the past, to control rural development in the interests of the large-farm and urban capitalist sectors.

In its attempts to deal with the problem of urban unemployment within the framework of neo-colonialism, the government had more room for manoeuvre. In June 1970, it announced a new one-year Tripartite Agreement, fairly closely modelled on the agreement of 1964–5. Compared with its predecessor, the second agreement was not a response to a major threat to political stability, such as that represented by the landless and unemployed 'roaming around the Rift Valley' at independence, nor was it needed to prime the pump of economic activity or revive foreign investment. Although 291,000 people registered as unemployed, many were people in employment hoping to find a better job, and many were women seeking to enter the urban job-market; and even if most of those registered had been people wholly without any means of subsistence, the problem would still not have been a critical one by the standards of many other underdeveloped countries. Moreover, although 40,000 people were given jobs under the agreement, private employers were unanimous in insisting that the true net effect of this was only to bring forward by some months increases in private-sector employment which were to be expected anyway.

But there was a significant difference in the way the second agreement was implemented compared with the 1964–5 agreement. In 1970 separate registers were made for unemployed school leavers who had passed through four years of secondary school, and virtually all of these, amounting to about 4,000 in all, were found jobs of the kind they aspired to – i.e. white-collar jobs.[34] It was not hard to see that here was a mechanism well adapted to containing the contradiction between foreign capital and educated youth by periodically ensuring that the latter were given priority in the job queue.

The other aspect of the contradiction between foreign capital and wage-workers, the level of wages, has already been touched on at several points.[35] The policy of the government was to keep

---

34. Based on interviews; for general statistics of the Agreement see *Employment, Incomes and Equality* (ILO, Geneva 1972), pp. 529–44. A useful review was also carried out by the FKE. The momentary appearance in Nairobi in April 1970 of a School Leavers' Association was highly significant. It disappeared with the implementation of the Agreement.

35. See especially Chapter 6, pp. 178–83.

down wage-levels so as to encourage foreign investment, maintain agricultural profitability in face of externally fixed commodity prices, and make African-owned enterprises profitable. This policy could be easily rationalized, as we have seen, either in terms of maximizing the growth in employment, or in terms of keeping down the urban–rural income-differential, or both.[36]

To achieve this aim seemed bound to involve conflict with the unions, and as we have seen, the FKE insisted that the government should take powers to curb the right to strike, so that a policy of direct control of wages could be enforced by the Industrial Court. These powers were taken by passing the Trades Disputes Act of 1971, but the government shrank from actually issuing wage settlement 'guidelines' to the Court. There may have been several reasons for this. It is doubtful if all members of the government realized the real implications of the policy towards which they were moving; the Development Plan published in 1969, for instance, stated: 'the Government considers that most workers have a right to expect regular gains in real income';[37] unlike the Ndegwa Commission, which frankly stated: 'what we would prefer to see is a [growing] wage bill almost entirely attributable to increases in total wage employment; in this case average wages remain relatively constant'.[38] There was also probably some reluctance to face the invidious comparisons and the rise in the level of political consciousness which are involved in any attempt to enforce an incomes policy in a highly inegalitarian society.

Moreover, the truth of the matter may well have been that *average* wage-rates were actually falling, owing to the growth of low-paid non-enumerated employment throughout the second half of the 1960s. In 1969/70 there were nearly 500,000 full-time or casual labourers working on smallholdings at any given time, with an average wage of about £24 per annum. This compared with an average of £69 per annum for 182,000 African employees in the large-farm sector, and £222 per annum for the same number in private industry and commerce. Not included in the

---

36. The assumption that there *is* a rural–urban income differential should not be accepted uncritically either, as C. Allen has shown in 'Unions, Incomes and Development', in *Developmental Trends in Kenya* (Centre of African Studies, Edinburgh 1972), at pp. 62–73, which reviews evidence that seems to have been rather neglected by the ILO mission on unemployment in Kenya that year.

37. *Development Plan*, 1969, p. 138.

38. Ndegwa Report, p. 39.

government's estimates, but of considerable importance, was the fringe, 'intermediate' or 'informal' sector of urban employment, in bars, charcoal delivery, non-enumerated domestic service, and so on, much of which paid wages well below the legal urban minimum.[39] Thus so long as wages stayed low in the export (i.e. the agricultural) industries and in the smallholding and non-unionized urban sector, where most African enterprise was located, why should the government invite political trouble by intervening further in wage settlements in the much more limited field of unionized commerce and industry? The unions could no longer force wages up by strike action. If wages rose, it was because employers preferred to pay for labour stability and harmonious industrial relations, or because the kind of labour they employed was relatively scarce, and they could meet the costs either out of their substantial profits or – as the government in effect did with the civil-service salary revision of 1971 – pass the cost on to the consumer.

But if the government was thus relieved of the necessity for a confrontation with the unions, it was at the expense of the growth of a highly impoverished and exploited employment sector, merging into the unemployed labour force, who provided a potentially powerful basis of support for the KPU.

IDEOLOGY AND REPRESSION

In practice, the government did not rely on being able to contain the contradictions which fuelled the opposition. In spite of official harassment, including the jailing of both Kaggia and his leading Kikuyu associate, Waiyaki, for holding meetings without permission, the KPU continued to have fairly wide-spread support and, in Central Nyanza, overwhelming support; in May 1969 this was conclusively demonstrated when a handpicked candidate of the regime obtained less than 10 per cent of the vote in a by-election at Gem, in the heart of Luo country.[40] Even in Kikuyu country Kaggia's support could not be discounted three years after his defeat in the Little General Election, especially since factional conflicts were rife in KANU as individuals and

---

39. In 1969 the statutory minimum for men in Nairobi was £106 per annum.

40. See J. J. Okumu, 'The By-Election in Gem', *East Africa Journal*, June 1969, pp. 9–17; on the harassment of the KPU see Suzanne D. Mueller, 'Statist Economies and the Elimination of the KPU', paper presented to the African Studies Association, Philadelphia, November 1972.

THE POLITICS OF NEO-COLONIALISM

groups struggled for control over patronage, licences, contracts, and other fruits of office.

In this situation a number of KANU backbenchers, including some Kikuyu MPs who had avoided switching to the KPU in 1966 but had been reflecting popular discontent by making populist speeches (for instance by calling for the long-promised ceiling to be imposed on the size of landholdings), began to fear that they might be deprived of renomination by the party leadership at the forthcoming general elections. Some may also have felt that unless they could dissociate themselves from the top leadership they might suffer the same fate as the party's candidate at Gem. They began to demand primary elections for the party nominations. This was publicized in the 'Ol Kalou Declaration', signed in April 1969 by twelve Kikuyu and seven other MPs, and it was soon clear that it had widespread support among KANU backbenchers. In face of this Kenyatta decided to agree to primaries. This created a new problem, however, because there was no register of KANU membership; primary elections would have to be open to all voters, including KPU sympathizers. If the primaries were fair, the outcome of both the primaries and the general election seemed distinctly unpredictable.

This was the situation when Tom Mboya was assassinated on 5 July 1969. It is very unclear where his murder fits into the picture. A government statement made by the Vice-President, Moi, suggested that it had been instigated by a Communist state in order to 'divide and seize' by removing the man who 'was certainly standing in the way of a form of "scientific colonialism" '.[41] An alternative theory was that someone had taken the opportunity to remove a dangerous candidate for the succession to Kenyatta, foreseeing that it would also reinforce the 'tribal' orientation of politics. All that is clear is that no motive was disclosed and that the man who was hanged for pulling the trigger claimed to have been put up to it by someone whose identity was never revealed; and that as in the case of the murder in 1965 of the radical Goan MP, Pio Pinto, some curious aspects of the testimony given in court were not pursued.[42]

The assassin was a Kikuyu; and in spite of Mboya's leading

---

41. *EAS*, 14 July 1969.
42. Attwood thought that Pinto's murder removed Odinga's best tactician (*The Reds and the Blacks*, p. 245: see note 22); the death of Mboya did the same for Odinga's opponents, but they were in no way lost without him.

role in the removal of Odinga from power, and the subsequent harassment of the KPU, his killing was seen by most Luo as an attack on the whole Luo people through the murder of one of 'their' most brilliant sons. There was a massive demonstration of support for Odinga as a symbol of Luo solidarity. A Luo crowd demonstrated against Kenyatta at Mboya's requiem service in Nairobi. The Kikuyu leadership responded by inaugurating a mass oathing programme among the Kikuyu, Embu, and Meru, and also part of the neighbouring Kamba. In the course of about twelve weeks virtually every adult Kikuyu took an oath 'to keep the flag in the house of Mumbi' (i.e. keep the government in Kikuyu hands); Kikuyu tribalism pitched against Luo tribalism. The oathing programme was finally called off in September shortly before parliament was due to reassemble. Later, it was generally described by educated Kikuyu as a failure, meaning that it had not proved capable of papering over the growing cleavages in Kikuyu society.[43] Momentarily, however, it helped to create a tense atmosphere (a good deal of violence was used against reluctant oath-takers) in which Kaggia was finally persuaded to give up the KPU. Announcing this on 1 August he said that 'in spite of all their efforts' the KPU had become less and less effective as a means of achieving the aims for which he had joined it, which were

> to see the freedom fighters recognised and rightly honoured for their gallant contribution to Kenya and [that] everyone – farmers, workers and businessmen – had their rightful share in the fruits of independence. I wanted to see the land given back to the tillers and all sons and daughters of the soil their right to education, work and medical facilities.[44]

His defection, together with virtually the whole of the rest of the KPU's Kikuyu leadership, finished the party's prospects in Central Province. Odinga was restrained in his comments, alluding to the pressure put on Kaggia and saying that he 'had succumbed to tribal sectionalism under the misleading label of Kikuyu unity'.[45] Kaggia replied by saying that 'it would be

---

43. The *Daily Nation* had, for instance, reported on 3 June 1969 that 'veteran politicians including several members of the defunct Kikuyu Central Association [the main nationalist movement of the inter-war years] have expressed concern over what they call political disunity in the Central Province which could lead to an explosive situation', and were seeking an audience with Kenyatta to find a solution.

44. *DN*, 2 August 1969.

45. *EAS*, 4 August 1969.

a tragedy for a politician of Mr Odinga's standing to appeal to tribal sentimentalities', and that he had stayed in the KPU up till then 'despite so many tribal tendencies in KPU which so many KPU members have been complaining about'. O. O. Mak'-Anyengo, a leading KPU trade-unionist, put his finger on what had happened when he pointed out that Kaggia and the others who had formed the KPU had done so because they had found that they could not achieve their aims through KANU, and added: 'Mr Kaggia has not told us the new method he has discovered to influence changes in KANU, which he could not use before the formation of KPU', and that 'One cannot expect a party to be as effective as it should be when it is denied even the right to convene a delegates conference, leave alone public meetings.'[46]

It was fairly clear that after three years of almost complete political frustration even the KPU leaders found the ideology of tribalism hard to resist. KANU officials could now claim that 'the KPU was now a mere tribal organization which would never have support anywhere in Kenya outside Nyanza Province'.[47] But this claim was not to be put to the test.

In October Kenyatta visited Kisumu, the capital of Luo country, on what was in effect a campaign tour. The centrepiece of the visit was the opening ceremony of a hospital. The crowd was hostile, and when Kenyatta in his speech launched a bitter and offensive attack on Odinga, who was present, the atmosphere became extremely tense. As Kenyatta's car left, the crowd pressed towards it; his bodyguard fired into the crowd, killing ten and wounding seventy. Five days later the KPU was banned and all its major leaders were detained.

With the KPU out of the way, the KANU primaries could be held without fear of the consequences. There was no other legal party, independents were not allowed to stand, and so whoever won a KANU nomination would automatically be declared elected to parliament. The primaries became in effect a general election in which anyone could stand provided he was not a recent KPU member, and they were fought almost wholly on the basis of clan and (in the towns) tribal support. The electorate merely 'circulated the élite' – about 60 per cent of the sitting MPs were replaced – in the hope of finding individuals who would be

---

46. Letter to the *Sunday Nation*, 14 September 1969.
47. *EAS*, 4 August 1969.

more energetic and successful in providing jobs and services for them. The Kikuyu ministers and their main cabinet allies were all returned. In other words it was an election which reinforced tribal forms of consciousness, and which disturbed nothing and changed nothing.[48] Twelve months later the new MPs made this clear by voting themselves a 25 per cent increase in their parliamentary incomes in the middle of the national wage-freeze imposed under the Tripartite Agreement.[49]

The final suppression of the KPU in 1969 coincided with the further development of the neo-colonial relationship, in which the government, co-operating closely with the interests concerned, undertook the nationalization (with compensation) of oil-refining, power supplies, and the banks, and embarked on an expanded programme of new joint ventures with foreign private capital. Both of these had been central planks in the KPU programme. The significance of the coincidence need not be overlooked. The KPU had been a response to the power of foreign private capital. The 'effect' was 'done away with', as Marx put it, while the cause was kept alive; the borderline between cause and effect, on the other hand, was simultaneously 'obliterated' by a series of measures in which the state apparatus and foreign private capital became much more closely intermingled.

But the suppression of the KPU showed that not everything could be done by political adroitness, especially with the passing of Mboya. From 1966 onwards a marked shift towards reliance on coercion and the suppression of dissent had been occurring, accompanied by a steady enlargement of the Kikuyu share in the means of control. At independence the army was predominantly drawn from the Kamba and Kalenjin and hardly at all from the Kikuyu. After the 1964 mutiny (in which junior officers and other ranks in all three East African countries briefly challenged their continued subordination to expatriate officers and the continuation of pre-independence pay structures), military training was reorganized with British assistance and a process of recruitment of Kikuyu was put in hand which was particularly important

---

48. On the elections generally, see G. Hyden and C. Leys, 'Elections and Politics in Single-Party Systems: The Case of Kenya and Tanzania', *British Journal of Political Science*, Vol. II, No. 4, 1972, pp. 261–92.

49. *EAS*, 8 January 1971. Actually, MPs' salaries were kept pegged while tax-free allowances were greatly enlarged to produce this result. The increase followed a hotly debated decision in June 1969 to pay ministers 'gratuities' worth 20 per cent of their salaries, backdated to 1962 (see *DN*, 6 June 1969 and subsequent issues).

in the officer corps. By the end of the 1960s Kikuyu officers with
high levels of education and training were beginning to reach
middle rank, and the days of complete dominance of Kamba or
Kalenjin commanders promoted from the ranks were numbered.[50]
Meanwhile a new mobile paramilitary force, the General Service
Unit (GSU), had been created under Kikuyu command, which
was independent of both the army and the police. Although in no
way a match for the army, it could be used independently for
political control in situations in which the army could not be
deployed without the risk of making it an arbiter of policy. For
instance the GSU was used to coerce the university students in
1970 and 1971, and was regularly used to remove squatters from
large farms, or wherever a show of force was thought necessary.
This apparatus of force was reinforced by greatly widened
definitions of sedition and subversion, the power to detain without
trial, the power to control all political meetings, the power to
make any political organization illegal by refusing it registration,
and so on.[51] There were also subtler, informal mechanisms of
control. For instance, a Provincial Commissioner did not hesitate
to say: 'People who criticized the government and yet had been
given loans to buy farms and open businesses would forfeit them.'[52]
The government also made clear to the press and to academics the
limits of permitted criticism.[53] A degree of populist rhetoric was
tolerated; but a settled opposition to neo-colonialism and a
determination to work against it was not.

Increased reliance on coercion, and the progressive enlargement

---

50. By 1967 Kikuyu officers formed 22·7 per cent of the officer corps, compared with
the Kamba who formed 28 per cent. (J. M. Lee, *African Armies and Civil Order*,
Chatto and Windus, London 1969, p. 110.)

51. On the legislative basis for political control generally see Y. P. Ghai and J. P.
McAuslan, *Public Law and Political Change in Kenya* (Oxford University Press,
Nairobi 1970), pp. 433 ff.

52. *EAS*, 21 October 1972.

53. This was well expressed in a speech given by an official of the Office of the President
to a Workshop on 'Coordination of Production, Dissemination and Utilisation of
Social Science Research Findings' held near Nairobi in January 1972, and published in the proceedings (which were appropriately entitled 'Harnessing Research'). Mr Sitati said: 'For any research to be useful, it must be bound by a code
of ethics, i.e. intellectual honesty and discipline . . . In some cases, a few scholars
have mistakenly assumed the role of critics, to expose what in their own mind are
follies of a Government or organisation. Such researchers are a liability to any
society. Any undertaking should aim at seeing a meaning in a situation and
evaluating it without biases . . . it is of paramount importance that the Government
and scholars work as a team with common goals and intentions.'

of Kikuyu control over the apparatus of coercion, reached a
further stage in June 1971, with the trial of thirteen men for
planning a *coup d'état*. Being charged with sedition rather than
the capital offence of treason, all thirteen agreed to plead guilty,
so that the evidence given in court consisted merely of the
prosecution's account based on their alleged statements. But even
allowing for this, it seems clear that the plot was extremely
faint-hearted and naïve. Its significance lay in what it revealed
about the perspectives of opposition in Kenya by 1971.

The plotters were a disparate group. The prime mover was a
former army lieutenant who had been jailed for his part in the
1964 mutiny, was subsequently released under a general amnesty,
subsequently served a jail sentence for forging and had also been
held in detention for (presumably) oppositionist political activities. The group of men he recruited was a motley one, until it was
decided to draw in some 'notables' with connections of the kind
needed to widen the plot. In spite of the fact that the original
group of plotters apparently had only a very vague idea of what
they were doing, they seemed to have had little difficulty in enlisting the support of a Luo university lecturer working in Uganda,
and – more importantly – a Kamba MP, Gideon Mutiso. The
lecturer, who was assigned the task of enlisting material aid from
the Tanzanian government, got cold feet when this proved to be a
fantasy. Mutiso, on the other hand, is alleged to have stated when
they approached him that he had already had conversations with
the Commander-in-Chief of the army, Major-General Ndolo,
which indicated that Ndolo (also a Kamba) was already enter-
taining the thought of a military takeover; and Mutiso therefore
entered into the plot – or, to put it more accurately, into the confused and extraordinarily casual conversations about a plot – as
some sort of go-between linking the group to the Army Commander.

The question then becomes why either Mutiso or the Army
Commander should have done this. The answer is probably fairly
simple. Down to December 1969 Mutiso had been a junior
minister in the government. But in September he had become the
first MP to attack the Kikuyu oathing programme who provided
specific proofs of it. He claimed that Kikuyu oath administrators,
with the help of the National Youth Service and the GSU and the
connivance of the Provincial Administration, had been forcibly
oathing both adults and children in his part of Kamba country.
Up to this point it had been left mainly to private individuals,

especially Christian church leaders, to denounce the oathing programme, in which large numbers of people were severely beaten and at least one, a clergyman, killed for resisting it.[54] By the time Mutiso spoke, the programme had been virtually completed; his reaction was against the extension of the programme to the Kamba; and it was widely rumoured that attempts to administer the oath to the army had also led to intervention from the army command – i.e. from Ndolo, no doubt supported by other Kamba officers.[55] Mutiso retained his seat in the 1969 election but was dropped from the government. When the other plotters approached him he is said to have told them that he was already under police surveillance.

His first exchange with the army commander, according to his statement, was about May 1970. Ndolo gave him to understand that he did not like 'what was happening', but later said that so long as Kenyatta was in power, he would not intervene. However, when Mutiso subsequently put the group's proposals to him, he allegedly said he had decided not to wait.

---

54. There was a parliamentary debate on 8 August, led by KPU MPs, in which the government denied that there was any significance in the stream of lorries full of people travelling to Gatundu, marked 'KANU PRIVATE', which were to be seen on all main roads in Central Province and also in Nairobi. Mr Mbiyu Koinange, the President's Minister of State, said people were going to express their loyalty to Kenyatta in the light of the demonstrations against him when he attended the memorial service for Mboya in Nairobi in July. Thereafter the Assembly was in recess. The daily press reported only public statements alleging oathing, such as those in this debate, and studiously avoided direct reporting of the movements of people involved, or investigating their significance. The Christian weekly *Target* alone dared to attack the government's denial as incredible, in view of facts which were public knowledge, and asked: 'If these visits were part of the usual visits by the wananchi to pay their respects to the President . . . why did Mr. Peter Gachathi, Director of Information, fail to send the cameramen from V.O.K. [Voice of Kenya] to record the visits in the same way as has always been done?' The editor of *Target* was later dismissed. By the middle of September meetings to condemn oathing and organize anti-Kikuyu opinion were being held in many areas of Kenya, and violence between Kalenjin and Kikuyu on two large farms in the Rift Valley had led to a special peace-making tour by Moi. It was at this point that the programme was called off, and from denying that there was any oathing the government now announced that 'instructions have been issued to the Police and Administration officers to investigate these allegations with a view to prosecution.' (Moi's statement, *EAS*, 20 September 1969). Mutiso's statement giving chapter and verse for the situation in Yatta, in Eastern Province, was reported in *EAS*, 19 September 1972, and he produced further evidence on September 25 (*EAS*, 26 September 1972).

55. See C. Legum and J. Drysdale, *Africa Contemporary Record: Annual Survey and Documents, 1969–70* (Africa Research Ltd, Exeter 1970), p. B 123. It should be noted that Ndolo had only taken over as Commander-in-Chief from a British officer in May 1969.

At this point we confront the most striking feature of the whole episode. With the possible exception of Mutiso, none of the thirteen men who were tried seems to have attached much importance to their political aims. Owino, the ex-lieutenant, allegedly told one of the others when recruiting him that the new government would consist of 'young and energetic people' and that 'all ministers are rotten'. Ndolo, according to Mutiso's statement, responded as follows when Mutiso mentioned that there were rumours of a plot to assassinate him (Mutiso):

> If there was a shot to you or any other leader it will be replied with many other shots because I think people have gone a little too far and in fact all that was needed now is a single mistake to be made either by detaining people of the Government party or one being killed because this will mean a violation of the Constitution since there is only one political party which is also the Government. Should a mistake be made I will take action.

There is something fairly authentic about this statement, even at third hand; it had begun to dawn on the Army Commander that the power of the regime was dangerous, perhaps even to himself and the army. He added:

> Let me tell you things have got to a stage when I think action must be taken. I have always hesitated to do anything while Mzee is in power, but I think I cannot let things go the way they are going. I would like you to do one thing for me. . . . Go and draft a statement listing all the things you know one can read as reasons why one has taken over the Government.

Mutiso drafted a statement, but all the court was told was that it contained 'eleven imaginary grievances'. As for the rest of the group, one was also an army officer dismissed after the 1964 mutiny, one was a former GSU police officer, a Kalenjin dismissed for 'general inefficiency' or, as he claimed, on account of the 'tribalism and nepotism practiced by Ben Ngethi, the Kikuyu commandant of the GSU'. One was a leader of a militant religious sect, the Legio Maria. Others declared they joined the group because they were unemployed and hoped to get money.

Granted the difficulty of knowing what credence to give to what the court was allowed to hear, it is all the same inherently unlikely that this diverse group had made any sort of radical critique of the socio-economic system. They thought that their grievances, imagined or real, could be remedied by a change of government. They saw that this could not be brought about by open political activity. Where they went wrong was in thinking that the opportunity for making such a coup existed; it would not have existed unless the army had been much more radically politicized and alienated from the regime than it actually was.

Thanks to the fact that the 'plot' scarcely rose above the cowboys-and-indians level the government was able to use the affair to extend still further its control over the state apparatus, while at the same time making much of its lenient treatment of the offenders.[56] The first plotters to be arrested agreed to co-operate with the police and implicated Mutiso; Mutiso's agreement to co-operate implicated Ndolo, who, however, was allowed to resign;[57] and a 'loyalty' demonstration was organized, in conditions of well-manipulated public excitement, in which the Kamba Chief Justice, who had been appointed two years before, was called on to resign and eventually felt it prudent to comply. With characteristic finesse the government did not replace the Army Commander or the Chief Justice with Kikuyu candidates, but the lesson of the whole episode – the effectiveness of the government's intelligence, the plotters' declared frustration at the 'reliability' of the GSU, and in general the government's strength as well as shrewdness in the handling of security – would not be lost on the new incumbents.

THE INSTITUTIONS OF THE NEO-COLONIAL STATE

In spite of its increasing reliance on coercion, the Kenyatta regime was still a predominantly civil one. Kenya had still some way to go before reaching a stage where, as in many Latin

---

56. It looks as if the plot, which was known to the government in January (according to Moi's statement to the Assembly, reported in *EAS*, 16 June 1971), was allowed to mature to the point where exposing it would be most helpful to the government, but before it threatened to constitute an unpredictable risk through the possible actions of Ndolo; and President Nyerere's decision to turn over to the Kenyan authorities the plotters who sought his aid may have forced the government's hand.

57. Ndolo was treated with remarkable lenience, perhaps because of his consistent expression of reluctance to act against Kenyatta personally. He retired to his 9,416-acre farm which he had acquired in Machakos, a latter day Cincinnatus. Probably no one in Kenya thought it odd that one of the meetings between Mutiso and Ndolo took place 'at his [the Army Commander's] shop at Emali'.

244 UNDERDEVELOPMENT IN KENYA

American countries, the population became 'prisoners of their own army', although this is probably the logical destination of bonapartism; but the state apparatus, as a system of domination, was extremely important. The expression 'state apparatus', however, is not very precise, even though it conveys a more useful general idea than terms which suggest that countries like Kenya exhibit a modified form of 'democracy', 'representative government', and so forth. The political institutions of the Kenyan state need to be more closely described.

These are clearly not the same as the institutions of the bourgeois (or 'liberal democratic') state, imitations of which were established by the colonial powers before granting political independence: constitution, elections, parliament, cabinet, political parties, elected local government, and so on. The neo-colonial state does not represent the interests of a dominant national bourgeoisie, and consequently these institutions, which were developed for that purpose, function badly, if at all. Their utility is largely ideological; in reality they tend to atrophy.

The most vigorous of them was the National Assembly. Its debates were, as Gertzel observes, often lively, and even 'critical'; but it was a strictly licensed criticism.[58] Individual backbenchers, and even some assistant ministers, regularly criticized unpopular government policies, for instance the local obligations of settlement-scheme farmers, the purchase of large-farms by ministers and other 'big' men, nepotism in the labour market, and so on; occasionally they even spoke of the dangers of class war and revolution. So long as they drew their parliamentary salaries and voted for the government's bills, and did not organize an opposition or criticize Kenyatta, they were tolerated as a useful safety-valve. The Assembly's real function was to serve as a town club for the politically active members of the petty-bourgeoisie (even the 1971 coup plotters discussed their plans there at one point), providing income and status (and hence credit), access to the bureaucracy (and hence patronage), and – for the skilful – the possibility of advancement.[59] Just occasionally a majority of MPs

8. Gertzel, *The Politics of Independent Kenya*, op. cit. (see note 17), p. 18; and compare C. Seymour-Ure, '*Private Eye:* The Politics of the Fool', *Political Quarterly*, Vol. 43, No. 3, July–September 1972, pp. 282–94. ('By tolerating the fool the King shows his own strength.')

9. Jay E. Hakes, 'Patronage and Politics in Kenya: A Study of Backbencher Membership on Statutory Boards' (Nairobi 1971, mimeo), makes the point that about half of the KANU backbenchers were likely to hold some extra-parliamentary govern-

resisted government policy; but on nearly every occasion this was because it threatened them personally.[60]

The party's decline was more obvious. Unlike parliament it was not provided for out of public funds, and so it was not even worth maintaining as a façade. From 1963 onwards its main organs ceased to function and its paid staff gradually disappeared as their salaries fell into arrears.[61] Fanon wrote: 'nothing is left but the shell of a party, the name, the emblem and the motto'. A senior KANU official said of it in 1971: 'The party functions only when an election takes place. Then all that remains of it is the song, KANU Yajenga Nchi [KANU builds the nation].'[62] It was hardly surprising. A mass party implies mass participation, and mass participation implies a programme for the masses. The compradors wanted neither, and so the party was discarded. From time to time the leadership undertook to 'revitalize' the party; these efforts were at best naïve, and came to nothing.[63]

Other components of the imitation bourgeois state fared no differently. 'Constitutionalism' was a significant part of neo-colonial ideology, and the Kenya Constitution was elaborately amended in 1966 to make it embrace the sweeping powers which the regime wanted in order to deal with the KPU. But the myth of constitutionalism wore thin; sometimes even the government seemed to lose interest in refurbishing it, for instance when the President was said to have 'ruled' (he had no decree power) that local-government elections due in 1972 were to be postponed to 1974.[64] In the struggle with the radicals Mboya had exploited the

---

ment appointment at any given time; and individual cases show that MPs critical of the government could quite often expect to be co-opted into supporting it by this route.

60. For instance, they resisted a change in the criminal law which included a widened definition of sedition which they feared might be used against them.

61. Statement by the then Organizing Secretary of KANU, John Keen, cited in J. Spencer, 'Kenyatta's Kenya', *Africa Report*, May 1966, p. 6; see also Gertzel, *Politics of Independent Kenya*, op. cit. (note 17), p. 58.

62. John O'Washika, MP, *EAS*, 3 July 1971.

63. An exercise to 'reorganize, revitalize and rejuvenate' KANU was begun by a committee set up by Kenyatta in April 1971. The committee's report was adopted, and a programme to enrol members and hold nationwide elections to party committees and offices was set in hand. It bogged down in factional conflict and manipulation of all kinds, and the elections due to be held in March 1972 were postponed till May, and by the end of 1972 seemed as far away as ever.

64. Statement by the Assistant Minister for Health in the National Assembly, reported in *DN*, 15 September 1971. 'He asked who could question this ruling.'

ambiguity in Kenyatta's position as both Head of State and head of the government, so as to represent all opposition to the government as disloyalty to the state, and after this few people in Kenya had any illusions on the subject.[65] The matter was succinctly expressed by a District Officer at Maseno, near Kisumu, in 1972: 'Freedom of worship is guaranteed within the Constitution, but this could be curtailed at any time when the Government deemed it necessary.'[66]

As for elected local government, quite apart from the farce of the 1968 local-government 'elections', it was emasculated by transferring its only important functions (responsibilities for primary schools, roads, and health services) to the central ministries in January 1971.

Even the cabinet had little significance in the neo-colonial state. It met infrequently. Executive power lay elsewhere. The real institutions of the state were Kenyatta and his court, the civil service and the armed forces, and the machinery of 'technical assistance' and 'aid'.

Kenyatta's court was based primarily at his country home at Gatundu, about twenty-five miles from Nairobi in Kiambu district; but like the courts of old it moved with him, to State House in Nairobi, to his coastal lodge near Mombasa, and his lodge at Nakuru in the Rift Valley. This corresponded to his dual roles of Kikuyu paramount chief and national leader of the comprador alliance.

The inner court consisted of a small group of Kikuyu politicians from his home district of Kiambu: Mbiyu Koinange, his brother-in-law, Minister of State in the President's Office; Njoroge Mungai, his cousin, Minister for Foreign Affairs; and Charles Njonjo, the Attorney-General. It was quite rare for Kenyatta to travel or appear without one or other of these three men. The outer court – those with good access, though in much less constant attendance – consisted of two distinct elements. First, the other Kikuyu–Embu–Meru leaders, who between them controlled the bulk of the remaining important ministries: Gichuru, also from Kiambu, Minister for Defence; Kibaki, from Nyeri, Minister for Finance and Planning; Kiano, from Murang'a, Minister for Local Government; Nyagah, from Embu, Minister for Agriculture; and Angaine, from Meru, Minister for Lands and Settle-

65. Gertzel, *Politics of Independent Kenya*, op. cit. (note 17), p. 71.

66. *DN*, 15 January 1972: I am indebted for this example to Dr H. Colebatch.

ment. Second, the leaders of the three main tribes allied with the Kikuyu: Moi, the Kalenjin leader, Vice President and Minister for Home Affairs; Ngei, the main Kamba leader, Minister for Housing; and Ngala, the main Coast Province leader, Minister for Power and Communications.[67]

To the court came delegations of all kinds; district, regional, tribal, and also functional. Most of them came from particular districts, often in huge numbers, accompanied by teams of traditional dancers and choirs of schoolchildren, organized and led by the MPs and local councillors, and provincial and district officers from the area. They gave displays of dancing and singing; the leaders presented cheques for various causes sponsored by the President and expressed their sentiments of loyalty and respect; and would finally outline various needs and grievances. In return the President would thank them, commend the dances and songs, exhort them to unity and hard work, and discuss their requests, explaining why some could not be met and undertaking to attend to others. An example of one of these meetings, chosen at random, will do for all – it is only necessary to realize that similar sessions occupied a significant part of Kenyatta's typical working week.

> President Kenyatta said at the weekend that it is a declared policy of the Government to have electricity and water supply everywhere in the country – 'but this cannot be achieved overnight'. President Kenyatta was addressing a large delegation at his Gatundu home which had come from Western Province branches of the Kenya National Chamber of Commerce, headed by the Kakamega branch chairman Mr. Elijah A. Anane. With the delegation were the Western Provincial Commissioner, Mr. P. K. Boit, the Assistant Minister for Home Affairs, Mr. M. Shikuku, traders, elders, teams of traditional dancers and choirs. In a brief reply to their memorandum the President said the Government was involved in many development projects, including road construction and water supply. On building of industries in their area, Mzee [the Old Man] said that it depended mostly on investors – but the Government would continue to encourage them to spread industries in areas such as Western Province . . . The President assured the delegation that he would thoroughly study their memorandum. He also paid tribute to

---

67. Certain leading Kikuyu officials and others outside the government ought really to be included with this list; e.g. D. Ndegwa, the Governor of the Central Bank; and B. M. Gecaga, Managing Director of British-American Tobacco Ltd, and Chairman of the University Council.

the delegation for their three donations. The first amounted to 1,000/- (£K50) for Gatundu Self-Help Hospital, and was presented to the President by Mr. Anane, while the second of 1,000/- for the national Famine Relief Fund was presented by the DC for Kakamega, Mr. Nyarangi, and the last of 2,000/- (£K100) for the Armed Forces Hospital was presented by Mr. Boit. Meanwhile, President Kenyatta received another delegation from Nyeri District, headed by the Central Provincial Commissioner, Mr. Simon Nyachae, the District Commissioner, Nyeri, Mr. Chomba, and including teams of traditional dancers and school choirs. In a speech to the delegation Mzee Kenyatta said he was very delighted to hear from Mr. Nyachae that the people in the district had cooperated with the Government in cross-breeding their cattle . . . President Kenyatta reminded the nation that Uhuru [independence] without hard work was meaningless. He urged wananchi [people] to be alert at all times and ready to defend Uhuru.[68]

Some delegations, especially those including foreigners, proceeded less colourfully, though possibly with larger cheques. On such occasions the issues involved would not be reported, for instance the visit of 'a group of businessmen', or the representatives of a particular international company, or of the KNFU (i.e. large-farmers). But few people came to court without a reason. The entrance fee was substantial; visits, however discreet, had a bearing on issues raised elsewhere, if not at the visit itself: franchises for local businessmen, the terms of a foreign investment, farm-gate prices, and so on.

The court system served several purposes. The district and tribal delegations, with their gifts and dances and protestations of loyalty, and with their marked element of competition for attention, both reinforced and integrated the ethnic dimension of politics, which flowed from and lent immunity to neo-colonialism. Kenyatta on these occasions was the Father of the Nation, 'making the people happy within the frame of bourgeois society'. At the same time it helped to systematize clientelism, providing a sequence and a protocol for the seeking of favours. It could also be used to symbolize the submission of tributary strata, such as Asians who came to receive 'life membership' of KANU or foreign firms bearing cheques for the Gatundu Self Help Hospital (already fully funded by the Ministry of Health).

However, the basic significance of all this attendance at court should not be lost sight of: it worked like this because it was Kenyatta alone, with the inner court, who could make any important political decision. The ministries in Nairobi had the job of formulating detailed policy, including long-range planning. But this occurred within a clear understanding that all politically sensitive and important issues must be settled by the President and his inner court, and that this could quite often happen without much, if any, reference to the ministries concerned: the second Tripartite Agreement of 1970–1, and the milk and maize price changes of 1971 are all cases in point. Such decisions emphasized the instrumental nature of the rest of the state apparatus; its subordination to the authority of the Leader was particularly complete.

On the other hand, the civil service, parastatal bodies and the armed forces were all-important to the court, and their willingness to play their role depended on two factors: first, the presence in a large number of key posts of reliable and highly capable Kikuyu, and second, on the whole public service being 'well gallooned and fed'.

From 1965 to 1969 the number of people directly employed by the Kenya government rose from 85,000 to 109,000, an annual increase of over 6 per cent, or roughly the same rate as the growth of total national income. Down to 1970 this was accomplished without any significant increase in pay scales. So long as this was offset by the extremely rapid promotion pattern which resulted from Africanization and expansion, it did not matter very much. But by the end of the decade this leeway had been used up. Conspicuous consumption by politicians and the steady rise in the salaries of top African executives in the private sector had begun to strain the patience of senior state officials. Consequently, as we have seen, the Ndegwa commission was appointed, and it tackled the problem of increasing public-service incomes in an instructive fashion. Since the public sector as a whole accounted for 40 per cent of all enumerated employment in Kenya, major pay increases for the greater part of it would be bound to have a large impact on wages and salaries generally, as well as place a heavy burden on public revenue. Pay increases should therefore be kept to a minimum. On the other hand, a discontented public service, especially in the higher ranks, was unacceptable. What could be done was to give only a modest pay increase (about 4 per cent for most grades) but at the same time lift most of the more important restrictions on civil servants engaging in private enterprise. The commission's recommendations on these issues (which the government adopted at once) involved an acceptance that in Kenyan conditions – that is to say, the conditions of neo-colonialism – the public service had to be paid on a quasi-prebendary basis. The higher civil service would be allowed to 'take their opportunities like other citizens', and so acquire a stake in the profits of the system.[69] The commission did not deal with the armed forces, but it was taken for granted that they would be dealt with no less favourably (though it is fair to say that in Kenya they had not so far been treated more favourably either).[70] As the Development Plan remarked: 'Above all, the forces must be unswervingly loyal to the Government', a message reiterated at every military parade addressed by Kenyatta or Moi, and undoubtedly complemented by all necessary practical measures to ensure it was complied with.

Finally, no account of the political institutions of Kenya in the 1960s would be complete without some mention of the machinery of 'technical assistance' and 'aid'. Previous chapters have perhaps made the general point about the impact of capital aid sufficiently. As regards technical assistance, there were some 3,600 technical-assistance personnel of all kinds in Kenya in 1971.[71] Of these, about 2,800 were employed by the central government. Seven hundred of these were fairly junior volunteers and a further 1,000 were people employed in the four main spending ministries – education, agriculture, health, and works (in agriculture they also occupied some important policy-making posts in the ministry). A further fifty-eight were employed in the Ministry of Home Affairs. Only a handful occupied posts in the main policy-making ministries, but they were particularly significant: thirty-three in Finance and Planning, twenty-four in the legal and judicial departments,

69. See Ch. 6, pp. 193–6 above.

70. On the basis of data cited in M. Lofchie, 'Social and Institutional Change', in Lofchie et al., The State of the Nations (University of California Press, Berkeley 1971), p. 279, Kenyan army pay in 1968 seems to have matched that of the police, which in turn was related to civil service pay scales generally.

71. All data in this paragraph are derived from J. R. Nellis, 'Expatriates in the Government of Kenya', Journal of Commonwealth Political Studies, Vol. XI, No. 3, 1973, pp. 251–64.

fifteen in Commerce and Industry, and six in the Office of the President.

These people worked for the government in Kenya like any Kenyan. There was no question of divided loyalties, even given the presence in Nairobi of what were (relatively speaking) large foreign diplomatic and aid missions of the countries which supplied them. This was because of the close harmony which existed between the governments of these countries (all Western except for Yugoslavia) and the Kenyan government. This was most obvious in the case of Britain, which supplied nearly 60 per cent of all technical-assistance personnel in Kenya, a fact which was underlined by the use of British-army personnel in Kenyan army training, and the regular presence in Kenya of units of the British army.[72] But it was not essentially different in the case of the USA (the second largest source of assistance, with 11 per cent of the total) or any other donor. The importance of the technical-assistance personnel in Kenya was not that they represented foreign interests. It was rather that they helped to harmonise 'comprador' interests with those of foreign capital. To this role they brought a distinct advantage; they were familiar with the basic institutions and mechanisms of capitalism, and could often provide extremely valuable help in devising remedies for the particular contradictions which beset it in the conditions of under-development. If the results often seemed to work rather obviously in favour of a privileged few, they could try in various ways to mitigate such effects.[73] In both respects their efforts had a significant impact in smoothing the transition to neo-colonialism and in winning the maximum breathing space for the consolidation of the 'compradors' ' position.

CONCLUSIONS

This chapter does not pretend to be a comprehensive analysis of Kenyan politics in the 1960s. Its aim has been to make the simple point that in a neo-colony 'politics' must be primarily understood

---

72. The appointment of Malcolm MacDonald as a 'Special Representative' of the British government in Nairobi (after his position as Governor-General was abolished when Kenya became a republic in December 1964) was also indicative of this special relationship.

73. This is based on discussions with many technical-assistance personnel whose views are, I think, rather well synthesized by G. Papanek in the paper already cited (Ch. 1, note 28).

in terms of the interplay of economic and social forces originally generated by colonialism; otherwise it remains ultimately mysterious.

The conventional view of post-colonial societies in Africa, which tries to divorce the study of their politics from the context of imperialism and underdevelopment, sees the mounting authoritarianism of post-independence regimes as an unhappy paradox which must be explained away. The explanation usually takes the form of listing various 'legacies' inherited from the past, especially 'tribalism' and its party-political expression, factionalism. On this view, tribal factionalism inside the party obliges the government to rely instead on the civil service, which is itself full of authoritarian legacies also inherited from colonial rule.

The trouble with this is that it does not explain why some 'legacies' are so persistent, while others disappear. It is only if politics is considered in integral relationship with social and economic change that this kind of false conundrum can be avoided. 'Tribalism' certainly acquires a vicious cumulative force of its own, but its genesis is recent, and can be traced to the emergence of specific material conditions, namely the creation of economic insecurity and competition for security, which not only continue but become more acute under conditions of neo-colonialism. To explain the 'colonial' character of a post-independence regime in terms of a 'legacy' of tribalism is thus to reverse cause and effect. It would be truer to say that tribalism is a product of colonialism, and that what colonialism produces, neo-colonialism reproduces.

'Tribalism' is a form of consciousness, but more than that, it is a specific form of consciousness through which the 'comprador' regimes in many parts of Africa exercise a 'civil hegemony', complementing the coercive use of state power. In Kenya, tribalism and repression developed simultaneously in face of the challenge of a socialist, or would-be socialist opposition. Tribalism served both to displace the emerging class-consciousness of the most exploited strata of society, especially in Kikuyu country, and to prevent the KPU from channelling emerging class-antagonism into a nationwide opposition movement. At the same time the KPU was prevented from organizing and finally suppressed. Because of the dominant position of Kikuyu in the government, commerce and the higher bureaucracy, tribalism could be made to seem more a non-Kikuyu than a Kikuyu obsession, at least until 1969; and thanks to the spread of tribalism, the regime was able to frustrate and suppress the opposition with only a minimal use of force. This was important, both because at that time the influence of the Kikuyu leadership over the army was still incomplete, and because the regime was very dependent on a steady inflow of foreign capital and a substantial expatriate presence, including an important tourist trade, both of which are sensitive to the use of force.

Kenyatta and his advisers were helped greatly by various mainly short-term factors, some of which were unique to the Kenyan situation; by the availability of European-owned land for transfer, partly to landless people but also to rich farmers, traders, civil servants, etc.; by the availability of Asian-owned trade for transfer to the African petty-bourgeoisie; by the anxiety of the British to finance the land-transfer programme, in the interest of its own nationals, and in general by the anxiety of aid donors to support the highly co-operative government of what they saw as a strategic state in the region; by the high rate of foreign investment which Kenya's regional position, in particular, attracted; and by the high rate of growth of output which was available from peasant farming in the short run once it was adequately serviced, thanks to Kenya's unusual mixture of tropical and temperate farming zones. They were also assisted by the tactical and ideological weaknesses of the opposition.

Before Kenya was far into the second decade of independence, some of these advantages would have been used up. New ones might always arise; but it seemed likely that Kenyatta's successors would eventually confront the contradictions of the situation with less room for manoeuvre and little if any of the personal authority which the Old Man had deployed so successfully.

CHAPTER 8

Contradictions of Neo-colonialism

The account of Kenyan history in the 1960s which has been put forward in this book has been the result of trying to answer a series of questions posed by underdevelopment theory: what was the nature of the impact of capitalism on the economies of pre-colonial Kenya; what was the nature of the colonial economy; how did that economy change with the ending of direct colonial rule; what was the role played by social classes in this transition, and in the subsequent course of political change. To the extent that my answers to these questions are valid, what do they collectively imply?

A RECAPITULATION

In the first place, the colonial economy in Kenya was highly monopolistic. Capital was appropriated from the African population through primitive accumulation (land alienation and forced labour) and through wage labour. Some of the surplus flowed to Britain as profits and also through unequal trade. The transition from colonialism to neo-colonialism was a planned one, aimed at preserving the greater part of the monopolistic colonial economic structure in the interests of large-scale commercial, financial and estate capital by coming to terms with those leaders in the nationalist movement – a majority – who represented the new petty-bourgeois strata which had been formed throughout most of Kenya under colonialism. This bargain was sealed in 1961–2 under the pressure of the crisis in the colonial economy. The critical issue was the terms of the transfer of mixed farms in the highlands from Europeans to Africans. The decision that the incoming Africans should pay for the farms at full market value underwrote the position of foreign capital in the remainder of the economy, and the protection of private property in general.

The neo-colonial system was consolidated in the years after 1963 by a combination of policies which had a common double thread running through them: on the one hand, the adaptation of the 'peasant' modes of production to the capitalist mode in new ways, and on the other, the establishment of the new African petty-bourgeois strata within sectors of the economy formerly reserved for foreign capital.

The settlement schemes were planned so as to protect the remaining large farm sector, financed so as to reinforce the regime's commitment to foreign property, and substantially abandoned when further settlement of the smallholding variety seemed no longer to serve the immediate needs of foreign – in this case essentially British – capital. The large farm sector was preserved even though its economically parasitic nature was increasingly admitted, both because its preservation was cheaper than settlement from the point of view of the British government, and because by the mid-1960s it had already become a substantial vested interest of the African petty-bourgeoisie, including many politicians and higher civil servants. The incoming African large-scale farmers were wholly dependent on state-administered foreign capital (as credit) and still more dependent than their white predecessors on monopolies, which they succeeded in extending through their political influence over agricultural prices and in other ways. Meanwhile throughout the rest of the country the systems of land tenure were converted to freehold private ownership: property relations were brought into line with the dominant productive relations so as to ensure that peasant production would be adapted to and would supplement capitalist production, not challenge it.

Foreign capital was on the whole little affected. A modest proportion – probably less than 15 per cent of the total in 1963 – moved out of mixed farming, partly abroad and partly into manufacturing, tourism and other 'growth' sectors. New foreign capital, largely belonging to multinational firms, moved into the same sectors from abroad. These sectors, and the long-established estate sector, remained almost wholly foreign-owned. Profits were high, as was the real level of the transfer of profits overseas. The government sought with some success to control foreign capital, to prevent it exporting surplus accumulated by the employment of domestic savings, to prevent it avoiding taxation and to make it employ Kenyan executives. The government also entered into a number of joint ventures with foreign capital and even bought virtually full ownership of the electricity industry. These measures, however, were conceived largely in the interests of Kenyan capital; their main immediate effects were a substantial outflow of capital (the purchase price of the government's share acquisitions) and a substantial expansion of credit from the government-controlled banks to Kenyan businessmen. The manufacturing sector remained overwhelmingly foreign-owned. Although the multinationals' Kenyan plants were not always as capital-intensive as their plants in Europe or the USA or Japan, the fact that they were producing for a limited and predominantly middle-class market still made them low users of labour and heavy users of imported inputs. A small section of the wage-labour force obtained large wage increases during the 1960s. The bulk of the wage-labour force, however, was paid as much as its weak bargaining position, in a situation of rising unemployment, enabled it to secure, i.e. low and barely rising real wages. The government's measures to curb the power of the trade unions reinforced this and the share of wages in national income declined and that of profits rose. Most of the country's wage-workers – about a million people in all – were 'super-exploited', depending for survival on supplementary income from family agriculture.

The Kenyan businessmen whom government measures sought to establish within the capitalist mode of production were principally small retail traders, bar-owners, small-scale transporters, builders, and the like. Their numbers expanded as Asian competition was progressively excluded and credit was channelled towards them on favourable terms. However the pressure from new entrants to 'business', added to shortages of capital and know-how, made their position precarious and what they sought was a protective symbiosis with large-scale foreign capital, or forms of state monopoly which closely paralleled the situation in agriculture. The growth of their numbers, coupled with their strong representation in the government and the higher bureaucracy, enabled them to secure extensive political concessions as well as assistance from foreign capital. At the same time the absolute position attained by African non-agricultural capital by the end of the 1960s only appeared striking in relation to its almost complete exclusion from the urban scene under colonialism; the effective share of the total surplus appropriated by African capitalists remained very modest.

The class structure which both determined and was determined by these developments was still relatively 'plastic' but its essential features were clear. The various petty-bourgeois strata represented by the majority of the political leadership at independence gradually gave rise to an 'auxiliary bourgeoisie' tightly linked to foreign capital. The consolidation of their position involved them in struggles with the mass of the population, the 'industrial peasantry', which took many varied forms: the most dramatic at this period was the decisive defeat of the 'radical' opposition which eventually crystallized in the KPU. Radical politicians among both the Luo and the Kikuyu expressed the hostility to all aspects of imperialism – including its neo-colonial forms – which had been generated during the anti-colonial struggle. They drew support from poor and landless peasants and workers, as well as from various petty-bourgeois elements – especially 'middle' peasants and small traders –who felt deprived of their proper share of state services, licences, contracts, etc. The main reason for the complete defeat of this alliance lay in its own internal contradictions. The political aims of the KPU leaders were essentially petty-bourgeois in character – a 'fairer' distribution of land, more help for the 'little man' in business, and so on – although they were given a socialist flavour both by the established rhetoric of African nationalism, and by the fact that their opponents were so closely identified with foreign capital. Their commitment to parlia-mentary and electoral politics made them easy game for a regime which did not scruple to alter the rules. More fundamentally, their standpoint made them look for support among an electorate the majority of whom were just in the process of being confirmed in the individual ownership of land, and whose interests were there-fore opposed to those of people whose plots were too small or who were landless. The result was a compromised programme, which eventually succumbed to tribalism. The decisive moment in the defeat of the KPU was not its banning, but Kaggia's decision to abandon it, which in the end only anticipated by about a year the decision of most of the other KPU leaders to exchange their release from prison for an agreement to rejoin KANU. In due course most of them were reabsorbed into the ruling alliance through a variety of salaried appointments.

These processes constituted Kenya's experience of under-development under neo-colonialism. The economy was far from static; during these years, although the poor remained poor, it is doubtful if they became, in aggregate, absolutely poorer. What the mass of the people experienced was, rather, a consolidation of their subjection to the power of capital. This was still overwhelmingly an alien power, though increasingly linked to the political power of domestic capital. It meant a continuation of the structure of exploitation and domination established by colonial rule, which for the vast majority of the population meant a continuing prospect of hard, unproductive labour mainly for the benefit of others, accompanied by growing inequality, insecurity, social inferiority and the virtually complete absence of political rights.

Yet there was nothing permanent or inescapable about this, in Kenya any more than elsewhere. Any impression of an unbreakable structure, locked in a stable equilibrium, is not based in reality but in the way the facts are interpreted. Speaking generally, after all, the evidence of events throughout the third world suggests the reverse: neo-colonialism is a structure of contradictions which elsewhere have progressively transformed relatively indirect and subtle forms of control into more and more direct forms, accompanied by more and more acute political polarization, leading both to military repression and to various forms of armed struggle. In Kenya at the end of the 1960s the contradictions of neo-colonialism had had little time to develop, but this does not mean that they did not exist.

THE ILO MISSION ON UNEMPLOYMENT

An awareness of contradictions underlay the work of the large and authoritative ILO mission on unemployment which visited Kenya in 1972.[1] They, however, were perhaps bound to assume that the problems which were generated by neo-colonialism – of which unemployment was one – could in fact be overcome within the existing social, economic and political framework. Since the argument of this book is that the contradictions of neo-colonialism make this impossible, a comparison of the mission's analysis with the one offered here should make clearer what these contradictions are.

Possibly to the government's initial surprise the mission began by rejecting the concept of 'unemployment' as its central concern. Instead it concentrated on the fact that the mass of the population, while working, were abjectly poor (the report called them 'the working poor'), while a small minority enjoyed highly rewarding employment. This situation, the mission thought, was due to a fundamental 'imbalance' of the economy, which it proceeded to analyse in some detail.

In the rural areas, the report pointed out, the main cause of

---

1. *Employment, Incomes and Equality* (ILO, Geneva 1972).

unemployment and of unrewarding employment was that many people had little or no land. Young people entering the labour force therefore sought work in the towns, especially Nairobi. But there, modern-sector employment had grown very slowly, thanks to the capital-intensiveness and limited markets typical of foreign-owned manufacturing plants, most of which were import-substituting in the strict sense, producing locally what had formerly been imported – i.e. relatively sophisticated consumption goods for the highly paid few. Employment in such concerns was well paid, and moreover offered especially high rewards to those with advanced formal educational qualifications. Consequently people had been willing to pay a very high price for schooling, and there had been a massive expansion of it, accelerating the flow of people to the towns where the jobs calling for education were to be had. But since there were few such jobs, most of the young migrants eventually found work in what the report called the 'informal sector', meaning economic activities which largely escape recognition, enumeration, regulation and protection by the government. In the towns this accounted for an estimated 28–33 per cent of all African employment.[2] Labour-intensive, competitive, using locally produced inputs, developing its own skills and technology, locally owned and controlled, the informal sector was in the mission's view the model of the kind of economy Kenya needed; but instead of being encouraged to the maximum it was restricted and harassed so that it too failed to furnish adequate incomes to those who were engaged in it.

In a historical chapter the report traced this complex of rela-tionships to the fact that at independence the colonial economy had been taken over largely intact, and that this economy had been structured to yield high incomes for the small white minority; and it also pointed out that the school system, the pattern of government spending, the fiscal and tax system, investment policy, and so on, reinforced this economic structure.

> Since independence, economic growth has largely continued on the lines set by the earlier colonial structure. Kenyanisa-tion has radically changed the racial composition of the group of people in the centre of power and many of its policies, but has had only a limited effect on the mechanisms which main-tain its dominance – the pattern of government income and expenditure, the freedom of foreign firms to locate their

2. ibid., p. 225.

offices and plants in Nairobi, and the narrow stratum of expenditure by a high-income elite superimposed on a base of
limited mass-consumption.[3]

Unless there is a major change in development strategy and
policies, and in the absence of effective and powerful redistributive mechanisms, the heavy concentration of income
is likely to continue and may be further intensified in the
future. A high degree of income inequality is a characteristic
feature of private enterprise economies in an early stage of
development. Further, these inequalities tend to be intensified
with the growth of the economy over long periods of time.
There are reasons to believe that such dynamic factors tending to perpetuate and intensify inequalities may be operative
in the Kenyan social and economic system.[4]

So far the mission's understanding of the problem seems not
very different from that of this book. The fundamental difference
emerges clearly, however, when the report turns from analysis to
making recommendations for rectifying what it sees as the basic
'distortion' which had produced this situation; for the mission
treated the situation as capable of being put to rights by a programme of reforms. This had two consequences. One was a series
of politically utopian recommendations. The other was, I think,
a misrepresentation of the modes of production in Kenya, and
their mutual articulation.

The basic thrust of all the recommendations was that if income
were distributed more equally the 'working poor' would not only
be richer (by hypothesis) but would also constitute a mass market
for the expansion of domestic manufacturing and services on
labour-intensive lines; an expansion which the mission saw as an
essential alternative to an unrealistic as well as undesirable dependence, under existing plans, on further massive inflows of
foreign capital.

The main redistributive recommendations were as follows. To
generate productive employment for the masses, the one per cent
of the population earning over £700 per annum (the rich) would
accept a substantial cut in their incomes immediately (through a
drastic improvement in tax collection, and a more progressive tax
structure) followed by a complete freeze for five years, and thereafter would forego any substantial improvement for a further seven

3. ibid., p. 11.
4. ibid., p. 97.

years, to 1985;[5] so that the real incomes of the 'working poor' and the wholly unemployed could be doubled, bringing them by 1985 at the latest up to roughly the level of the legal minimum wage adopted for Nairobi in 1966. This was called 'redistribution from growth'; after the first impact of increased taxation on the rich they would give up any further improvement for ten to twelve years while all economic growth was channelled into investment designed to raise rural incomes and foster the 'informal' sector of urban employment. This would also be accompanied by a large-scale redistribution of land from large to smallholdings, and a re-direction of services like extension and credit towards the mass of really small farmers, together with a varied package of pro-grammes for every district and division on the lines of the Special Rural Development Programme; a complete restructuring of the educational system to provide basic (mainly vocational) schooling free for every child, with an immediate move to a regional re-distribution of school places; much tougher terms for foreign investors, with a progressive revision of all existing grants of pro-tection, tightened company taxation, and so on.

The character of these recommendations becomes clearer if they are seen in terms of the various groups whose interests they would affect. To put it in a nutshell, the people who had fought their way to positions of power and wealth in the Kenyatta regime – minis-ters, MPs, councillors, KANU office-holders and their various clienteles – were to agree to surrender a significant part of the advantage they had gained for themselves and their families. To begin with, they would start paying income tax, or start paying much more income tax, as a result of a drastic tightening of collec-tion (the mission cited evidence suggesting that over 50 per cent of those liable to pay income tax were not assessed), and making the tax progressive. Those with large farms who were seriously in arrears with payments to the AFC or ADC would have their farms taken away and redistributed in smallholdings to the landless. In the longer run, landowners would have to agree to a land tax which would make it essential to sell off land which was not being profitably farmed. The better-off smallholders, teachers, traders and the like who had obtained the larger low-density plots in the Million Acre settlement schemes would be put under similar

---

5. For people with incomes between £200 and £700 a year the mission proposed that increases should be kept below 3 per cent annually: those with less than £200 should get 3 per cent more per annum.

pressures to subdivide and sell off a large part of their holdings so that this could be redistributed in smaller plots. Those traders, distributors, transporters, owners of service enterprises, in fact all African businessmen who had succeeded in breaking into some more or less protected area of activity, where a more substantial and secure profit could be made, would have to give up their new-found protection so as to give encouragement to the unregulated and competitive (in the mission's terms, 'informal') sectors from which they had recently escaped.[6] Higher civil servants and company executives would accept a five-year freeze of salary scales (though the mission thought that their annual increments might keep their real earnings level with inflation), and minimal improvements for seven years beyond that. The areas of the country best provided with services, notably Kikuyu, Embu, Meru, and Machakos, were to give up their lead so that services elsewhere could be brought up to a comparable level. Last but not least, foreign enterprises would pay higher corporate taxation, drastically reduce their profit remittances, and shift away from the capital-intensive technology and imported inputs usually supplied by their parent companies without a significant loss of enthusiasm for investment in Kenya.

The obvious puzzle presented by these proposals is what incentive the mission thought all these groups – the heart and soul of the alliance of domestic and foreign capital – might possibly have for making such sacrifices. Apart from anything else, there was at least a family resemblance between the mission's package of proposals and the essentials of the KPU's former programme. The KPU had not of course worked out a programme as fully or with as much sophistication as the mission; but then the mission did not, for its part, seem to have pondered the significance of the suppression of the KPU. What did the mission think would induce the Kenyatta regime to do in the 1970s what it had not only not done, but had destroyed its opponents for advocating, in the 1960s?

From the report itself it is hardly possible to answer this. In several places the mission cited the principle of 'growing incomes,

---

6. This was the general theme of the mission's many detailed recommendations for cutting down on protection and monopoly profits by a revision of tariff and import quote restrictions, by the effective abolition of restrictive licensing in trading and transportation and of the oligopolies handed out by the KNTC – see especially Chapter 12. But the mission's recommendations for assisting the 'informal sector' tended to gravitate in an opposite direction.

equitably distributed' from Sessional Paper No. 10 of 1965, as if that formula reflected something more than the homage vice pays to virtue. Here and there one detects the spirit which Marx noted among the French democrats in 1849:

> The democrats concede that a privileged class confronts them, but they, along with all the rest of the nation, form the *people*. What they represent is the *people's rights*; what interests them is the *people's interest*. Accordingly, when a struggle is impending, they do not have to examine the interests and positions of the different classes. They do not have to weigh their own resources too critically . . .[7]

At other times, the mission seemed to suggest that whatever their short-term disadvantages, its proposals were in the long-term interests of the regime. In a final chapter called 'The Cost of Inaction', it wrote:

> We realise that in many cases action along these lines may be difficult – politically, administratively, financially and psychologically. It may represent a break with familiar traditions and offend or hurt sectional interests. But when the cost of action is weighed we plead that the cost of inaction may be also considered. . . . Moreover, the cost of dealing with problems may be much higher once they pass the threshold of what is considered intolerable, since the opportunities of dealing with them by rational and consistent methods and by national consensus may be greatly lessened . . .
>
> The frustration of younger people in search of opportunities – frustration instilled by their present preparation for life – may lead to alienation and intolerable tensions . . .
>
> . . . the problem may become insoluble in future, whereas it can still be avoided by timely action.[8]

But the mission did not make clear what 'intolerable' meant in this context, and the hard fact remained that the 'cost' of inaction, in the future as in the past, would evidently be borne by the 'working poor', not by the leading supporters of the regime. Or did the mission believe that the government's power ultimately depended on the support of the 'working poor'? Perhaps a clue lay in the mission's remark that it was 'not the first group to see parallels with Latin American experience, in which inequality becomes deeply locked into the structure of the country and only the most

---

7. *The Eighteenth Brumaire*, op. cit. (see Ch. 7, note 1), p. 278.

8. *Employment, Incomes and Equality* (note 1), pp. 327–9.

drastic remedies can change the situation'. But if the mission hoped to induce the government to adopt egalitarian measures out of fear of revolution they were careful not to say so explicitly.

The mission's thinking about the motivation which the government might have for implementing its proposals was unclear; the reason for this lay, however, not so much in particular illusions about the nature of the regime, as in the limitation of its whole approach. It saw clearly enough that within the existing socio-economic arrangements the problem of unemployment was certainly insoluble. But its thinking was cast within the logic of a social science whose central concepts ultimately embodied bourgeois interests. What it saw, therefore, was not the contradictory reality, but only an 'imbalance'; not a struggle of oppressing and oppressed classes, but only a series of particular 'conflicts of interests' which the 'leadership' would resolve, if only from enlightened self-interest, in favour of the common good. The mission saw that poverty and unemployment were connected with 'income inequality' and that this in turn was linked to the role of 'foreign capital' (in the sense of foreign companies producing capital-intensively for narrow markets of relatively affluent consumers). But it did not see that these in turn were an expression of, and a condition for, the power structure in Kenya and in the international capitalist system as a whole. They wrote of social or political forces antithetical to their own proposals as 'interests' or 'obstacles' which would have to be overridden or overcome, as if there were some further 'interest', independent of these and more powerful, which would respond to its appeal.[9] But the political power of the compradors, and the political impotence of the 'working poor' were also integral parts of the structure of underdevelopment.

Once this is grasped, the central weakness in the mission's analysis can be discerned throughout its argument, and not merely in the utopianism of its recommendations.

For example, although it devoted a chapter of its report to the historical context of the problem, the mission's conception of history was narrow. It saw the contribution of history as one of explaining how the inequality of incomes established in the colonial period (under 'the influence of the colonial government and the European settlers') came to be carried over into the post-

---

9. See for instance the reference to 'sectional interests' in the passage quoted on p. 263.

independence period. Basically its explanation for this was that for the African leadership, conditioned by years of exposure to the European reference-group, 'the political aim of taking over the economy became merged almost imperceptibly with individual aspirations to take over the jobs, positions and life styles which the economy made possible'; 'the immediate problem appeared to be to take over the economy, not to change it'.[10] The historical context thus became reduced essentially to the reporting of an understandable mistake which, once perceived, could be corrected. How and why the Europeans became established in Kenya in the first place, the relatively epiphenomenal role played by the 'settlers' proper in the penetration of the country by foreign capital, the adaptations of foreign capital to the transitions of independence and to changing world conditions, the emergence of new comprador interests – in a word, the *continuing* forces which produced and reproduce the problem of unemployment in Kenya – were not discussed. Nor were the mechanisms which continually reproduce inequality; inequality was discussed as something which perpetuated itself by mere inertial force, rather than as constantly *developing and evolving* as the result not merely of continued old policies, but of new policies adopted since independence which extended inequality in fresh ways.

Consequently what the mission saw as centrally wrong in the situation was a vicious circle of extreme inequality of incomes leading to a distorted pattern of demand, i.e., very narrow markets for sophisticated goods and services capable of being provided only by protected, capital-intensive concerns using advanced foreign-owned technology and imported inputs, with a consequent further stagnation in the domestic rural and informal sectors, and a further reinforcement of income-inequality. What they wanted was to break this vicious circle by a redistribution of income, giving rise to a wide market for goods and services of a relatively simple kind that could be produced by an expanding locally-owned, labour-intensive industry using local inputs. But the mission also assumed that this change must take place within a capitalist framework. They imagined the rapid expansion of an autonomous local capitalism, reformed and free from contradictions. If the measures they recommended for achieving this were unreal it was because the goal itself was unreal. The contradictions of capitalism could not be so easily resolved.

---

10. *Employment, Incomes and Equality* (note 1), pp. 87–8.

In the mission's thinking a key role was played by the concept of the 'informal sector', which it regarded as a major conceptual advance.[11] The 'informal sector' consisted, according to the report, of economic activities characterized by ease of entry into the activity concerned, reliance on indigenous resources, family ownership, smallness of scale, labour-intensiveness and 'adapted technology', skills acquired outside the formal school system, and unregulated and competitive markets. The question was, the mission said, why this way of doing things provided such low incomes for those who followed it. The answer, it believed, was threefold; first, the low incomes of those it catered for; second, official discouragement, owing to a 'pejorative' official view of the value of such activities; and third, lack of demand from the 'formal sector', public and private. Therefore it proposed that besides increasing the incomes of the poor the government should turn from harassing to fostering the 'informal sector', and should also start placing official orders with it, and inducing firms in the private ('formal') sector to do likewise. From being the Cinderella of underdevelopment the 'informal sector' could thus become a major source of future growth.

But what, after all, is the 'informal sector'? In illustrating the concept the mission generally referred to self-employed craftsmen and the like in the towns: 'a variety of carpenters, masons, tailors and other tradesmen, as well as cooks and taxi-drivers, offering virtually the full range of basic skills needed to provide goods and services for a large though often poor section of the population'; 'the carpenter at work behind his dwelling, the tailor inside an unmarked mud and plaster hut, or the *matatu* [illegal taxi] driver who is out earning fares'.[12] Although the mission's interest in the 'informal sector' was primarily in its labour-intensive character, it seldom referred to the fact that it consisted also and predominantly of wage-workers; and this also enabled them to write as though the *wholly* unemployed were 'outside' the sector altogether. Yet what

---

11. The mission recorded a debt in their thinking about the 'informal sector' to 'a number of sociologists, economists and other social scientists in the Institute of Development Studies at the University of Nairobi' and added: 'One begins to sense that a new school of analysis may be emerging, drawing on work in East and West Africa and using the formal–informal distinction to gain insights into a wide variety of situations' (p. 6). Such a development might well express the class outlook of some academics in this situation, but perhaps the mission's demonstration of where such a 'school' would lead may encourage the emergence of a more radical approach.

12. ibid., pp. 5 and 225.

stands out about the so-called 'informal sector' is that most of what it covers is primarily *a system of very intense exploitation of labour*, with very low wages and often very long hours, underpinned by the constant pressure for work from the 'reserve army' of job-seekers. The mission noted evidence that in 1970 the lowest-paid workers in Nairobi worked the longest hours, with about 30 per cent working over sixty hours per week. On smallholdings in the rural areas in 1968 wages were in some places as low as 50 cents a day, and the rate 'most often given' was between 1/50 and 2/- a day.[13] The 'informal sector' was in fact a euphemism for the particularly intense forms of exploitation to which the articulation of the capitalist and 'peasant' modes of production gave rise, as Engels observed 100 years ago:

> Competition permits the capitalist to deduct from the price of labour power that which the family earns from its little garden or field. The workers are compelled to accept any piece wages offered them, because otherwise they would get nothing at all and they could not afford to live from the products of their agriculture alone . . .[14]

Or, as the mission put it, ' . . . the bulk of employment in the informal sector, far from being only marginally productive, is economically efficient and profit-making . . .'[15]

The mystification of the 'informal sector' also resulted in a degree of self-contradiction. According to the mission, one of the keys to increased employment lay in effecting *links* between the 'informal sector' and the 'formal sector' – i.e. the protected, monopolistic sector of the capitalist mode of production – by increasing the latter's demand for the 'informal sector's' goods and services. Yet the links binding the 'informal sector' to the 'formal sector' – links of mutual dependence and mutual antagonism – could hardly be more intimate. What the 'informal sector' does is to provide the 'formal sector' with goods and services at a very low price, which makes possible the high profits of the 'formal sector'. Smallholders provide cheap food crops, pastoralists cheap beef, traders cheap distribution, transporters cheap communications; the owners of workshops making shoes out of old tyres and stoves

---

13. Mimeographed draft of J. Heyer, D. Ireri and J. Moris, 'Rural Development in Kenya' (Institute for Development Studies, Nairobi 1969), p. 167.

14. 'The Housing Question', Marx–Engels, *Selected Works* (Moscow 1962), Vol. I, p. 553.

15. *Employment, Incomes and Equality* (note 1), p. 5.

out of old tins, the sellers of charcoal and millers of maize; all of them provide cheap goods and services designed for the poverty life-style of those whose work makes the 'formal sector' profitable, and enables them to live on their wages.

So what did the mission really mean when it called for links to be made between the 'formal' and the 'informal' sectors – apart from diverting attention away from the central contradiction involved in all these activities? It meant that the sort of links which the monopolistic, mainly foreign sector had *not* previously found it profitable to have with small-scale African firms, and which the government itself had hitherto had with foreign firms, should now be added to the more fundamental links which already existed between foreign capital and the government on the one hand, and the rest of the economy on the other. Provided the new goods and services which foreign capital would be asked to procure from the 'informal sector' were cheap enough to compensate them for what they would lose in not buying from their own sources of supply abroad, no doubt it would be happy to collaborate. But this could only happen if, in addition to 'informal' wage-rates remaining extremely low, a good deal of regulation and protection were introduced to govern these transactions. The mission, for instance, envisaged special training schemes for 'informal' producers entering into arrangements to supply goods to 'formal sector' enterprises, together with state loans for new plant, long-term purchasing contracts and the like; what would still be 'informal'–i.e. 'competitive' – about the activities involved in this process would evidently be only the wages paid.[16] Consistently enough, the mission's discussion of trade-unionism ('industrial relations') did not even entertain the possibility of an antagonism between workers and employers, let alone regard it as being of central importance. It even wrote that in the rural sector 'it is hoped [it did not say by whom] that increased trade-union activities may help to bring about an improvement in the working and living conditions of rural workers . . . [trade unions] could exert effective pressure when necessary to protect the interests of *small farmers, casual workers and landless labour* . . .'[17]

In a word: by talking of two 'sectors' the mission saw a *duality* (the word is theirs) where there was a *unity*, i.e. between the mass

---

16. For instance, the mission recommended: 'the *de facto* policy of awarding [government] construction contracts to enterprises paying less than official minimum wages could be made official . . .' (p. 230).

17. ibid., p. 259 (italics added).

CONTRADICTIONS OF NEO-COLONIALISM

of very low incomes in general and the very high profit-levels of the larger, mostly foreign firms; and ignored a vital contradiction, i.e. between the employers and the workers within the so-called 'informal sector'. The effect of the mission's proposals for 'linking' the two 'sectors' (even in the improbable event of its recommendations on income redistribution and the circumscription of foreign capital being implemented) would be primarily to transfer business from high-wage foreign-owned firms to low-wage African-owned firms, and to enable a new stratum of the African petty-bourgeoisie to transcend the limitations of the competitive market and achieve a measure of protection among the ranks of the auxiliary bourgeoisie.[18] Because of the more intensive use of labour by small African firms than by large foreign ones, the problem of *un*employment might be relieved.[19] It was not clear how the problem of the 'working poor' would be. On the contrary, the real meaning of the mission's proposal about the 'informal sector' was that exploitation should be spread more evenly.

Nor was it clear how, after the initial redistribution of income was brought about, the problem of inequality and unemployment was not to reappear. The mission's treatment of this point was brief, and can be quoted in full:

> It cannot be emphasised too much that our strategy is based not on permanent transfers of income to the lowest income group through redistribution from the top, but on investment to provide the unemployed and the working poor with the basis for earning reasonable minimum incomes the levels of which can be raised over time. Initially, the target would be to double the present average income of the lower income group by giving an income to the unemployed and raising the incomes of the working poor. Our hope and expectation is

18. One problem not adequately discussed in the report is the extent to which consumer tastes have already been moulded by advertising and conspicuous consumption by the rich, so that any substantial increase in the incomes of the working poor would expand demand for 'formal sector' products (such as bread, leather shoes, bicycles, etc.) rather than for craft-produced cheap goods.

19. This is on the assumption that the steps recommended against the excesses of foreign firms with regard to surplus transfers, etc., and other measures, would not reduce the overall growth rate assumed by the mission of a minimum of 6½ per cent per annum. The mission's judgement that their recommendations would not on balance do this seems well supported, but with an important proviso: this would depend on the balance of their proposals being faithfully reflected in the balance of the measures adopted. If they were implemented selectively, and especially if the redistribution of income were much less than they recommended, balance-of-payments constraints and other problems might well reduce the overall rate of growth so that the level of *un*employment was not much affected.

that once this has been achieved the economic system which will have been created as a result of the new strategy will continue afterwards to make for more equal income distribution and an economic growth which is the healthier and faster for being more widely shared and more equitably distributed.[20]

It would be interesting to know what mechanisms the mission thought would operate in the Kenya of the late 1980s to keep raising the 'reasonable minimum' income levels of the poor, and how the 'economic system' would continue to 'make for more equal income distribution'. The mission also wrote that 'an employment strategy can be sustained only on the basis of a national consensus, when all concerned feel that they benefit fairly'. No example was given of such a consensus about the fairness of the benefits of the distribution of benefits under a capitalist system.

The truth seems to be that the mission brought to its work a broadly 'social-democratic' outlook according to which governments should govern in the interests of the majority. The mission, however, had to address itself to a situation in which the regime actually rested on the support of foreign and domestic capital. The mission hoped to influence it in an egalitarian direction. But the effect of putting forward an analysis which ignored the contradictions of the situation was that it might be used to legitimize the essential features of neo-colonialism, by representing them as compatible with the progressive, reforming programme suggested by the mission. The historic function of Sessional Paper No. 10 of 1965 on African Socialism had been to formulate a 'developmental' ideology adapted to 'comprador' interests. The ILO report indicated how this might next be modified in a populist direction. The result was a new government statement, Sessional Paper No. 10 of 1973 on Employment, which stated that 'in most cases, proposals in the [ILO] report reflect, or are consistent with, current government policies'. Although this new document was rather general in the commitments it made, its main thrust was clear enough. Most of the mission's recommendations on the informal sector would be adopted. Those on the redistribution of income and assets would be adopted wherever they did not seriously offend the established interests of capital, i.e. very circumspectly, if at all, as regards the salariat and the large-scale farmers, for instance, though with more vigour as regards unionized labour; while the government declared itself determined to

20. ibid., p. 114.

give priority in all its policies to the 60 per cent of households earning less than £60 per year, and above all to 'those who are absolutely landless and without work and pastoralists in semi-arid and arid areas', and to try to 'provide either a wage job or land to everyone by 1980'.[21]

The government's claim that the ILO mission's recommendations largely reflected its current policies contained an element of truth: so long as 'populist' policies (such as the SRDP) were compatible with the general interests of the various forms of capital on which the government's power rested they would continue to be adopted, since they strengthened the government's relative autonomy. And for foreign capital, the growth of small-scale domestic capitalism, capable of absorbing the excess growth of the labour-force and preventing the development of absolute pauperization, was desirable on both economic and political grounds. Where the ILO mission differed from the government, was that it was much less sensitive to the interests of the middle and higher bureaucracy, and of the large-scale farmers and the auxiliary bourgeoisie and those pressing to join them; interests which depended on multiple forms of protection and monopoly and were thus basically opposed to the changes which the mission had in mind.

CONTRADICTIONS OF NEO-COLONIALISM

This difference, however, concerns what is, perhaps, the central contradiction of neo-colonialism, in its essential meaning of a system of domination of the mass of the population of a country by foreign capital, by means other than direct colonial rule. By its nature such dominance requires the development of domestic class interests which are allied to those of foreign capital, and which uphold their joint interests in economic policy and enforce their dominance politically. This system is however unstable. The underdevelopment which begins with colonialism (if not before) and continues under neo-colonialism implies limits to growth and a growing polarization of classes as the exploitation of the masses become more apparent. To avert this, foreign capital seeks a redistribution of income internally (on the general basis exemplified in the ILO report) so as to expand domestic markets and hence production and wage employment. But any substantial redistribution of income is at the expense of the owners of domestic,

---

21. *Sessional Paper on Employment* (No. 10 of 1973, Nairobi), p. 68.

mainly small-scale capital – i.e. the domestic allies of foreign capital. In the Kenyan situation, too – and this seems likely to be true elsewhere in Africa – a redistribution of income needed to be accompanied by a dismantling of domestic monopolies if it was to have a sustained effect on the growth of internal demand. But these monopolies were also very important to the interests of the domestic petty-bourgeoisie and auxiliary bourgeoisie who, far from wishing to dismantle it, pressed for its extension. They would have much preferred to see a reduction in the level of protection accorded to foreign capital, and in the level of capital exports by foreign firms. The one solution jeopardized the alliance between domestic and foreign capital, and the other threatened the continued inflow of foreign capital on which the neo-colonial economy depended.

Where a domestic bourgeoisie is relatively strong it may, in theory at least, opt to pursue a policy of economic nationalism, with various 'populist' programmes aimed at securing the support of particular elements among the workers and peasants, and at the expense of some elements of foreign capital. But in Kenya, once the opportunities for adopting populist measures at the expense of Asian commercial capital (and settler large-farm capital) were exhausted, the continuing dependence of the African petty-bourgeoisie and auxiliary bourgeoisie on foreign capital seemed more likely to lead to a policy of wage controls and of land distribution which would as far as possible redistribute income between different sections of the 'industrial peasantry', rather than between the middle classes as a whole, and workers and peasants as a whole. In that case there would be a gradual intensification of the exploitation of labour, with the risk of a growing politicization of the masses. At the same time the conflicting interests of domestic and foreign capital, and of different sections of domestic capital (large-scale farmers, small-scale manufacturers, importers, rentiers, etc.) would tend to weaken the alliance of the different interests supporting the regime, with potentially serious consequences in the succession crises to which any 'bonapartist' government is necessarily prone.

The sort of structural constraints with which the ILO mission was mainly concerned were symptoms of such contradictions, and could not be removed unless the contradictions were resolved. Moreover, focusing on such constraints leads to rather uncertain conclusions when they are abstracted from the antagonisms between classes. The mission, for instance, seems to have been particularly concerned that Kenya was about to encounter a serious balance of payments problem, which could not be solved by any realistically foreseeable level of capital inflows, and which would lead to a declining rate of growth, rising unemployment, and hence perhaps to political unrest which could have further repercussions on foreign investment, tourism, etc. An interesting early paper by one of the members of the mission went a good deal further than the mission's final report in developing this line of thought:

> It would seem safe to predict that the present strategy of development incorporates the necessary and sufficient conditions for the following characteristics to emerge within the next 25 years:
>
> (a) agricultural stagnation resulting from adverse terms of trade, urban migration and low rates of surplus and re-investment, leading to urban food shortages and structural inflation;
>
> (b) continual balance of payments crises requiring dependence upon foreign finance to a growing degree, and perhaps to repeated devaluation;
>
> (c) non-competitive domestic industrial sector with powerful trade unions, resulting in employers and unions forcing up import and food prices, further feeding inflationary tendencies; and
>
> (d) increased urban migration as agricultural terms of trade deteriorate, resulting in explosive growth of shanty-towns around Nairobi.
>
> In brief, the present strategy provides the ingredients for secular stagnation, and must be seen as an underdevelopment strategy. It seems quite possible that Kenya can achieve this state much more rapidly than Latin American countries have managed to do.[22]

Yet although such fears may have been justified, a very large number of other factors enter into the total situation, making all such models of rather doubtful value as guides to policy. Population pressure might be absorbed by further land transfer from foreign owners, by irrigation to bring more land into production, and by a continuing reduction in plot sizes made possible by improved technology. Export markets for many crops might greatly

---

22. John Weeks, 'Imbalance Between the Center and the Periphery in Kenya: A Diagnosis and a Strategy', n.d., mimeo, p. 8. I am grateful to Dr Weeks for an opportunity to consult this paper.

expand, and the terms of trade, which moved sharply against Kenya in 1973–4, might improve later; new policies and new technologies might expand the use of labour in manufacturing more rapidly than in the past; and so on. In other words, models of this kind are not crystal balls which hold the secrets of the future; and for the same reasons it would be dogmatic and mechanical to assert that neo-colonialism and underdevelopment must inevitably lead to revolutionary change in Kenya as a result of inevitable social and economic crisis.

On the other hand, it is equally dogmatic, and highly misleading, to regard the social and political system which had emerged in Kenya by the end of the 1960s as 'stable'. The post-independence years were exceptionally favourable for the consolidation of neo-colonialism. Even so, those years had witnessed some intense class struggles. The initiative in these was taken by the African petty-bourgeoisie (against settler and Asian capital, and against wage-workers and the poorer peasants) and by large-scale foreign capital (against organized labour). In the course of these struggles the power of the state was used forcefully to give the petty-bourgeoisie the various forms of protection it wanted, to subdue the unions and to progressively eliminate political opposition. The result was a structure of social control, based on clientelism, and of ideological domination based on a mixture of tribalism, 'free enterprise' ethics and 'development' doctrines; reinforced by a restrained but effective system of repression, in which organized opposition was outlawed. The 'stability' of Kenya in 1971, on which it was so frequently congratulated by western journalists, was therefore an appearance which resulted directly from the assertion of state power by the currently dominant combination of classes, and did not reflect the underlying reality of increasingly sharp social and economic contradictions.

It was, in fact, obvious to everyone that when Kenyatta, then in his seventies, left the political scene, the problem of succession which is inherent in bonapartism would reveal these contradictions again. The balance of forces within the ruling alliance, which reflected Kenyatta's special position in the country, would be upset and, in the ensuing struggle for power, class forces which had been repressed would quite likely be released. This could apply to the organized workers, to landless and unorganized rural workers and to the urban unemployed, whose struggles for the time being were manifested largely in indirect forms, such as absenteeism, illegal squatting, crop theft, organized urban crime, and so on. It would apply in a different way to the army, where the immediate question of succession was likely to be settled.

On a longer view, however, the forces which would ultimately combine to transform the social and economic order in Kenya were – like those which produced underdevelopment – regiona and international, as well as national. Developments in neighbouring countries, especially Tanzania and Uganda, and elsewhere on the continent – particularly in the liberation struggles in southern Africa – would have very important consequences for the future course of struggles inside Kenya. So would the vicissitudes of the international capitalist system generally, as the long boom of the 1950s and '60s began to give way in the early 1970s to a period of uncertainty, monetary crisis and the risk of recession.

The resulting processes of change which would be generated in Kenya would, however, certainly be prolonged, and meanwhile it is true that academic studies can contribute little to the effort to achieve new strategies of development grounded in the interests of the mass of those who are currently the victims of underdevelopment. Perhaps the most such studies can do is to try not to obscure the structures of exploitation and oppression which underdevelopment produces, and which in turn sustain it.

Appendix

Selected social and economic statistics for Kenya

a) Population

(i) By race (to nearest thousand)

	African	Asian	European	Other
1962	8,365	177	56	38
1969	10,733	139	41	30

(ii) Main towns ('000)

	Nairobi	Mombasa	Nakuru	Kisumu	Thika	Eldoret	Nanyuki	Kitale	Malindi	Kericho	Nyeri
1962	267	180	38	24	14	20	10	9	6	8	8
1969	509	247	47	32	18	18	12	12	11	10	10

(iii) Tribes

	Kikuyu	Embu	Meru	Luo	Luhya	Kamba	Kalenjin	Kisii	Mijikanda	Somali	Masai	Taita	Other
millions 1969	2·2	0·1	0·6	1·5	1·5	1·2	1·2	0·7	0·5	0·3	0·2	0·1	0·5

Source: Statistical Abstract 1971

b) Main exports (percentages)

	Coffee	Tea	Petroleum products	Sisal	Meat	Pyrethrum	Hides & skins	Cement	Wattle bark & extract	Sodium carbonate	Other
1964	32·7	12·9	4·6	12·8	4·6	5·2	2·7	1·7	2·3	1·5	19·0
1970	31·1	17·7	11·4	2·6	4·0	3·0	2·3	2·3	1·6	2·3	21·7

Source: Statistical Abstract, 1971

(c) *Gross Domestic Product at constant (1964) prices by sectors*

	K million		per cent of total		Average annual rates of growth
	1964	1970*	1964	1970*	1964–70*
Agriculture	51·97	69·11	15·80	14·26	4·9
Forestry	1·88	2·80	0·57	0·58	6·9
Fishing	0·85	1·26	0·26	0·26	6·8
Mining and quarrying	1·46	2·50	0·44	0·52	9·4
Manufacturing and repairing	34·17	53·24	10·39	10·98	7·7
Building and construction	6·82	16·18	2·07	3·34	15·5
Electricity and water	4·84	7·10	1·47	1·47	6·6
Transport, storage and communication	24·52	41·54	7·46	8·57	9·1
Wholesale and retail trade	32·98	48·18	10·03	9·94	6·5
Banking, insurance and real estate	9·85	18·31	3·00	3·78	10·9
Ownership of dwellings	13·34	14·46	4·06	2·98	1·3
Other services	11·90	20·34	3·62	4·20	9·4
Private households (domestic services)	2·94	3·66	0·89	0·76	3·7
General Government	42·47	73·08	12·91	15·08	9·5
Total monetary economy	239·98	371·76	72·97	76·71	7·6
Non-monetary economy	88·89	112·86	27·03	23·29	4·1
Total monetary and non-monetary	328·87	484·62	100·00	100·00	6·6

* Provisional

Source: Economic Survey 1971

d) *Pattern of trade: Visible imports and exports*, 1970, by value (K£ '000)*

	Exports to	Imports from
Tanzania	14,752	5,938
Uganda	16,698	10,048
Rest Africa	9,158	1,833
UK	14,847	41,459
W. Germany	6,817	11,197
Rest W. Europe	13,303	24,501
E. Europe	1,952	3,476
USA	6,357	11,906
Canada	1,805	796
Middle East	2,272	14,292
India	2,735	3,104
Japan	1,225	15,196
Other	11,135	14,266
Total	103,056	158,012

* Excluding re-exports

Source: Statistical Abstract 1971

(e) *Comparative statistics*

	Populations 1969 (millions)	1969 GNP per capita ($)	Average growth rates of real GDP 1960–70 %	Aid receipts 1965–70 ($ millions)	Aid receipts per capita 1965–70 [4] ($)
Kenya	10·5	136	5·1	455·83	43
Uganda	8·3	118	6·7	184·67	22
Tanzania	12·9	96	4·3	269·53	21
Zaire	17·0	98	2·6[1]	679·83	40
Ivory Coast	4·2	300	7·9[2]	330·02	78
Ghana	8·7	256	2·6	334·20	38
Africa (average)	—	150	1·7	—	—
India	536·9	89	3·7	6,804·99	13
Latin America (average)	—	475	5·4[3]	—	—

[1] 1959–70   [2] 1960–68   [3] excluding Cuba   [4] based on 1969 populations

Source: UNCTAD: Handbook of International Trade and Development Statistics 1972

Index

African Socialism, Sessional Paper o
1965 on, 60, 72, 208; and
nationalization, 131, 223; appealed to
by ILO report, 262–3; as 'comprador'
ideology, 145, 221–3, 224, 270
African Workers' Federation (AWF),
48–9
Africanization, of large farm sector,
marketing boards, etc., 103–5; of
foreign companies, 122–4, 147; of
FKE, 140; of trade, 150–9; of road
transport, 159–63; of construction,
163; of manufacturing, 164; of
shareholding, 164–5
Agricultural Development Corporation
(ADC), 65, 104, 261; and large farm
purchase, 88–9, 96, 100
Agricultural Finance Corporation
(AFC), 65, 71, 91, 92, 102, 104, 105,
261; finances sale of large farms to
Africans, 82, 85, 93–5, 100
aid, 65, 250; technical assistance, 250–1;
for land registration, 70; for first
settlement schemes, 74, 78–9, 81–2;
for new schemes after 1970, 84, 86; for
large farm purchase, 88–9
Akumu, Denis, 143, 215
armed forces, 238–9, 250–1, 253
Asians, 33–4, as indigenous bourgeoisie,
38–9, 119–21; entry into
manufacturing, 44–5; share purchases
by, 129; transfer of trade to Africans,
151
Assembly, National, 244–5

balance of payments, 77, 87, 130–1
banks, commercial, monopoly among,
35; and agricultural credit, 71, 100;
acquired by governments, 130
Blundell, Sir Michael, 42
bourgeoisie, English in India, 4; role in
neo-colonies, 10, 26–7; African

entrants to, 51, 165–9; 174–8;
resident European and Asian, 174–5;
class consciousness of African,
176–7; predominance of Kikuyu
in, 202; Fanon's views on, 210–11;
see also class structure, classes,
strata
bureaucracy, higher, 193–8; Marx's
views on, 209; growth of, 249; method
of rewarding, 249–50
'businessmen', 177, 195

Cabinet, 246
Campbell, Sir Colin, 218–20
capital, xiv, 2, 3, 17; protected by
monopolies, 35; conflict between
forms of, 39, 55; flight of, 58; inflow of,
118–19; transfers of, 137–8; interest in
income redistribution, 271–2; see also
investment, surplus
capitalism, 2–7, 9, 10; 'autonomous'
development of, 17, 19; 'periphery'
and 'peasant production', 64–5, 171–4;
international system of, 1–2, 8–25
passim, 72, 84; African, in trade,
150–9; in transport, 159–63; in
construction, 163; in manufacturing,
164; shareholding, 164–5; in
agriculture, 91, 97, 101, 115; in trade,
156, 171–4; monopoly capitalism, 7,
10–13, 14; see also monopoly
Central Organisation of Trade Unions
(COTU), 141–2, 143
class structure, 16; of Kenya, 170–206
passim, 207–9
class struggles, 19, 20; in Kikuyu
country, 204–6, 214–15
classes, xii, 9; role of in underdevelopment theory, 20; formation, 173, 177,
183; and rural socio-economic
differentiation, 186–92; and
contradictions, 271–5

Gatundu, 98; Self-Help Hospital, 249
Gichuru, James, 57, 61–2, 246

Harambee, Settlement Scheme, 75
Housing Finance Company of Kenya
(HFCK), 194

ideology, 234–43 passim; of private
enterprise, 145–6; 'comprador', 220–3
imperialism, xv, 5, 7, 20
import substitution, 13–14
India, 2–7
Industrial and Commercial
Development Corporation (ICDC),
145, and foreign capital, 131–3; loans
to African traders, 151, 167, 201; to
African manufacturers, 164, 167, 201;
Investment Company, 164–5
industrial relations, see unions
industrialization, 3, 13–15, 18; prevented
in Kenya under colonialism, 33, 41;
growth of, 119; see also investment,
manufacturing
'informal' sector, defined, 259; criticised,
266–9
investment, foreign, welcomed, 61;
inflow of, 118, 146–7; joint ventures
with Kenya Government, 119, 131–3;
control of, 125–8; effects of, 135–46;
see also multinational companies
Ireland, 6–7

Kaggia, Bildad, 215; resignation from
government, 219; loses seat, 225;
jailed, 234; leaves KPU, 236–7
Kalenjin, support for KADU, 212–14;
for Moi, 274; and land purchase
228–30; in army, 238–9
Kali, J. D., 215
Kamba, support for KANU, 212, 214;
oathing extended to, 236, 240; and
army, 238, 240–3
Kenya African Union (KAU), 48–9
Kenya African Democratic Union
(KADU), 56, 58, 60; relations with
KANU, 212–14
Kenya African National Union (KANU),
65, 216, 248, 261; and land transfer
formula, 56–8; accepted by foreign
capital, 59; class character, 60; forms
government, 61; KANU 'A' and 'B',
206; relations with KADU, 212–14;
divisions in, 213–15, 220–3; primary
elections in, 235, 237–8; institutional
decline of, 245

Kenya Association of Manufacturers,
(KAM), 139, 145
Kenya Coffee Producers' Union
(KCPU), 103, 104
Kenya Cooperative Creameries (KCC),
36, 103, 105; and 'quota' abolition,
111; and milk price, 111–13
Kenya Farmers' Association, (KFA), 36,
39, 103, 104
Kenya Federation of Labour (KFL), 54
Kenya Hardware Distributors'
Association, 155
Kenya National Farmers' Union
(KNFU), 96, 102, 104, 248; and maize
price, 108–10, 112
Kenya National Trading Corporation
(KNTC), 152–5
Kenya People's Union, 141, 216, 224;
manifesto, 224–5; harassed, 226;
Wananchi Declaration of, 226–7;
banned, 237; resemblance of ILO mis-
sion's proposals to programme of, 262
Kenya Tourist Development
Corporation (KTDC), 132
Kenya Wines Agency Ltd., 132, 154
Kenya Wines and Spirits Distributors'
Association, 154–5
Kenyatta, Jomo, 62, 65, 75, 83, 118, 201,
219, 220, 244, 253, 261; leader of
KAU, 48–9; of KANU, 62; views of,
57, 62, 179–80; policy towards white
settlers, 62; accepted by foreign
capital, 59; and large-farm interest, 98,
229; role in raising maize and milk
prices, 110, 112–13, 249; and
'tribalism', 206; relations with foreign
capital, 221; and 'radicals' in KANU,
224; attacks Kaggia, 225; agrees to
primary elections in KANU, 235;
attacks Odinga, 237; power of, 245;
'court' of, 246–9; succession to, 274–5
Kibachia, Chege, 49, 60
Kikuyu, 31; pre-colonial social structure
of, 189; as landless squatters and wage
workers, 46–50; educated, 50; traders,
early efforts to assist, 51–2; and land
transfer formula, 56–7; and class
conflict in Emergency, 50, 62, 214; and
land purchase, 90, 228–30; and
shareholding, 165; pre-colonial
relations with other tribes, 199; and
uneven development of capitalism,
200–3; support for KANU, 212;
alliance with Kalenjin leaders, 228–9;
and oathing, 236, 240; and armed
forces, 238–9

slum clearance in, 179–80; profits from property in, 194; 'home' city of Kikuyu, 202
Nairobi Chamber of Commerce, 58–60
Nakuru District Ex-freedom Fighters Organization, 92–3
Nandi, 67
Nandi Hills Declaration, 229–30
National Construction Corporation (NCC), 163
national income, 74; growth to 1964, 40–1
nationalization, 238
Ndegwa Commission, on public service, 193, 195–7; and wages policy, 233; and private enterprise by civil servants, 249–50
Ndolo, Major-General, 240–3
neo-colonialism, concept of, xiv, 25–7; transition to in Kenya, 37, 50–62, 73, 76, 78; consolidated, 216–20; contradictions of, 254–75 passim
New Kenya Group, 45, 54, 56; and neo-colonial strategy, 42–3; support for KADU, 213; disappears, 62
Ngala, Ronald, 213, 247
Njonjo, Charles, 246
Nkrumah, Kwame, 26

oathing, 236, 240
Ol Kalou Declaration, 235
Odinga, Oginga, 220, 228; advocate of help for African traders, 52; and trade unionists, 141,'179; in KANU government, 216; outmanoeuvred, 224; Kaggia's defection from, 236–7
Oneko, Achieng, 216, 220
OPEC, 12

partnerships, African, formed to buy large farms, 91; African, with non-Africans, 157, 162
'peasants', 10, 11, 39, 64, 77, 88, 91, 99, 115, 166, 183; meaning of, 64 n. 4, 170–1; and capitalist production, 190; differentiation among, 184–92; Marx's views on, 209; and landowning, 225, 226–7
petty-bourgeoisie, 51, 174–8; salaried, 177–8; see also traders
Pinto, Pio, 235
plantations, see estates
plot, of 1970–71, 240–3
population, 40
prices, agricultural, and large-farm

interest, 105–14; Costs and Prices Committee, 113; see also monpoly
primitive capital accumulation, 2, 7, 8, 9, 168
profits, 118, 129, 134; of foreign companies, 136–7; see also surplus
property, private, 2, 43; in land, 56, 66–73
public sector, expanded, by joint ventures, 119, 128, 131–3; by purchase of controlling interest, 130–5

railway, 28, 34; protection removed, 160–1
ranches, 39, 42; left in foreign hands, 63
regionalism, 213, 216
relations of production, 9; rural predominant over urban, 181; capitalist, in Kikuyu country, 204; see also classes
reserves. African, 37, 64, 66, 74, 76; relabelled, 70
revolution, 7, 16–17, 29, 20; problems of, 22–4
Rift Valley, 64, 90, 91; and white settlement, 28–33; and of squatting, 48, 217–18; and competition for land, 57, 214, 228–30; Kikuyu role in towns of, 202
Rogers, Sir Philip, 53, 59
'rural development', 208, 230; see also Special Rural Development Programme

Seroney, John, 229–30
settlement schemes, 73–84, 90, 96, 100, 101, 115–16, 216, 227; nature and scale of, 73–6; proposals to terminate, 27–8, 83–4, 88–9; indebtedness of, 78–80; economic effects of, 82–4, 86; Kikuyu share in, 201; later programme of, 84–5, 88–9, 228; see also settlers
settlers, white, 28–40 passim; found dispensable, 42–3, 55; and squatting, 46–8; production by, on areas made into settlement schemes, 76; see also land transfer, farms; African, on settlement schemes, 74–84; evictions of, 79, 102; see also settlement schemes
Sifuma, Peter, 104, 112
Singh, Makhan, 49
socialism, petty-bourgeois, 215, 221, 224–7; bourgeois, 221–3, 270; see also African socialism
Special Rural Development Programme (SRDP), 230–2